Tana Douglas was sixteen when she took her first job as a roadie with AC/DC. Now recognised as the world's first female roadie, Tana has worked alongside some of rock'n'roll's biggest names in a career spanning three continents and more than thirty years. Tana currently resides in Los Angeles, California. *Loud* is her first book.

LOUD

TANA DOUGLAS

ABC
BOOKS

© Robert Ellis

© Alain le Garsmeur

This book is dedicated to every young girl
who has ever dared to dream of MORE!

And to all those road crew who took that leap of faith
when they were told one day: 'Come on, it'll be FUN!'

CONTENTS

Prologue   1

 1. Father of Mine   3
 2. White Rabbit   15
 3. Darling Nikki   30
 4. Born to Run   36
 5. She's Got Balls   52
 6. It's a Long Way to the Top   75
 7. Girl, You'll Be a Woman Soon   97
 8. California Dreamin'   121
 9. London Calling   139
10. Rockin' All Over the World   152
11. Lust for Life   171
12. Who Are You   192
13. What Is Life   208
14. Crazy Train   223
15. God Save the Queen   234
16. Ghost in the Machine   246
17. Empty Garden   262
18. Under Pressure   280
19. There Goes the Neighbourhood   296
20. Are You Gonna Go My Way   312
21. For What It's Worth   325

Epilogue   331
Postscript   332
In Memoriam   333
Playlist   335
Acknowledgements   338

PROLOGUE

A STRANGE FEELING HAS come over me. It's six in the morning as I pause to take it all in. Behind me things are already loud, hectic, even chaotic – to the untrained eye. There's a row of massive semitrailers spewing their loads out onto the backstage area. It'll be okay for me to take just a moment while I wait on the rigger to unload his boxes. I usually let this feeling pass as I'm not here to look, I'm here to work.

This time feels special: it's a turning point in my career. How did I end up here, on the most revered stage of the world's touring circuit? Beyond lies a vast, empty cavern shaking off the last tentacles of the night's mist. In a few short hours, eighty thousand punters will be here, paying homage to their musical heroes while being transported to rock'n'roll heaven, as only a great live show can do.

In this time of dramatic change in the music industry, finally the road crew are coming into their own and being recognised for their skill sets. This crew here today are considered among the best. And here I stand, the only woman in that crew. When you can sell out London's

Wembley Stadium, you've made it! When you work for the band that accomplishes that feat, you've also made it! Not bad for a girl who started out as a fifteen-year-old runaway in Brisbane, Australia.

It's August 1979 and I've been in London three years. I'm lucky enough to have worked for two of the four bands on the bill. Today I'm working for The Who but there was a time not so long ago that I worked for AC/DC. Way back in the beginning, in Australia, when we were all just getting started.

It's going to be a long, hard day, but I already know it will all be worth it when The Who and Friends roar in. Plus, I get to reminisce with my old friends in AC/DC. These are the kinds of things that keep us, the crew, coming back: the bonds we build among ourselves, and the bands we work for. There's only one thing a band member relies upon as much as their bandmates, and that's their roadies. We are there 24/7 for them, and they know it. Lifelong friendships are made in this Industry of Music. If it doesn't kill you, it's one hell of a way to make a living!

1

FATHER OF MINE

YOU MIGHT BE WONDERING, 'What on earth would cause a young girl to run away from home and choose a life of rock'n'roll?' It was as if I'd been training for it all along. Running away was what I knew from an early age.

When I was four, I was taken from the only home I'd known in Brisbane in the middle of the night. My mother abruptly awoke me and my half-sister. 'Here, put these on and don't make any noise,' she told us urgently. We sat side by side holding each other, wide-eyed but silent, hurriedly dressing as directed, while our mother grabbed handfuls of clothing and shoved them into bags. She whispered, 'Do not wake up your father. We are leaving, we can never be happy here.' As children, we'd thought we were happy.

No further explanation was given. We were just gone, leaving my father asleep in bed.

This would become our new normal. We would turn up in a town, stay a while, then pack up and leave in the middle of the night. If you've ever worked for a travelling production/concert tour, that is pretty much how it's done. As young children, we played along with it being an adventure, but we soon realised something was wrong and begged to be able to stay put – it was scary to be always leaving. There is no childhood memory of 'home'.

Living with my mother was like holding your breath too long. She couldn't bear to be alone, so she constantly collected people and lovers. Anything so long as she didn't have to be quiet – 'the quiet' scared her. Her impromptu company would keep the dark at bay, until it didn't. Then she would slide into fits of depression. She sought alcohol as an answer.

I remember late one night, several towns away from Brisbane, sitting up alone watching a movie on TV, deliberately scaring myself as small children do. *The Three Faces of Eve* was on. That was my mother's name, Eve, and the bad woman in the movie was acting a lot like my mother did. Just as it ended, Mum came crashing through the front door. Dishevelled, still pretty, but overshadowed by a sadness. Thankfully, she was alone; neither my sister nor I wanted any more uncles. It could be my bedtime now I knew she was safe.

After several more towns we ended up in Melbourne, about as far from our starting point as we could get. This was where my sister, now in her mid-teens, plotted her escape from growing, unwanted attention from our mother's boyfriends. Within a year she was free.

Being left behind brought about changes I couldn't even have started to imagine. I was resentfully thrust into my sister's position in the household and expected to act accordingly. In my mother's eyes I was a wilful child, and it was my fault Amber had left. 'Look what you've done! You've chased your sister away! Now you'll do her chores as well.' These were the words thrown at me by an enraged mother who'd seen her second household income disappear.

A mother unaware that, together, my sister and I had scrimped and saved enough for my sister to leave, all the while keeping her secret safe.

I was now eleven years old, and this was when the physical abuse escalated. My mother was out of control, and neither of us could continue to pretend things were okay. After one particularly severe session with a belt buckle, I'd got myself to school, but I was in a bad way. I'd locked myself in the outside toilets. The teacher was insisting that I join the class. 'Tana Douglas! You march yourself into that classroom right NOW and take your seat!' Due to the severity of the beating, every movement of my loose summer dress felt like fire rushing across my back. I couldn't sit and was embarrassed by the thought of my plight being made public. I was yelling through the toilet-stall door, 'NO, I won't! I won't ... I can't ...' then I just started sobbing. I'd tried so hard not to, but I'd had enough. My yelling enraged the teacher at first, but when I broke down she finally figured out what was going on and sent me to the nurse. I could see in her eyes that she now understood why a child who showed such promise had just shut down and no longer participated in class. The school contacted child services.

Enter my father. I knew instinctively that the decisions being made about me, without me, but in front of me would put an end to my mother's reign. Since the incident at school, I'd been spending my nights cloistered in a facility for endangered children. Each day I watched a battle play out over me. Or was it really about them? From my corner position, I looked across that cold, sad room. There she was: stoic, unmoving, plotting ways to save herself. Her hair and make-up were perfect as she sat poised with her hands in her lap, knees together and ankles crossed off to one side, as if in a photo shoot. She didn't see me; she didn't care to. I'd betrayed her. She asked quietly for a cup of tea. I knew what she really wanted was a glass of whisky.

I looked to the other side of the room at my father. His appearance was different, heavier in build and sadder around the eyes. This was his chance. He finally had her cornered; she wouldn't slip away into the night this time. He was a large man in an immaculately tailored three-piece suit, similar in appearance to a well-known American comic of the time, Jackie Gleason. Unlike my mother, he would make eye contact with me, with a hint of reassurance, but mostly with the look of someone who may have just bitten off more than they could chew.

I would have to wait and see what lay ahead without having any idea when so much as a polite smile might next cross my face, when I would next get to breathe. I wanted all these adults to stop looking at me 'that way' as if they knew me, knew what I'd been through. I wasn't going to tell everything that had happened. I just couldn't.

Since my sister's departure, music had become my talisman. It was the only constant in my life, and never beyond my reach. My escape from my mother would come at night. Once alone and in my bed, head under the covers, I could turn up my little radio, listen through my earpiece and be carried away by whatever story the singer was telling. It gave me the feeling that something else was out there, something better. The songs I gravitated to were those describing unknown places – ones that sounded a little dangerous. Eric Burdon of The Animals sang 'We Gotta Get Out of This Place', and that became my anthem as I too was determined to get away. It was my secret – I'd sing it out loud only when I was alone. Like my sister before me, I didn't want to get caught out. I would sing it at the top of my lungs while I worked my way through the flat doing both my chores and those I'd inherited from my sister before my mother returned from work. To the neighbours, it probably sounded like a cat was being murdered. I didn't really understand all the lyrics, but I clearly understood the urgency and hung on the line that refers to a better place for me and you.

This world of music gave me hope, an inner strength, a peek at something I wanted to become a part of. From those early days I saw it as a destination that I could choose to go to, something bigger than the options shown to me so far. Somewhere I could belong. I never saw it as noise coming across the airwaves. I came to rely on it as sustenance for my soul. It was all mine, and I didn't share it. When a song I didn't like came on the radio, it would only last the three minutes, then it would be over and something better would come on; or if I didn't want to listen anymore, I would just turn it off. It was better than real life – you can't turn real life off.

* * *

While I'd escaped into Radioland, the final steps were being made for me to return to Brisbane with my father, who, in anticipation of my arrival, had moved in with his mother. In all fairness, being landed with a very angry, bordering-on-feral eleven-year-old surely wasn't what he'd envisioned. Be careful what you wish for, father of mine. He and my grandmother quickly decided that boarding school would be best for me: a calm, safe and structured place to make up for the years of chaos. I'm sure he also hoped it would rub off some of my rough edges. I immediately resented being shipped off and interpreted it as him trying to get rid of me.

To my mind, that was what parents did. This got me off to a rocky start at my new school.

My father had chosen Glennie, a Church of England school for girls located west of Brisbane in Toowoomba. This large town is in an area known as the Darling Downs, which lay between what was considered 'The Outback' and 'Civilisation'. The Glennie girls were a mix of sheep farmers' daughters, white kids whose folks lived in Port Moresby, a few city girls, and the somewhat pampered day girls. All the parents hoped that the school would produce well-educated and balanced young ladies who would go out confidently into our flourishing nation and become good wives to successful businessmen or better. While the cities were flourishing, the country folk, however, were being decimated by drought, so they saw Glennie as a chance to get their daughters off the land.

My favourites were these girls: they were the salt of the earth. They'd had a hard time of it from these constant droughts, which gave them a certain strength. During school holidays, I visited some of their homes way out west, around St George, Tara and Meandarra. We'd spend the days horseriding through their massive properties that traversed hundreds of miles and housed tens of thousands of livestock. But conditions were tough, and the girls' families were just trying to survive day to day. I remember a seemingly endless expanse of dying livestock, and a farmer telling me he couldn't afford the bullets to put them out of their misery – an eye-opening experience for a young child. I would join in musters to round up any sheep still strong enough to be moved, and we'd come back to the farmhouse covered in red dust I could taste in the back of my throat. I would wash it off in a bucket of water taken from the property bore that smelt of sulfur. Tiny frogs jumped up out of the toilet bowl when I peed.

Having witnessed their life on the land, I could understand why these girls had been sent to Glennie. But for the life of me, I couldn't figure out why I was there. I found the strict daily routine very confusing, to say the least. While living with my mother I'd pretty much looked after myself, coming and going as I pleased, using whatever means necessary to stay out of her way. I would stay with friends for days on end until their parents finally sent me home. I'd adapted to keeping a low profile and taken on the attitude of a moving target. Here in these hallowed halls of my boarding school, all of that changed. God was everywhere, and I wasn't sure I wanted the company.

Glennie was a large, rambling property with two main residential structures, and in my second year I moved to the main building with the upper grades, where everything was bigger and somehow even more formal. I felt like the runt of the litter: after changing schools so often while living with my mother I had somehow skipped two years. I would turn twelve in April. My classmates were all at least two years older than me, but I fought both the school and my father, taking an aptitude test to stay in that class as it meant I was two years closer to leaving school. I was feeling alone, feeling different, sure the other girls would notice I wasn't like them. I didn't care for the things they did, like who had the nicest clothes or wore make-up, or even who'd been kissed by a boy; I was too young to relate to any of that. It seemed unimportant. And I hated the feeling of hurtling headlong into that dull existence when somehow I knew there was so much more to life.

When you're left to raise yourself, you grow up rather quickly and without knowing what's age-appropriate. I was

Here I am at Glennie. In the front row of three girls, I'm the one on the left. It was 1971 and I was in Year 11. I would turn 14 that year.
(COURTESY OF THE GLENNIE SCHOOL)

smoking cigarettes that the day girls would bring in, raiding the school kitchen in the middle of the night, and sunbaking naked on the rooftops – those were my ways of fitting in. I would mastermind whatever illicit adventure our group of boarders chose. My saving grace was the few hours we had to ourselves on Sunday evenings: I would spend that time in the rec room listening to as much music as I could squeeze in. It turned out that a small group of us shared a love of music, and this was how I got to relate to my classmates without getting into trouble.

* * *

I soon discovered Janis Joplin. The album was *Cheap Thrills*, and the song that set her apart from the likes of Joe Cocker, Leon Russell, Marvin Gaye, Al Green, The Zombies, The Beatles, The Stones, and even Cat Stevens and Carole King, was 'Summertime'. The others were great, but this girl was pure, raw emotion. Janis was taking no prisoners. *Now we're talking*, I said to myself. *Finally, a girl after my own heart.* And wow, what a girl!

Within a short time of my discovering Janis, word spread across the schoolyard that she was soon to perform at a place called Woodstock. I'd never heard of it, but I decided I would convince my father to let me go. I didn't know exactly where Woodstock was in relation to Toowoomba, but surely it wouldn't be such a big deal. When I practised my pitch with a friend, she mentioned it probably wasn't a good idea, but my mind was made up. 'It's a one-of-a-kind cultural experience,' I planned to tell my father. 'And if you let me go I will never, ever ask for anything ever, ever again. And I'll get better grades. I promise.' Seemed like a fair deal to me.

My father came to visit that weekend. Over dinner off campus, I could tell he was taking his role in my life very seriously. I was full of great expectations for our meeting. I presented my well-rehearsed speech. 'Dad, this is my once-in-a-lifetime chance to hear Janis Joplin. All the girls at school are talking about it. I just *have* to go!'

With the main course completed and my pitch over, there was an extremely long and deafening silence while our dessert was presented with great pomp and ceremony – and set on fire. It was a bombe alaska, and it wouldn't be the only thing to bomb that night.

My father took a long, deep breath, then finally spoke. 'Bear,' he said, using his pet name for me, a constant source of embarrassment, 'do you know where Woodstock is?'

I squirmed. 'Well, no, not exactly.'

'And do you know what goes on there?'

'They play music? I think it's kind of like a fair?'

I could feel the mood changing. My father knew exactly what Woodstock was all about: tie-dye, pot smoke and rock'n'roll. Radicals. Hippies! This just wouldn't do for his recently rescued daughter.

After a lot of begging and pleading and more promises that I'd improve my grades, the matter was firmly put to rest, although I did try one last desperate plea. 'Dad, if I don't see Janis play at Woodstock, I'll never, ever have another chance!' But, of course, he didn't budge.

My journey into this world of music was inspired by this woman, Janis Joplin. (ELLIOTT LANDY/REDFERNS/GETTY IMAGES)

My prediction sadly came to pass: in October of the following year, Janis was found dead in her hotel room in Hollywood from a heroin overdose. Woodstock went on without me.

* * *

I spent a lot of time plotting my exit from Glennie. It took me a couple more years, but I finally persuaded my father to let me start my final year at a state school in Brisbane. Now it was my turn to be careful what I wished for. I found it hard to relate to my new classmates, who had a completely different attitude to my age difference than the Glennie girls had. So I didn't settle into my new school, not at all. Alas, my education came to a screeching halt.

School was out forever. What to do now?

Every city has an area to which young people gravitate. In Brisbane in the early 1970s, the city square was full of youngsters selling candles and incense and playing live music. A Krishna temple was nearby, offering free vegetarian food, which was new to me, and more live music. Just as word had spread about Woodstock a few years earlier, a new buzz was spreading through the city square – everyone was talking about the Nimbin Aquarius Festival of music and arts. Nimbin was obtainable, a town not too far away, just across the border in New South Wales, practically my backyard compared to Woodstock. Nothing was going to keep me from this one! I needed a plan, although this time I didn't think it wise to let my father in on it. Things weren't going well for me on the home front. Living under the same roof as my father and grandmother was complicated, to say the least.

Back when my father had gained custody of me, I had fantasised that my grandmother would be a kindly old lady. Sadly, that was not the case. With my father off at work one day, she had summoned me to afternoon tea and taken that opportunity to make me aware of her house rules. Until that moment my stay in their household had been uncomfortable, but I hadn't realised it was conditional. Her opening statement was, 'I do not want you here, but your father is insistent. So, you will do as I say. You will be polite when I introduce you in company, otherwise you will be seen and not heard. Oh, and under no circumstances, ever, call me Grandmother. Call me Suze.' This was the most she ever said to me in one sitting. I decided I preferred it when she stayed quiet.

I once overheard her saying to a friend, 'You know, it was her mother who ruined my son's life! She is going to be nothing but trouble, that child.' My grandmother knew I could hear her – she was looking right at me. At times like that, I amused myself by imagining her toppling headfirst down the back staircase, an accident that just couldn't be helped. Another fantasy was of her and my mother locked in a room together. Yes, there would be blood!

My fantasies were fleeting distractions, and my only ally in the household was a father clearly out of his depth. I needed to get away and the Nimbin Festival was looking good.

2

WHITE RABBIT

IT WAS 1973 AND I was fifteen. I left that house without so much as a goodbye, joining up with four young people to head off to the promised land of freedom and music. I was a skinny, gangly kid, no boobs, all arms and legs. I hid behind a mass of long hair with only one eye visible to anyone who talked to me. My clothes of choice were kaftans or a skirt with a scarf as a top. Shoes were optional, although I brought a pair of sandals just in case a formal occasion arose. I never got into the whole not-washing-clothes thing that was widely accepted in this hippie lifestyle, but if I couldn't access hot water for a while, I was willing to make the sacrifice. Everything felt brighter, shinier, more welcoming, and I liked this feeling of being a part of something, no longer just an onlooker who might get caught staring.

My group's transportation for our adventure was a gold Cadillac, fins and all, from the US of A. She was immediately christened the Gold Top in honour of a type of hallucinogenic mushroom we were planning to try.

This mode of transportation proved quite expensive. Money was tight, but, as luck would have it, the family of one of my Glennie schoolfriends owned a petrol station in Tweed Heads, on the New South Wales border. I was sure they'd be happy to see me and help us out, and the journey would be saved. It was obviously meant to be. My little group arrived at some time during the night, and we knocked on doors and windows until we roused my friend and her family. Once they figured out they weren't being robbed by a bunch of hippies, I was greeted by my friend and her somewhat wary parents. They were happy to put us up for the night, feed us and even throw in a tank of petrol – under the condition that we didn't run off with their daughter.

Before arriving at our destination, we made a slight detour, this one to collect our Cadi's namesake: gold top mushrooms. We surely didn't want to arrive in Nimbin empty-handed. Who knew what the supplies would be like in the local fields with so many people converging on the one spot? Once north of Byron Bay, we started pulling over to pick our special mushrooms. It was a beautiful drive up the incline through a belt of coastal rainforest with fields of cattle dotting the landscape into the hills ahead of us, while behind and below were glimpses of the Pacific Ocean glistening in the sunlight. With a break in the rain and the sun shining through, to me it symbolised a washing away of my past and a bright new beginning.

Before getting back into the Cadi for the last leg of our journey, we each ate a few of our harvest for the day. We then followed the long and winding road all the way to Nimbin. The combination of rain and sunshine made everything sparkle and pop, bringing out the many colours of the tropical growth along the roadside. I snuggled in the back seat with my head on the open window's ledge, looking up at the sky and taking in the scents carried on the wind. Damp hay had never smelt so good. This was it! My time had finally come. The Turtles' 'Happy Together' was playing on the car radio, and we all sang along.

My first impression of Nimbin was straight from the pages of one of those fabulous Victorian-era books about fairies in the garden. The road through town, still moist and shimmering as if covered in diamond dust, was hemmed with rainbows, butterflies and mushrooms on either side – all artworks on buildings, of course, but in my state of mind the town truly was Wonderland. Snatches of music were wafting into our Cadi from the fields below, and I decided to find its source as soon as we arrived.

The Nimbin Festival had been dreamt up by a group of university students who wanted to combine cultural exchange, music and art, to build peace, harmony and tolerance. It seems I wasn't the only one who felt robbed by missing out on Woodstock. When I arrived, the festival was still three weeks away, due to start on 12 May, and would last for ten days. The final attendance was several thousand. A lot of like-minded people for a misfit teenager to come across, and along the way I lost track of my travelling companions. I stayed in one of several abandoned farmhouses and settled in to the rhythm of the place, glad not to be camping in a field in the rain.

This was when I started playing guitar. In one of the houses, I found an old nylon six-string. I took it apart, cleaned it, brought it back to life. That part was easy – learning how to play it was harder than it looked. One of the girls, Pippin, came to my rescue. For a few days she watched me take off with that old guitar before she called out, 'Come over here, Tana, and bring that thing with you.' She then asked me two questions. The first was, 'Do you know how to tune a guitar?' and the second, 'Aren't you left-handed?' I hadn't really put together the whole tuning thing, so I was happy to learn, and it turned out I needed to restring the guitar for my left hand (learning all this came in handy down the road!). I was off and running. Being left-handed, I picked it up rather quickly. I figured out if I sat opposite someone playing guitar, I rarely had to glance down at my fingers. Neil Young's songs were the easiest. 'Heart of Gold' was only four chords: E minor, C, D, G. I learnt a lot of Neil Young.

This handful of people with their instruments was like a private club that knew something the rest of us didn't. They did: they knew music, and I wanted to know it too.

* * *

One day in the midst of the festival I came across a guy walking along a wire high up between two points. The way he moved was hypnotic. He was Philippe Petit, the French tightrope-walker who had a reputation in Europe for his impromptu, death-defying performances. His Nimbin appearance was sponsored by the Australia Council, but they were unaware of the event that was to follow, the main purpose of his visit to our shores, which would involve a trip all the way down to Sydney. As the Nimbin Festival drew to a close, my friends in the farmhouse spoke about heading to Kuranda in the mountainous rainforest just outside Cairns in the far north of Queensland, the marijuana-growing capital of Australia. But I was fed up with everything being damp from the rains – I needed to dry out for a bit.

When I hooked up with Philippe Petit's troupe, little did I know I was about to become part of my first production. (JOHN O'GREADY/SYDNEY MORNING HERALD)

Having never been to Sydney, I opted to head down there with Philippe and his crew. I was also hoping to take part in whatever they were up to. I'd watched them rigging and adjusting his tightrope, which reminded me of tuning a guitar, and I was curious about the whole set-up. When they let me in on their plan to rig a steel cable for Philippe to walk between the two towers of the Harbour Bridge, I was in! For the first time, I was becoming part of a production crew. I would be with the group on the ground charged with taking the film footage of the stunt to a safe place, so it couldn't be confiscated by police when they inevitably arrested Philippe and his camera operators.

The stunt was well planned, with blueprints and rigging plots for the bridge, and talk of wind factor, torque and access to rigging points. I had no idea what these things meant, but I wanted to. And I was amazed by the way these workers could organise a traffic-stopping event without being noticed, especially at such a major thoroughfare and tourist attraction.

On the day of the performance, I watched the city come to life, shaking off the night as the golden glow of a new day spread over the harbour. Ferries loaded with workers were scurrying across the water, and as the traffic started to build … it happened! Bonjour, Sydney!

It took a while for Sydneysiders to realise what they were witnessing. By the time the police arrived, Philippe was over halfway across on his first pass, and the morning commute was in chaos. I couldn't keep my eyes off him, squinting into the sunlight at the silhouette of his tiny figure dressed in black with a shock of carrot-coloured hair. It was exhilarating to think I'd contributed to this. People were getting out of their cars to watch, while others were in an

'I'm late for work' mode, not even aware of what was going on above them.

The police weren't sure what to do, but they did know they weren't going up after him. 'He must be mad! Some crazy Frenchman. Is this what they get up to over there in Europe?' They directed traffic as best they could. Philippe's crew members on the bridge made it clear to everyone present that if they interfered with the rigging at all, Philippe would fall to his death.

Just as the police were relieved to see he'd started his return crossing, he suddenly stopped midway and lay down on the wire. It was inspiring and totally awesome. I left with that vision, as it was my cue to join the cars below, ready to have the film dropped off the side of the bridge to us, with our exit route free from the traffic jam above. Mission accomplished. I'd just done my first gig!

I promised myself that one day I'd come back to Sydney to see what lay beyond that bridge. For now, it was time to make my way north to join my friends in Kuranda.

* * *

'Come sail the Pacific Seas with me, Tana!' said my new friend Paul, who'd just bought a boat. Not an offer you get every day.

The charted course would be north to the Great Barrier Reef then on to Cedar Bay, right past Kuranda. The vessel, a trimaran, was like the ones used by Polynesian tribes, so Paul felt we'd be blessed by the Polynesian gods. You gotta love hippies! Irrelevant were the facts that we weren't Polynesian and didn't know how to sail. Regardless, I said, 'YES!' I loved the ocean, had just learnt a bit about rigging, and I could cook. What could possibly go wrong?

On the day of our departure, it seems the Polynesian gods were busy elsewhere. After several false starts and near misses, we cleared the Sydney Heads. Finally, we were out at sea, no land in sight, with a mass of stars above. I lay on the deck feeling the roll of the boat over the ocean swell while taking in the salt air. I yelled up to those stars, 'I am the luckiest girl alive!'

When we docked at Coffs Harbour for provisions and a change of crew, I mentioned to Paul it might be best if he took some more-experienced sailors on board, and maybe I could meet up with them further north (once they'd figured out what the hell they were doing). I left my sea legs temporarily and started hitchhiking to Kuranda.

It's a long drive from Coffs to Cairns – I had allowed four days to hitchhike – and along the way I picked up odd jobs to pay for food and gas. When I got to Maryborough just north of Brisbane, some locals told me that a fruit and vegetable cannery was hiring day labour, which sounded perfect.

The next morning, I turned up to work along with the group of young hippies I was with at the time. We decided it would be a great idea to take some mushrooms to help pass the time. We were put in the part of the factory where the fruit is sent down a huge metal ramp before being sliced on a conveyer belt and then dropped into cans. Just as the mushrooms started to kick in, thousands of bright-red shiny beetroots started pouring down this ramp. They were bouncing and jiggling all over the place, with the odd one flying off onto the floor.

I thought it was the funniest thing I'd ever seen. 'Look! They're making a break for it!' I shouted, and everyone started laughing.

After about thirty minutes of uncontrollable laughter that seemed contagious, as everyone in the factory was also caught up in the moment – who knows what they were on? – the foreman appeared. 'What the hell's wrong with youse drongos?' When he saw that three of us still couldn't stop laughing, he gave us the less taxing job of watching the canned goods go into boxes for the remainder of the day.

First thing on the morning of the second day, the foreman pulled us aside and asked, 'Are you going to be able to keep it together today? No more wacky weed?'

We mumbled promises to behave and ran inside. I spent that day wishing we hadn't finished all our mushrooms, while deciding that factory work wasn't for me.

* * *

I finally made it to Cairns, my last stop before Kuranda. The house for the night was a large, wooden structure with a tin roof and wraparound veranda, suspended on long, gangly legs made of solid tree trunks. This served two purposes: to keep the floods out during the wet season, and to discourage deadly crawling things from entering. I was exhausted when I curled up ready for sleep, not worrying about what the night may bring.

In the wee small hours I was woken by yelling and loud banging. Suddenly the room was overrun by several uniformed policemen rousting our group from slumber. The head cop was a gruff but also rather comical-looking character with his floppy hat and too-tight shirt with buttons that gaped from the strain of too many home-cooked meals. His uniform was completed by khaki shorts and knee-high socks – a precursor to the Crocodile Hunter, without the muscular physique or charming smile. It was a raid. Our arrival, it seems, had coincided with his decision to rid his tropical paradise of 'the great unwashed', a term the country folk of Australia unanimously used when referring to the hippie population. We were bustled out of the house and down the rickety staircase in the dark. I felt the rain on my face and could see the geckos rustling back down the rails to avoid being squashed by uncaring boots.

The cops had discovered a fancy pipe from India with a hand-carved wooden stem and an engraved brass bowl in my shoulder bag. It was a keepsake from Nimbin with which I only smoked tobacco, but these men wouldn't for a moment consider that a young girl would smoke a pipe – even with the pouch of tobacco in plain sight.

We were all taken to the local jailhouse, which was being pushed well beyond its capacity with an additional thirty or so guests; it seems the hippie-dragnet had extended across the whole town. I was told the clientele usually numbered around two to three people at most.

Another soul ensnared in this net was a friend I hadn't seen since Nimbin, known as Preacher Barry. When he was led past my cell, I called out, 'Hi, Preacher Barry!'

This confused the guards, who now thought they had a real preacher in custody.

'Hello, my child,' was his response, followed by, 'Don't be afraid, my child. God works in mysterious ways.' With that he winked, smiled, reached through the bars to cradle my head in his hands, and kissed me gently. That was the preacher up to his old tricks – I'd just been dosed with an acid trip. He worked his way around the cells, blessing and dosing the other cellmates as he went. This was how we passed our first night of captivity: tripping on acid, singing, dancing and making music from anything we could. The camaraderie kept my fear at bay.

By midmorning most of my fellow detainees had been released, run out of town, or charged with something and sent off to a real jail. I was standing my ground, refusing to give my name or any information when questioned. This wasn't only because I'd done nothing wrong and knew it wasn't right for them to imprison me – I also didn't know how news of my age would play out in this part of the country. I didn't want my father's first news in months of his wayward sixteen-year-old daughter to be that she was locked up a couple of thousand kilometres from his home; I'd hoped instead to share with him the wonders of my travels. My associates, unaware of all this, saw my silence as an act of defiance against 'the Man' and hailed me a hero.

The police chief had no idea what to do about me. Over days that turned to weeks, he would get bored on the night shifts and wander by my cell. 'So, Jane of the Jungle,' he once said to me, 'what do you see in these hippie types?'

'They aren't just hippies, they're musicians and artists, and most of all we are free!'

'Argh, not today, you're not! You're all crazy! I don't get it.'

He had also noticed my cassette player in my bag. On his next night shift, the chief brought in a cassette tape purchased on a recent trip to New Zealand. He'd become enthralled with Māori music, but his wife wouldn't let him play it in the house. 'So, Jane,' he said to me, 'what if I get you batteries and you let me play my tapes?'

'What's in it for me?'

'You can play your music during the day when I'm not here. How's that?'

I nodded – this meant I could listen to my tapes of Janis Joplin, The Animals, The Stones and Jefferson Airplane to help break up the boredom.

His wife must have also been grateful, as she started adding extra food like bread, cheese and even a lamb chop to his dinner box to be given to me. But this didn't change the fact that I wasn't talking, and eventually I was sent up in front of a judge as a Jane Doe.

The courtroom looked like something out of a 1950s noir film set in the Florida Keys, with a sleepy local judge on the bench. Before proceedings started, the first words that bleated out of my mouth were, 'My name is Tana Douglas, and I'd like to complain about my treatment. I am a minor who has been held in a men's jail for over two weeks. I am scared, and I want to call my father!'

Well, that sure got the judge's attention. The whole room erupted, and after much aggravated gavel-banging everyone was hurriedly cleared out. It was time for me to have a tete-a-tete with a judge suddenly not sure of his immediate future. After a lot of fumbling, fidgeting and quoting of laws I knew nothing about, it was decided that the fair town of Cairns would pay for me to fly to Brisbane: a one-way ticket, under the condition I wouldn't come back. Ever!

The legal advice I'd followed had come from none other than Preacher Barry. God surely does work in mysterious ways.

Getting out of jail felt good, but returning to Brisbane was daunting to say the least. I was about to get my first glimpse of who my father really was.

As the plane door opened and I stepped onto the rolling staircase, there he was in one of his immaculate three-piece suits. He cast an imposing figure at over six feet tall and weighing 105 kilos. Not a hair on his head was out of place. It must have been over 43 degrees Celsius on that tarmac, but there he stood with a hint of Old Spice on his person. He greeted me with a little disappointment and an attempt at stern disapproval, but mostly relief and genuine happiness.

Back at the house, after he'd chastised me about running away for Suze's sake (fortunately, she had no idea of what I'd been up to), he and I sat down alone to have a conversation about 'the evils of marijuana use'. I don't think this chat went the way that either of us had envisioned. After he stated the obvious about it being illegal, leading to incarceration or worse, I informed him that I only smoked tobacco in my pipe, and the police were just being arseholes.

We soon came to an agreement: I would stop smoking a pipe, and he would try pot before he made up his mind as to how evil it truly was. Now this was going to be interesting ...

I went out and scored some Kuranda Heads pot, and the humour wasn't lost on him. After dinner, when we were sitting together at the highly polished walnut dining table, I presented the bud. It was a surreal feeling with my grandmother sleeping in the adjacent room.

He looked at it closely, while I explained about the different strains being grown in Australia. I was surprised by my father's curiosity and his openness to the whole procedure. Rolling joints had become my specialty since Nimbin, so I proceeded to de-seed it, rub it so it burnt evenly, then build a nice five-paper joint with a filter. I didn't want him to think we were heathens – nothing but the best. I placed the immaculately rolled joint on the table in front of him and asked if he would like to do the honours.

After serious consideration, he declined. 'I will watch, if you don't mind.' He probably thought it prudent to stay in control of his faculties enough to save me in case the experiment went south.

So, I moistened the joint then lit it by rolling it gently in the flame.

'Just like a good cigar,' my father observed.

I explained that he would need to inhale to get the effect, and we passed it back and forth a couple of times without a word.

Then he started to giggle quietly. 'I don't know what you kids see in this stuff that's worth going to jail for.'

I reminded him I hadn't had any pot on me when I was arrested. I then asked what had made him laugh. He said he'd thought of this girl he'd once known who was so full of life and expectations that he'd fallen in love with her. I hoped he was talking about my mother, but knew he probably wasn't, and I didn't want to ruin the moment by asking.

While we finished the joint, we sat in the lounge room watching Harry Nilsson's animation *The Point!* on TV. My father said he'd been wanting to see it – maybe he was a little more turned on than he was willing to admit. I related to the movie; I too was on a journey looking for my 'point' as I also felt different from everyone else. By the end of that very strange and wonderful evening, he came to the decision that smoking pot really wasn't that bad, but I had to promise to be careful. We were also never to mention that night again.

My father bought me a couple of cassettes: The Stones' *High Tide and Green Grass*, *Pearl* by Janis (he remembered), and Creedence Clearwater Revival's *Cosmos Factory*. He'd chosen these albums himself. I was impressed – it was all good stuff.

We had an understanding that I would be leaving again soon. This time, I said goodbye.

Next stop: Kuranda via Cairns. Well, let's be fair, it was the only way to get there from Brisbane! I decided to hitchhike alone, but I didn't share that with my father. When I arrived it was like coming home. Familiar faces were happy to see me, the girl who'd stuck it to 'the Man', and here was the live music I'd been missing. Being a part of this made sense to me.

The group gave me a boxer puppy that I named Arrow after the dog in the Harry Nilsson movie, in honour of the time I'd just spent with my father.

I stayed in far north Queensland for one season only. While it looked like paradise, it didn't provide an easy lifestyle. Living off the land in a tropical rainforest isn't for the faint of heart – snakes and crocodiles are more adept than a bunch of city kids growing pot. I jumped at the opportunity to travel back to Sydney with Pippin, my friend from Nimbin, and her dad, especially as they had a little terrace house in Paddington, a suburb adjacent to the notorious Kings Cross. Arrow would travel with me.

My days as a hippie were coming to an end, but I wouldn't have changed them for anything. The group had been nothing but gracious to me, taking me as they'd found me. I'd needed that.

Their parting warning was 'Stay away from Kings Cross.' Hmm, interesting!

3

DARLING NIKKI

IN LATE 1973, AUSTRALIA was regarded by the rest of the world as a quaint little country ten years behind everywhere else. What the rest of the world didn't know was that Australians were bred of a hardy stock. At the very least we were tenacious and, if provoked, we were capable of being downright feral. Two hundred years after being lumped together as a Nation of Convicts, we defiantly embraced that title, wearing it like a badge of honour.

My move to Paddington was a dramatic change from Queensland. It erased all the easygoing nonchalance of the rainforest and replaced it with a hustle mentality. Now my focus shifted to making money. It didn't matter if that meant selling kerbside art, handmade candles or – more financially appealing – pot or acid: it was all about moving the product. I probably stayed in that house for longer than I should have, but I was comfortable manoeuvring through the nearby streets of the Cross, so that meant I went in on a daily basis, to sell drugs.

I got to know the trannies, working girls, dancers, spruikers, pool hustlers (that's how I learnt to play pool) and various hooligans who called this place home. I was transfixed by these loud and colourful people. The women dressed like peacocks with their extremely short mini-skirts covered in sequins and topped off with lots of make-up and cheap fur coats; they screeched just like the birds. The men strutted with gold chains draped over open-fronted shirts, tucked into tight pants – sometimes too tight for the body on parade – finished off with pointy-toed boots that weren't only a fashion statement but could deliver a good kicking.

Of all the accessories, the boots got the most use. But even after figuring that out, I kept coming back.

Early on, I had a run-in with a pimp who was a particularly nasty piece of work. He was known for dealing hard drugs and running girls. He reminded me of the children's song 'Never Smile at a Crocodile'. His plan, he would brag to anyone who would listen, was to add me to his stable of working girls – one way, or another. These girls were very young and vulnerable and it was obvious they were regularly beaten by him and controlled by the drugs he fed them. I felt for them, and the blankness I saw in their faces reminded me of my childhood. I wasn't the only one to be haunted by demons. This gave me a strange sense of belonging and kinship. I would try to get them to run away, not realising that running had brought us all to this place.

I guess I still hadn't developed the means of finding out what was age-appropriate. In a very short time, I had immersed myself wholly in this environment, building friendships with a few of the old-school locals. Carl, who ran the pool hall and just about everything illegal on the streets, had taken a shine to me. He was a first-generation Polish immigrant and resembled a character from a Rembrandt painting of peasant farm workers I'd seen in school. When he figured out I was a natural pool player, he teamed me up with one-armed Ernie to hustle any tourists unfortunate enough to stumble across our path. We must have been quite the sight: a young girl wearing a scarf for a top, a miniskirt and Army Surplus jungle boots, with her faithful dog by her side, and a Korean War vet with half an arm missing and a bum leg. Without even noticing, I was becoming one of these colourful characters in the Cross. That's when it gets dangerous, when you think you belong.

Another local, a snappy dresser, was Terry the Kid. It was rumoured he had ties going all the way to the top of the Cross's underworld. This seemed to be the case, as once Terry took me under his wing, I became hands off! He was the first adult I could talk to about anything, and we would talk for hours. He would really listen, and never judged. Friendships are built on such things, no matter how odd the couple. Whenever Terry found out I liked something, he would go out of his way to make it happen – whether it was flaming desserts, swimming in the ocean at night, or horses. And there were plenty of things going on with Terry to keep a young girl's eyes wide open: backroom card games, gambling at the track, hustling, nice dinners, and wild penthouse parties with all the beautiful and famous people rubbing elbows with the Sydney Mob.

But my psycho pimp hadn't forgotten about me as easily as I'd let him slip from my mind.

Very late one night, Terry dropped me at the schnitzel place in the Cross. All the usual suspects were there, hanging out. The story going around was that the pimp's youngest girl, Nikki, had disappeared. We all knew she had nowhere else to go, and as he'd beaten her badly the last time she'd tried to get away, we were worried for her. Since her disappearance he'd been acting irrationally.

As if on cue he appeared, nasty as ever, with his too-tight red pants and his slicked-back, greasy dark hair. An imposing figure for someone so short. Oh, yes, and wearing the boots.

Seeing Terry wasn't around, he charged at me from across the restaurant. He grabbed me by my hair and dragged me kicking and screaming to the street. I saw the look in the punters' eyes and knew two things: everyone in that restaurant was afraid of him, and I was on my own. Now I was afraid too. He showed me a gun tucked in the waistband of those tight red pants and told me I was going with him, and if I didn't shut the fuck up he would shoot me 'right here, right now'. I didn't doubt him for a second.

I followed him meekly through the empty back alleys of Kings Cross. In the predawn hours the city was in limbo while it waited for the street sweepers to come through, washing away the sins of the night. I shuddered as the cold morning air reached the panic sweat on the back of my neck.

We ended up in a crusty bedsit. This, he told me, would be my home from now on. I was now his property.

I looked around for a means to escape. It was a small, dirty room with a mess in the corner that could have once resembled a kitchen area and a single bed in the opposite corner. He threw me onto the bed that smelt like my future and pinned me there. In my mind I heard my mother's voice: 'You'll never be good for anything but making a living lying on your back.'

This had an unreal effect on me – I knew I'd rather be dead than have her be right. It spurred me to action. *This can't be happening! This isn't going to happen!* I realised I might have one shot at this, so I stopped struggling, took a deep breath to compose myself, then spoke in as calm a voice as I could muster. I told the pimp what he wanted to hear. Spoke to him like I'd watched his girls do. 'You're right, Daddy, you are the man. Let's do some drugs to take the edge off. If you just let me, I can relax a little, and you can do whatever you want.'

As for any good junkie, the word that stood out to him the most was 'drugs'. And with me no longer struggling, the atmosphere in that room seemed strangely calm. Now his focus had shifted. This whole kidnapping incident turned out to be a spur-of-the-moment thing that had made him overdue for a hit. Starting to get a little shaky, he was more than happy to believe what I was telling him.

He cooked up a hit while half-heartedly continuing to tell me how my life would be from now on. 'I'll give you this hit, but then it comes out of your earnings each night.'

I nodded while I kept coaxing him on, even trying a smile, saying, 'Daddy, we need more than that if you're going to keep me happy.' I'd never done heroin or used a needle to take anything, but I'd seen how junkies were: greedy.

He snapped at me, 'I always go first. You wait!' When he took that larger hit all in one, he was momentarily too high to move. He was sitting with his back to me on the edge of the bed, at that nodding phase only a user knows, the moment of total surrender that happens immediately after the payload starts coursing through the blood directly to the brain.

This was my chance. I raised my right knee up to my chest and pushed against the wall, and with all the force I could muster I kicked him in the back of his neck. There was a *pop* as he fell forward.

As I bolted for the door, he yelled a final threat at me. 'If you fuck me over, they will never find your body either!'

I ran like hell to the pool hall, where I told Carl everything. He took me to a safe house. No argument from me – I needed to get out of the Cross as soon as I could and not look back. Whatever I was looking for, I could now see that it didn't lie in the streets of Kings Cross. What was it that I was searching so desperately for, that I would put my life in danger to find it? Was I even worthy of anything better?

My encounter with the pimp had left me feeling dirty and scared. It had been too close for comfort, and I knew whatever decision I made next would have an effect on the rest of my life.

Nikki's body was never found. No charges were ever laid. But the Cross has its own rough justice, and someone knocking off the working girls brought unwanted attention. My almost-pimp disappeared not long after my exit from the Cross; his body was never found either. Rumour had it he'd taken up permanent residence in Sydney Harbour. I wished he'd been killed for what he'd done to Nikki, but that wasn't the case: he was just a mad dog who had to be taken care of, so order could return to the streets. There was no justice for Nikki, only business as usual.

4

BORN TO RUN

IT WAS TIME FOR me to take control of my life. I had no idea what this meant or how I could accomplish it, I just knew that if I didn't make a change now, I might never get off this dangerous ride I'd found myself on.

My first step was to leave the share house and stop selling drugs. Then to distance myself from the dangerous people I'd become close to. I'd met two girls on my travels through the Cross, whose lives were very different from what I'd been exposed to, so I moved in with them. These girls were all about clubbing, and they wanted to show me the ropes. They knew all the doormen, owners and A-listers – and all of this, I was quickly finding out, was normal for a couple of motivated young women.

I was about to have my first club experience. When Saturday night finally arrived, we walked the short distance through the Cross and down William Street. On that walk, for the first time I saw clearly what I was leaving behind, and I was grateful I'd survived it. I casually nodded recognition to some but ignored most of the faces. That was my goodbye. I was moving on.

Then I was standing outside a single-storey venue with its bright, flashing, arc-shaped lighted front. How had I never noticed it before? Inside, it seemed smaller than the hype my flatmates had given it for a solid week, and just a little more worn-out than I'd expected. But it was still wonderful. This was my first encounter with the Whisky a Go Go.

An American funk/soul band was playing that night, so the place was packed. As if a starter's pistol had been fired, both girls were off and running: hugging one person while waving to another, blowing kisses across the room. Their transformation was something to see. I would soon find out this was called 'working the room'.

I've always been a shy person, which may sound strange for someone who up till this point had often done extremely spontaneous things with strangers. I think what drove me to take all those risks was a fear that if I stopped moving, I would just disappear. Now, I was happy to hang back and watch the scene unfolding before me, a technique I use to evaluate a room and get my bearings. I found I liked to watch these club goers; there was an ease to them, an air of confidence. They interested me, and I wanted to feel what they felt. I needed to find a way to make this my future. I wasn't interested in becoming someone's girlfriend – I wanted to be involved in the scene.

The people who devoted their lives to the music industry stood out to me. I'd seen them in restaurants, bars, even on the streets. I could always pick them out in a crowd, as if there was some secret handshake that until that moment I hadn't known I knew. They moved easily through the Cross but weren't a part of it; I could just tell they were a part of something else, something bigger.

Within a short amount of time I noticed one guy who stood out from the rest. When he appeared, everyone in the group

A chance encounter at the Whisky a Go Go in Sydney would change my life. (CITY OF SYDNEY ARCHIVE)

that had gathered turned to acknowledge him. I watched him interact with them – then suddenly he left them, walked right up to me and said, 'You came down with the girls? My name is Swampy, are you okay? Do you need anything?'

I was a little taken aback but managed to mumble, 'No. I'm okay, thank you.'

'Do you like American music? Are you a fan of the band?'

'I have no idea who the band is. I like all music, but most of all I'm curious to see what the show's going be like.'

Swampy took my hand and led me to an area where two guys were working with some sort of technical-looking control panel – it turned out to be the front-of-house sound console. Swampy told me, 'Stand here for the show. It's the best place to watch from. I'll check in on you soon. If you want a drink, just ask the guy with the dark hair behind the bar. Tell him you're with me.' He quickly headed towards the backstage area.

There I stood, waiting for the show to start, wondering about the person who'd just placed me there. Swampy (whose real name I would learn was Wane Jarvis) presented like a living, breathing Marlboro Man, with his perfectly pressed faded denim shirt and jeans accessorised with the leather belt and cowboy boots, topped off with blond curly hair and a summer glow. He could have stepped right out of one of the billboards that shone brightly in Sydney wherever the young money ventured. I was once asked, 'If you could live anywhere, where would it be?' My response was 'A Martini & Rossi ad'. I never bought the drink, but I wanted to go to the exotic places on their billboards. The living, breathing Swampy, I would learn, was way more substantial than his counterparts in those ads.

I had a great time that night. Even after my constant barrage of questions about the show and how it all worked, Swampy invited me back for the second and final show the following evening. I jumped at the opportunity – finally, music back in my life again!

I'd found myself fascinated by everything that was happening onstage. For the first time I realised there was a lot more up there than a bunch of guys playing music. People offstage were working with the band to make everything from the sound and lighting to guitar changes happen. I couldn't take in enough of what I was witnessing; I had to learn more. I knew right then and there this was what I'd been looking for. I had a strange feeling of knowing something I didn't yet know and waiting for the penny to drop – for it all to fall into place, to make sense.

What I also learnt from that first night is that there's strength in knowing the details and getting it right. When Swampy discovered I was about to try my first alcoholic beverage ever, he had a cocktail created for me by the barman he'd told me to go to earlier that evening. Even though the club was packed, the barman stopped what he was doing to create a drink for me. As I'd never had alcohol before, the men turned it into a bit of a game.

Swampy asked me, 'Do you like sweet or bitter?'

'Sweet,' I said.

The barman reached behind himself, pulled a bottle off the rack and added some to a long tall glass with ice in it.

'Do you like creamy or fizzy?'

'Creamy, mostly, but fizzy too.'

'Tea or coffee?'

And so it went until we had an original cocktail. We called it a Strawberry Blonde: one part vodka, one part Tia Maria, Coca-Cola, cream, with a drizzle of cherry brandy over the top. Making everything perfect is what a good roadie does. And, yes, it was perfect!

* * *

I arrived the next evening after the band had started playing. What had sounded great the night before was now very different, not good at all. I took up my position at the front-of-house console beside Swampy and asked him, 'What's happened?'

'The sound man has happened! He's got a problem with his sound that he really needs to fix.' Swampy called out in the direction of a very flustered crew member, with a telling look that let the guy know he'd be in worse trouble if he didn't get it together.

It turned out that the front-of-house sound guy had overindulged the previous night and wasn't coping with what had happened earlier that day. He'd turned up to the venue with the band right before the show was due to start, not realising that the club's cleaners had given his sound console a little wipe-down – in the process changing all his settings from the previous show. He was now struggling to fix it. Note to self: stay calm under pressure and always check your equipment.

I didn't stay that night for the quality of the show; I stayed to see if the sound guy would get it together. While others were complaining, I found this whole fiasco fascinating. Up until now, I'd had no idea this was how the live concert thing worked. I just had to learn more. Whenever Swampy had a moment that night, I asked him more about his job and how everything worked. 'What does it mean when the singer keeps pointing to his ear? It doesn't look like a good thing.' Then, 'Who is the guy that keeps bringing things onstage, then leaving, but not playing an instrument or anything?'

Swampy's answer to that question was: 'He's the roadie.'

That was the first time I heard the term 'roadie'.

'What's a roadie?'

Swampy briefly explained the term, then told me that he and his crew were off to Melbourne the next day with the band. If you did this job, not only did you get paid, but you got to travel as well – nice!

* * *

After my two nights at the Whisky a Go Go, things quietened down for a week or so. One of my new roommates was missing her home town of Melbourne and she was broke. Her parents wouldn't send her any more money. She mentioned that some friends of hers in a band called Fox were coming up to play a gig, and she thought they might give her a free ride back to Melbourne. This band had a hit song and was enjoying a modicum of success.

The venue was all the way across town, and we only arrived in time for their last set. They sounded pretty good and seemed like a nice enough bunch when I got introduced. We hung around having a couple of drinks after the show, and at first it was fun, but then it was getting later and later, and the subject of her getting a ride hadn't been brought up. I felt a little restless and the longer everyone sat there drinking and chatting the less likely it seemed they'd make it out of the club let alone the eight hundred kilometres or so back to Melbourne.

I finally broached the subject. 'So, guys! What about giving Chrissy a lift?'

The room went quiet. After a lot of fidgeting and sideways glances, Peter Laffy, the lead guitarist, said, 'If the crew get loaded out of here in time –' pointing to the stage '– then she can go back with them tonight. Otherwise, forget it.'

I looked in the direction of the stage – there were two guys staggering around and looking the worse for wear. I couldn't figure out what, if anything, they were getting done.

I had an idea. 'What if I give them a hand?'

The band members all smiled – well, laughed really – and said, 'Sure, why not!' as they continued to nudge and wink at each other while calling to their crew, 'She's going to come give you guys a hand with the gear.'

So, with a couple of pointers on what equipment they felt was safe for me to touch, which came down to the drum kit,

I got started. Me jumping in added momentum to the load-out – a guy roadie does *not* like to be shown up by a girl – and the three of us efficiently packed away the gear. After the guys explained the correct way to coil a cable, I was also allowed to help there. When it came time to load the truck, they were surprised by my strength and once again let me help. With the truck doors closed, off they went down the road with Chrissy sandwiched between the guys in the front seat.

Fox band members: (left to right) Neil Hodgson, Peter Laffy, Les Oldman and Michael Upton. The very first band to hire me in Australia. Thanks, guys! (NATHAN BRENNER)

A short time later, Fox came back to Sydney one crew member short and called the flat, asking if I wanted to come to the shows, and if I would help out with the gear. Sure, why not? If I did this right, maybe I could get out of the Cross at last. I liked the work and could see a glimpse of myself becoming a part of this group. If I did it right, maybe even relocate to Melbourne and keep working for them. Well, I did it right, and they offered me my first job as a roadie. They hired me to do backline, which meant looking after all the equipment onstage. I was officially now part of a two-man crew.

I needed a place to stay in Melbourne, so I tracked down my mother and offered to pay rent. She had a nice penthouse apartment, but she was alone. 'The quiet' still scared her, so with the offer of cash and company she said yes. I was stronger now, and she knew that if we were ever to rebuild any sort of relationship, we'd need to start somewhere. With me working nights and her days, I hoped we could make it work, at least until I had a better idea of what my new job entailed.

I got the hell out of Sydney and, from humble beginnings, my career was launched.

* * *

With my arrival in Melbourne, everything in my life changed drastically once again. I was settling in to work as a roadie, even though the extent of my relevant resumé was as follows: I had drummed in my primary school marching band, I had tuned and restrung guitars, I had helped pack up a drum kit, knew how to coil a cable, and I'd now worked a few paid gigs as a roadie. Also, I could roll a really good joint! But these limited skills were now coming in handy, even though Peter Laffy rarely let his guitar out of his hands.

It helped that nothing scared me. If I was told to do something, that was what I did. I was constantly looking and learning, and I was getting to know a lot of the A-team crew guys who worked for other bands. At the last show Fox had played before we'd left Sydney, I'd run into Swampy and he'd introduced me to a bunch of the crew guys on the other show, which helped when I got to Melbourne. Anyone can lift boxes, most people can drive a van, and some can learn how to plug in all the equipment – the real difference between a roadie and a wannabe was a mental one. There was a 'member of a club' mentality. To belong, you had to commit to the lifestyle. You had to commit to the band. You had to commit to making the show happen, no matter what the personal cost. And you had to be able to think outside the box. Oh, and the band had to like you! They needed to be able to trust you would do the job and have their back.

That club member mentality bound us roadies together and made us a crew – and, at the same time, separated us from everyone else. Belonging to this crew would be what separated me from the girls and women who turned up at the shows wanting to meet the band and often settled for meeting the crew. Aside from me, no women were turning up to load the gear.

It took a while for me to adjust to the job at hand, and a while longer before I even had time to consider the fact that there weren't any other female roadies. I didn't ever ask anyone about it, as I was worried that if I brought attention to the fact I was the only one, then maybe I would be thrown out of my new club. I dressed like the boys! Drank like the boys! Even swore like the boys! Most importantly, though, I worked hard like the boys! I didn't go into this field with the view that I was doing anything special or unusual; it was all about the music and a feeling of belonging. For all their gruff exteriors, these wild men had a gentler, more protective, side that they would deny vehemently, but I'd seen it, so I knew I would be safe here.

I was unaware of the recent global feminist movement in which women were burning their bras and standing up for equality in the workplace. I never wore a bra, but nonetheless I was striving for equality on a daily basis, without politics on my radar. I was just looking for a safe place to land. It was the call of music once again, changing the course of my life.

Swampy said he wasn't at all surprised to see me working for a band; he said I was a natural, that he was happy for me. And when I arrived in Melbourne already knowing some crew guys and already having a job, nobody saw me as a threat or even bothered to ask how long I'd been doing this. I never told anyone about my experiences in the Cross, where I'd come from, or how I'd ended up here.

Everything was changing so fast. What I didn't realise was that it wasn't only from my perspective – the entire structure of the music industry worldwide was changing right at that very moment. Big things were about to happen. This also helped me take my position as a female roadie: everyone was busy looking out for themselves, not wondering about me.

* * *

While a band needs a good manager, in those days they couldn't survive the long haul without a great booking agent. A band had to play live to get a following, and a great booking agent would get them national shows that would increase their press coverage and fan awareness, which could translate to a record deal and hopefully a substantial amount of money negotiated by a manager. New bands would argue about which was more important: a manager or a booking agent, hoping not to have to pay both. A good manager would guide their careers, while a good agent would work them within an inch of their life. Having both was ideal. This, however, was the era of the booking agent.

Fox was working at least three, sometimes four, shows a week, but this wasn't a lot by 1970s Australian standards. They weren't getting the momentum they'd hoped for. This was when the cracks in the band started to show.

Every Monday I'd go into the booking office, Premier Artists, to pick up the gig list for the week. Mondays were usually a no-show day and became a bit of a social event for roadies as we could all catch up on what was going on with each other's bands. On one of these visits I was approached by an agent named Bill Joseph, who asked if he could have a word. When he got me off to one side, he said, 'Would you be interested in working for a different band, Tana?'

I nodded.

'Then come join me in my office.'

I followed him upstairs to discuss the possibilities. The music industry can be brutal, and Bill came right to the point. 'I know you like working for the guys in Fox, but they aren't going to last. Bookings are slowing down, and I don't know how much longer they'll be together.'

'But they do really well at the shows!' I replied, trying to stand up for them – as if my feelings could change their future.

'That's great you're loyal to them, I'm looking for someone loyal, but when they finish, what are you going to do? Who's going to give you another gig? It's always better to go from one band to another without any downtime. Downtime can kill you.'

I hadn't thought about that before – I'd presumed we would just keep rolling along. This was a bit scary. For the first time I saw how it could all come crashing down around me. I'd made some friends among my fellow roadies, but did that mean they would give me a job over one of their old mates? Over another guy? I didn't want to find out.

To call Bill Joseph just a booking agent doesn't do credit to his substantial contribution to the Australian music industry. So when he spoke, I listened. The job offer could have been for any of the big-name bands: Billy Thorpe, Skyhooks, Split Enz, Little River Band, Ayers Rock, The Dingoes, Daddy Cool, Buster Brown, Lobby Loyde – the list goes on. He told me about a band that was moving from Sydney to Melbourne, just like I had. I'd never heard of them.

Bill said, 'The two blokes who formed the band are brothers around your age, and they're really into family. We want to make them comfortable being away from home, and I think this job would work well for all of you. We're setting up a house for them and their crew to live in, so everyone is together – that way there are no distractions.'

The fact that I could live away from my mother was a big selling point.

Bill added that he wanted me to start as soon as possible and, as Michael Browning's business partner in their management company TPM, he put me forward for the gig. The Boys had just arrived in town from Sydney – as part of the contract they'd signed, they had been expected to relocate to Melbourne. Lansdowne Road, East St Kilda, would become their base. They were raring to start playing live the music they were recording back in Sydney at Albert Studios. If I was in, he would call his partner into the room:

the man who would eventually take them out of Australia, Michael Browning. The band was AC/DC.

Michael also had an office in that building, known as Mushroom House, the hub of the Melbourne music industry. I took the name as a good sign from my hippie days and felt right at home. It was where another Michael's career got established: a Michael Gudinski, who founded the Mushroom Empire and ran the largest booking agency in Australia: Premier Artists. In fact, several of today's most recognised names on the business side of the Australian music industry came out of that building. I was in good company.

Michael Browning and Bill Joseph were very different people who would serve two very different roles for AC/DC. Bill was the money-man, a behind-the-scenes old-school kind of guy, who had also managed Bon in his early days with the Valentines. A fatherly type who I liked a lot. Michael was a hustler who got out there to make sure it all happened; he was smooth, a charmer. He'd managed Billy Thorpe and the Aztecs, and he owned, with Bill, one of the hottest clubs in Melbourne, the Hard Rock Cafe. He fit the bill to take AC/DC to the charts.

After meeting with both men, I was on board. AC/DC were still in the process of recording their first album, *High Voltage*, at Albert Studios in Sydney. If I was in, they needed my commitment now. I was to be the band's first backline roadie with this new configuration, which would mean looking after all the stage equipment, instruments and vocals for Bon when rehearsing. I'd set up the equipment for the live shows and wrangle Angus and his cable during the shows, making sure he and Bon didn't get tangled up. Between shows, I'd make sure – on our tight budget – that the brothers had strings. I would even find a way to set up their first drum sponsorship through the local drum shop Billy Hyde's. There was also to be no questioning what was expected of us, schedule-wise. Just do it. That part wasn't negotiable. Fine by me, as I couldn't get out of my mother's place soon enough. Each roadie and band member would be paid a weekly wage of $60 for food and incidentals; everything else would be covered by management. I felt like I'd just won the lottery – no rent to pay, away from my mother and a $60 wage! I would be the only crew person to live in the house with the band for the first few months until Ralph became our second permanent hire. The plan was that the Boys would continue to travel back and forth to Sydney to complete the recording, while also playing shows around Melbourne to test the new material.

I'm sure Michael already knew he could use the fact that I was a female somewhere down the line, and he did. He would also solidify his position of band manager by

The AC/DC the world first got to know: (left to right) Malcolm Young, Bon Scott, Angus Young, Phil Rudd and Mark Evans. London, 1976.
(MICHAEL PUTLAND/GETTY IMAGES)

working closely one on one with Malcolm coursing the band's future.

The next step was for me to meet the band. They were in town for the next day only, then heading back to Sydney to continue work on the album. This would give me a week to finish up with Fox, get my few belongings from my mother's penthouse and move in for their return.

Right after that meeting, Michael drove me to a house in East St Kilda where I would meet the Boys.

5

SHE'S GOT BALLS

IT WAS AUGUST OF '74 and summer was still a distant promise when I first pulled up outside the unassuming single-storey brick home on a tree-lined street in a quiet middle-class suburb of Melbourne. The house was large with several bedrooms but nothing special, maybe a little scruffier than its neighbours with a couple of rosebushes and a hedge as reminders of a time when its garden was cared for. None of this bothered me. I hadn't come to see a garden – I'd come to meet the band. Standing there for that brief moment, scuffing my shoes on the cracked footpath, waiting for Michael Browning to lead the way, I had no inkling of what waited for me beyond that ordinary front door.

In the entryway to the house there was a sense of a more glorious time that had passed. We'd let ourselves in, and Michael led me around a corner to the living room. I held back as he walked up to the group of six men casually standing around a table towards a kitchen area at the back. As a greeting, Michael placed his hand on the shoulder of a tall, blond guy in his late twenties, while shaking the hand of the one who appeared to be the other's business partner, a shorter guy of similar age with dark hair. These two were Harry Vanda and George Young, respectively. I guessed they were in charge, as Michael had gone to them first. He called over his shoulder, 'Tana, come meet everyone.'

The conversation stopped as they all turned to look in my direction, their smiles so big that I didn't feel nervous.

Brother George, as he was referred to by the inner circle, took the lead. 'How are you doing? Tana, is it?'

'Yes!'

'Come closer,' he said. 'We won't bite.'

And they all laughed, breaking the ice.

'You've an accent,' I said as I walked over.

'Yeah, we're all Scottish. Well –' pointing to the tall blond guy '– except Harry; he's Dutch, but he may as well be Scottish, as he's family.' Then George introduced me to one of the two guys who were closer to my age. 'This is Malcolm; he's my younger brother. He plays guitar and is the one who writes most of the music.'

In those early days, writing was a formula that started with Malcolm coming up with a riff and feel for a song, even an entire song's rhythm section. Then it would get worked over, expanded upon with George's guidance, then Angus would add his lead parts. Finally, Bon would be called in to add the lyrics that defined the feel of the song. (The three brothers would work closely together like this when working on Vanda/Young music also, for the likes of Stevie Wright and Jon Paul Young.)

I looked to Malcolm, who was standing with his hands shoved in his pockets, his shoulders slightly hunched. He did a little shuffle with his feet as he took a step forward. Then he looked up, a big smile spreading across his face.

He reached out, shook my hand and said, 'Hi Tana!' tilting his head slightly to one side. The body language before the handshake, I later learnt, had been Malcolm doing a quick evaluation to see if he thought he could trust me. The Youngs always screened people before dropping their guard.

Then it was the other guy's turn. 'Meet Angus, our youngest brother. He plays lead guitar.'

Angus, who was smoking a cigarette, looked like he'd just woken up – literally. (I would come to know that he always looked that way on a day off.) He followed Malcom's suit, stepping forward in a more reserved, but still friendly, way, after putting down his cup of tea and cigarette. Then with a distinctive, gravelly voice, he said, 'Yeah, hi, how ya doing?'

Bon Scott reached over between George and Harry. 'I'm not a Young or young –' Bon humour '– but I am Scottish! I'm the singer, and I write the naughty lyrics,' he said with a sly grin, slightly raising one eyebrow. He added that he was 'the old man of the group'.

Peter Clack was introduced as the drummer, and then Harry Vanda got a more formal introduction as the other half, with George, of the production team for *High Voltage*.

With these introductions over, they didn't stand on ceremony; they all started talking and smoking cigarettes at the same time. There was a buzz in the room as though they were on the brink of something big.

So that was the end of my job interview. I'd recently turned seventeen, and I'd just had my first encounter with the heart, soul and driving force of AC/DC. Of course, I didn't know much about the band yet – they were only just starting out and hadn't played any shows in town.

We all moved to take seats in the living room where we kept chatting.

Malcolm told me, 'We had a version of AC/DC that played gigs in Sydney mostly, and then we did some in Adelaide, where we met Bon!' nodding in his direction. 'And even one show in Melbourne, where we met Browning.' They always called Michael by his surname. 'It just didn't work out with those other guys. Our manager and singer sucked, and after getting stuck in Perth, we called it quits.'

The two members to survive that line-up were here in front of me looking for a fresh start.

'It's time for us to get serious,' Malcolm said. 'We need to steer away from a pop image. We want a harder edge. We want to play rock'n'roll. Bon can bring that.'

Angus added, 'We're all close, and we like to work that way.'

I told them, 'You can count me in!'

The Young clan had a history in the Australian music scene: George had been a founding member of The Easybeats with Harry, and both had tasted international success with that band. But I was too young to know the backstory, or those of Bon's earlier bands. I was just taking these guys at face value, and I liked what I was seeing. I had no concept of the talent standing right there in that room just chatting and joking. What I saw clearly, though, was their conviction about what was to come.

Later that day the brothers picked up guitars and started working together. Malcolm and Angus played parts with George and Harry talking them through the process for their next studio session, 'Try this chord here. Yeah, that sounds good.' Bon wandered off with a pen and notepad, disappearing into another room; he would reappear when called to contribute lyrics. That was how 'Soul Stripper' and just about every song was written.

I knew I wanted to be a part of this. I liked them right away. I was in!

I learnt that once they'd completed *High Voltage*, we would start a rigorous schedule of live shows to support the album. Until they found a permanent bass player, George would fill in where possible. They would also need a new drummer. Peter would play drums for shows until they found someone.

* * *

Not long after this meeting, and while still recording, we started rehearsals at Lansdowne Road. We converted one of the front bedrooms into a designated space that was in constant use day and night. Mal would stand in on drums or bass so they could work on the songs as they got more familiar with playing them live. They would all do whatever it took to get the music to where it needed to be. Bon would even jump in on drums if the brothers were working on guitar pieces. Malcolm and Angus would spend hours huddled together in the living room working on tracks until they were just right; they never settled for near enough. They had a clear plan and weren't going to let anything distract them from it, and you were either on board or not. I was 110 per cent on board, so I got on with looking after all the stage equipment and instruments; my job didn't include cooking or cleaning.

At our first meeting, Mal and Angus had asked how I would feel about living in that house on Lansdowne Road, and I'd said it would be great. They had also asked if my mother would be okay with it, and I assured them yes. But it seemed they were still concerned about this, and not because they had any idea about my real age – they wanted my mother's permission purely because I was a girl. So, when they returned from Sydney, I organised for the band to have a meal at her apartment on the St Kilda Esplanade; she could tell them herself that everything was okay. What struggling band is going to turn down a free meal?

While my mother may have been a lot of things, she also happened to be a good cook and a generous host. She loved being the centre of attention. After a lot of great food and plenty to drink, I was deemed free to move in to the house. And after an incident in which the barbecue burst into flames, the band all agreed that this would probably be safest for me.

The funniest thing about that meal was watching Bon flirt with my mother, ostensibly to convince her to let me live with the band. He was definitely a ladies' man, and I'm sure he was just trying to wind me up that day – he loved to wind me up.

From then on it was official: Lansdowne Road was my new home, and AC/DC my new band. Little did the Boys know that my mother was glad to have me gone. She'd done well for herself since I'd fled her home those years prior, and God forbid I cramp her style or let slip I was the youngest of four children.

* * *

Those Lansdowne Road days were a very busy time indeed. Creativity was bursting out of every room. There was no time to waste: with *High Voltage* now finished, the hunt was on for a rhythm section to enable us to start touring in earnest. George played bass on several shows in those early days, but he had other commitments. We were constantly working on new material. We were either rehearsing or sitting around the stereo playing all the music that each of us loved. The band used it to get to know each other better. As new members joined it was a way to get them on the same page musically for the direction Malcolm wanted to go. Bon was mad about Alex Harvey, Free and Elvis, while Malcolm and Angus were into old-school blues and rock'n'roll like Chuck Berry and Jerry Lee Lewis, and we all enjoyed a smattering of Bad Company along with ZZ Top's *Tres Hombres*, but the blues was best. I think they let me play stuff that I liked just to make me feel a part of it.

I learnt a lot about music from those early days at Lansdowne Road. During one of these sessions, Malcolm and Angus played Elvis Presley's 'Heartbreak Hotel', a song Malcolm used to play in one of his earlier bands. I cringed. They asked me why, and I told them, 'I do not like Elvis, or his songs.' But my only experiences with Elvis were those hideous movies; I'd never heard his earlier blues/gospel-influenced songs. They obviously thought I'd lost my mind and had spent way too long in the rainforest. Malcolm turned up the next day to set me straight with an album that he wanted me to hear. It was *Insane Asylum*. The singer was Kathi McDonald and the song was 'Heartbreak Hotel'. Mal knew I liked Janis Joplin, so he figured this was something I would relate to because Kathi had worked with Janis and they had some stylistic similarities. He sat me down and said, 'Listen to this and tell me what you think.' When the track finished, I looked over to him. He didn't have a smug 'I told you so' expression; it was more a 'Yeah? You get it!' look. I learnt two things that day. The first was that a song can have many lives, and the second was that Malcolm truly loved music and cared enough to show me how one song can resonate with different people through different versions. A good song is a good song. The album was mine to keep.

Something changed after that day. We spoke a lot from that time on. I'm not sure if it was just getting to know each other better or if Malcolm was getting homesick and missed the closeness of family. But I was becoming someone he could talk to, let his guard fall a little around, without affecting the dynamic with the other band members. These conversations weren't to do with the songwriting but more to do with the people we were starting to get to know who would come to the house, or what I thought of Browning – we only ever called him Browning – or how the rehearsal had sounded. Never anything about other bands we'd be playing with. As a crew person I would have closer dealings with other bands and their crews, but that stuff didn't matter to Mal. He rarely interacted with outsiders.

It was a tight circle, and that was how they wanted it. The juggernaut was about to hit high gear with no looking back. No stopping it.

Browning had started booking shows immediately, even before the album was finished. It was now urgent that we find both a drummer and a bass player. George and Harry had started working with their old singer from The Easybeats, Stevie Wright, on what would become a trilogy of songs called 'Evie' (Parts I, II & III), and the finished product would relaunch Stevie's career. Harry had already returned to Sydney to hold down the fort at Albert Studios.

These were the formative years. They not only set the standard for my lifelong work ethic but also my commitment to AC/DC. This included being present at the selection of the line-up that would pull all the pieces together to build the iconic sound of the AC/DC the world first got to know.

It was the end of 1974 and we had a show booked in Adelaide, Bon's old stomping ground. We needed to rent a truck to get the gear there. Now, this was a slight problem, as I didn't drive yet. We decided to hire someone to drive, who could also help with the gear, and I put the word out to see who'd be available. As it turned out, a drummer who'd played with both Lobby Loyde and Angry Anderson's Buster Brown really wanted a shot at auditioning for AC/DC. I was given this information by Karen Sullivan, who was managing Buster Brown at the time. The drummer's name was Phil Rudd. Phil and I came up with a plan: he would drive the truck, while I'd make sure he just happened to be playing Peter's drum kit when the band arrived at the venue for sound check so they would hear him. The rest, as they say, is

Angus, Mal and George Young at Albert's. This tried-and-true writing process created their hits. (PHILIP MORRIS)

history. Phil was hired when we got back to Melbourne and he moved in to the house.

I think Phil is a prime example of how the different parts of a band feed off each other to become great. Yes, he was a good drummer, or he wouldn't have got the gig. Yes, he was young, just starting out in his field, but in a different band would he have evolved into the drummer he became? I firmly believe that the sum of all parts allows each of the individuals to accomplish greatness. What they do with it is up to them. Some can't go the distance.

Now we only needed two things: a bass player, and someone who could drive the truck.

I was watching Mal's vision become reality. Part of that involved honing Angus's persona, and not just as an amazing guitar player. Mal wanted to get away from the satin and the outfits they'd worn before they decided rock'n'roll was best, and place the focus on Angus. 'Just make it interesting. Keep 'em watching! Go crazy.' That was Mal's take on it, and Bon added, 'Don't worry about me, I'll get out of your way, and Tana will keep an eye on the cables, so we don't get all tangled up.' Malcolm knew this persona would give Angus more say in the band. While they'd often spoken about it at home, none of us saw it until they hit the stage – that was when Angus came into his own. He does need to be given full credit for portraying the world's most out-of-control schoolboy. Angus in those days was rather reserved, even shy in a way; the moment he put on his school uniform, though, he had no fear. He gave me many a worrying moment early on, when it was my job to watch out for him on stage, by clambering up on anything and everything he could. Once he started wandering through the audience, we knew we'd created a monster.

The equipment in those days was set up by us at each venue, using whatever we could to find a way to make it all fit. This might include putting a couple of small round bar tables side by side to hold the PA speaker cabinets. The idea being to keep these cabinets off the stage so Angus would have more room to run around – of course, he had other ideas and saw them as more terrain to bound up onto. When a manic guitar player was added to one of those stacks, it became a teetering tower with me at the bottom trying to hold it all together. I would try to give him a heads up before he went onstage: 'Angus, the PA today is really shaky. It might not be a good idea for you to climb on it.' Yeah, that worked as well as 'Can you keep your guitar volume down a bit onstage, as Bon's vocals need a little help to get over the wall of sound?' All I'd get would be a two-second warning during the show, when Angus would throw me one of his wicked grins from a sweaty and snot-covered face to let me know that whatever he was about to do, I'd just have to keep up and hopefully not let him get hurt. It was like herding cats.

With all this going on, and Bon stepping up to interact with Angus, the AC/DC style was emerging. Give credit to Bon – not many lead singers would willingly share the spotlight in the way he did. 'Hey, whatever it takes,' was his answer to most things. There were egos involved, but the chemistry won out. And I think for Bon, these onstage antics brought him closer to the Youngs, helping to bridge the age gap.

* * *

I was there for a lot of firsts with this band. The first of many appearances on *Countdown*. The first hit single, to be followed by the first hit album: *High Voltage* launched on 17 February 1975. From the first pub gig to the first shows with 1200, 2000, 5000, 16,000 in attendance, and all in quick succession, and all a thing of beauty. These milestones would quickly become the everyday.

We'd been gigging for a few months now, playing everything from school halls to ice-skating rinks for the kids, to pubs. Lots of pubs.

* * *

In January 1975 I got the news that we were booked for our biggest show yet: the Sunbury Pop Festival. Since 1972 it had been held on the Australia Day long weekend, which had

Fifa Riccobono, down at Angus's right side, always looking out for her boys.
(PHILIP MORRIS)

become the three days of the year that Aussies spent watching bands while getting very drunk and rowdy, usually in the mud.

The introduction to the festival of international bands had started with Queen a year earlier and been met with mixed to negative reactions. The promoters were of the mind that if there wasn't a major band from somewhere else, the festival wouldn't cut it; in fact, it had done quite well without it for the first couple of years. Australia as a nation still had the mindset that anything Australian was somehow inferior.

AC/DC was booked to play right before Deep Purple, who were down to close the show as the international headliner. Our plan was simple: to blow Purple off the stage and properly introduce all of Australia to AC/DC a few weeks before the record went on sale.

Great plan, but not quite what happened.

Sunbury was a bust. It was pretty much rained out, and attendance was down from 24,000 the previous year to 16,000. The weather was miserable and the crowd wasn't feeling the love. Word had got out to the Deep Purple camp about the mood of the audience and the fact the sky could open up at any time. To add to their problems, some local band was threatening to blow them off the stage – that would be us.

There have been many different accounts of what happened that day. From my point of view of being right in the thick of things, it went something like this.

George Young was in town to play with the band for the Sunbury show, as they didn't want to take any chances by rushing to pick a bass player. I also think he was really looking forward to playing with his brothers to such a large crowd.

We arrived at the festival site some sixty kilometres outside of Melbourne and, apart from the mud, at first it looked like it could be fun. The band went backstage to the dressing-room area while I headed for the stage – I needed to get straight to work getting all our backline equipment ready for when I was called to set it up. But as soon as I started heading for the stage, I was stopped by security. He was a big guy, and I guessed not all that happy with his position as he looked a bit grumpy. 'You can't come back here, little lady,' he told me condescendingly.

'It's okay, I'm with the band,' I naively replied.

'Well then, you had better go find them, because you can't be here.'

That was when I realised he didn't believe me. 'No, you don't understand, I'm AC/DC's roadie.'

'I won't tell you again!' He folded his arms across his chest as he took a step towards me.

Just then a loud voice from up on the stage called down to the security guy. 'No, mate, for real! She's their roadie, you have to let her up here.' I'd been saved by Scrooge, one of the crew guys I knew through Swampy. Only after his say-so, was I allowed onstage – my word meant nothing. There were often these awkward moments when I'd have to convince someone that I really should be there, that this was in fact my job and I wasn't there to pick up musicians.

With that out of the way, my focus for the day was purely on the stage, the equipment, and making sure we got a fair shot at performing. I checked the running order for the bands to know when we were meant to go on. Once the stage was cleared of equipment from the band before us, I started to set up our gear. The whole idea was to be quick, so the crowd didn't get any more restless.

'You ready, Tana?' asked the stage manager.

'Yeah. Go ahead and mic it.'

No sooner had I said that than I was sent word to strike it, take it all down. Had I set it up too soon? Was there meant to be another band on before us? I was just told to strike it.

I went looking for the Boys to see what was happening. It turned out that Deep Purple had been having second thoughts about waiting to close the show, and now they wanted to go on next. What with the weather and all, yeah right! Michael Browning, the band and Brother George were standing off the side of the stage, huddled in a group.

'What's going on?' I asked.

AC/DC were standing their ground, saying they would play the spot they'd been booked to play. Browning told me, 'Don't worry about it, just go back and set up the gear.'

Back I went to do it all again. Now, the part of the job I was most uncomfortable with in those early days was going onstage when an audience was present. Eventually, they would figure out I was a girl and start whooping and hollering; it was always embarrassing to me. During this second set-up, a bored, restless and drunk audience did just that. 'Look, it's a sheila!' one heckler called, while another thought he was funny with, 'Don't hurt yourself, little girl.' I hated it but just got on with the job, pretending I couldn't hear any of it, hoping it would be over soon.

Not so, I'm afraid. Again, I got the word to strike it all. This was bullshit! I went towards the back of the stage where AC/DC were arguing with a bunch of men who turned out to be Purple's management and crew. What now? Purple were demanding to go on next, and AC/DC were having none of it. 'We're going on next, as that is the spot we were booked to play.' It was George's voice I could hear over the others. Purple's management not only wanted us to go on after them, they wanted us to wait until after they had removed all their equipment, including sound and lighting. This would mean we would be lucky to go on before two in the morning – after everyone had left. Everyone was yelling, and then the shoving started. One of Purple's crew knocked Angus, and it was on.

Unintentional or not, it didn't matter at this point. The Youngs had a very strong clan mentality, which was part of what I loved about them. You did not mess with one of their own.

The next thing I knew, George was swinging. I jumped in and got between him and some English guy on Purple's crew – I'd agreed to be loyal to the band, and I wasn't about to let the Boys get beaten up by anyone.

Then it just erupted. Lots of men jumped in, while security tried to break it up. In the middle of it all, AC/DC were standing back to back, still refusing to budge. Browning, looking a little flustered, hustled the Boys away, and I heard a 'Fuck this!' yelled out as a parting gesture.

Purple got what they wanted that day: they got rid of AC/DC, as the Boys refused to play last. But AC/DC got all the press. None of the Australian bands at the festival got paid anyway, as the promoter went bust after paying Deep Purple. AC/DC had shown they weren't about to be pushed around by a bunch of Poms who they saw as well past their prime. They would do it their way. I admired them for that.

AC/DC had created a stir, the first of many, and the album was about to hit. This should have been Browning's first warning sign as to who was really in control of the ship.

* * *

Our search for another roadie who could drive and help with the gear was resolved when Bon suggested a good one from his days in a band called Fraternity. We'd tried a few, but none had stuck, so Ralph was hired. Again, keeping the circle tight. One down, one to go: we still needed a bass player.

The album release was only a couple of weeks away, and we'd already auditioned a bunch of guys. There were certain requirements involving both talent and personality – and, of course, they had to look the part. Each audition had two rounds. In the first, the applicant didn't even get to plug in, he just talked to Malcolm and Angus about what music he liked, how he approached playing, and where he saw himself fitting into the band. This was a set-up for failure to the unprepared – which was great, as it minimised the amount of bad bass-playing we encountered. Bon would stay clear of this process, saying, 'It doesn't matter to me, I'm just the singer, it's up to Malcolm and Angus.' Phil was there keeping time, the human metronome; he fit in perfectly, and his style was the driving force they needed. They were like a roomful of Energizer Bunnies.

By the time Mark Evans turned up, we'd seen all sorts. He looked right, he wasn't too tall and he could play how they wanted him to. After he'd left round two of his audition, we all sat around talking about whether he would work.

Browning turned to me and said, 'Tana, you're a girl, what do you reckon?'

I thought for a minute. 'Well, he's the right height, he's young, he can play without trying to take over – can he sing?'

Mark hadn't sung anything at his audition, and in my mind we really needed someone who could sing backing vocals. Not Malcom's strongest suit, I'd always thought.

Again, Browning pushed me. 'Yes, but is he good-looking?'

This embarrassed me: I didn't like to talk about the band members in that way. 'I don't know, I guess,' was the best I could come up with.

Browning was all about the image – but in all fairness, that was his job. The band took care of the rest. Me, I was all about the music and getting the best possible outcome for the band.

* * *

The Australian music scene in the '70s revolved around the pub circuit. One of Melbourne's most notorious pub venues was the Matthew Flinders Hotel, a rough-and-tumble beer garden that held about a thousand punters and had a late-night liquor licence – not always a smart combination for the average upcoming band, as many a bottle had been hurled at the stage by a disgruntled punter. And while Angus was technically of the legal drinking age and could be in a bar, management had decided to run with the underage schoolboy hype; as far as the press and the public were concerned, he was underage. The funny thing was that Angus was a teetotaller, so either way the joke was on them. We, on the other hand, couldn't understand how he was such a high priority on Australia's Most Wanted List for eating chocolate, drinking milk, smoking lots of cigarettes and playing guitar. His infamy was the clever ploy of a good management strategy.

Because of all the publicity around his schoolboy image, there was frequently a police presence at those early shows. Everyone had been told to 'lock up your daughters' – eventually the name of one of the band's albums and tours – but this was ridiculous to us. Of course, it was great press.

Jovan Promotions Presents:

THE SUNDOWNER
GEELONG HOTEL

8pm - 11·45pm   Price Includes Supper

Fri. 20th June	Sat. 21st June
RED HOUSE ROLL BAND	JETS
$2.00 - $1.50	$2.00 - $1.50
Wed. 25th June	Thurs. 26th June
AC'DC BEECH $2.50 - $2.00	HOT CITY BUMP BAND MOBY DICK $2.00 - $1.50
Fri. 27th June	Sat. 28th June
MADDER LAKE BUSTER BROWN	RED HOUSE ROLL BAND

It was here in the Matthew Flinders one night that it looked like it could become a problem. I'd spotted some plainclothes policemen during the show from the front-of-house sound desk and, at the end of the show, they started making their way towards the backstage area.

'Whoa! Hi, guys! What can I do to help you?' I called out as I ran to catch up with them.

'We need to speak with this lot,' they responded.

'Sure, I'll take you back there soon, but right now Angus and the others will be getting changed. I'm sure you understand we can't go yet, me being a girl and all. There's no way out of the dressing room without crossing the stage, so we can all wait here.' They agreed after I went into great detail, as to how sweaty and cramped the space was in the broom closet the pub called a dressing room. 'You want a drink while we wait?' I asked one of the policemen innocently. 'Could be a while.'

'Yeah,' he answered, but insisted, 'Let me get it, though.'

I ordered then quickly drank a large Jack Daniel's and Coke, which the policeman dutifully paid for. Yes, you heard it here: he paid for it, and I was seventeen.

When I'd finished my drink, I let him know what he'd just done. 'So, I guess you're here to bust Angus for being underage? Well, he's not, it's all a publicity trick – but I am. Thanks for the drink, guys!' And I walked off to start the load-out of the equipment now I knew the Boys were off the hook. These are the skills that aren't in the job description. Whatever it takes!

* * *

It wasn't all wine and roses within the band – there were fights. But not the silly ego trips that most bands have.

Conflicts usually broke out when they were having a hard time getting something right musically in a rehearsal, or in the early stages of writing a song. Malcolm was a perfectionist: near enough was never good enough.

One time, Malcolm and Angus were in the living room working on a song in which the guitar solo wasn't coming together.

Malcolm became frustrated. 'Do it the same way you did it last time.'

Angus seemed a little distracted. 'I don't know, it'll be fine.'

To Angus's surprise and mine, Malcolm got up and stormed out of the room. 'If you can't be bothered, then neither can I.' As he left, arguing back over his shoulder to Angus, he accidentally slammed the neck of his beloved Gretsch guitar into the doorway. He continued to his room and slammed the door.

'Oh, SHIT!' That was the best I could come up with.

I'd never seen the brothers fight like this, resulting in something of value getting broken. The odd shove and back and forth, but not serious like this.

After what seemed like an eternity, I asked Angus, 'What should we do?' – meaning him.

Angus said he thought it would be best if we let Mal cool off a bit. The original argument no longer mattered: by smashing his guitar, Mal may as well have broken his right arm. Then Angus turned to me and said, 'I think you should go see if he's alright.'

What? I thought. *ME?*

Angus said, 'It'll be better if you go, as he isn't mad at you.'

Yet ... was my thought. I felt bad for both of them though, so off I went to see if Mal was okay.

Roadies are frequently put in positions when interacting with a band member can involve the plea of 'don't shoot the messenger'. This can clarify the brutal truth that a roadie is often sacrificed to save a relationship between band members – not Angus's intention, but important to remember when getting maybe a little too close to your bosses.

I quietly knocked on the bedroom door, half-hoping Mal didn't answer. I looked back over my shoulder to where Angus still sat on the couch watching and prompting me to knock again. This time I said, 'Mal, it's Tana. Can I come in?'

When Mal let me in, I was shocked to see his guitar lying on his bed with its head hanging off to the side.

The first thing I said was, 'It can be fixed! We'll find someone to fix it.'

Mal knew more about guitars than I did, so he knew it could be fixed. What was upsetting him more was the fact that he'd lost control. 'I shouldn't have lost my temper,' he said. 'We're not going to get anywhere if we don't stick together.' He'd gone to a very dark place, and he didn't want to go there again. 'This fighting is no good. We need to have a united front.'

The two of us sat and talked in that room for a long time. Mal sat on the end of his bed, leaning forward with his elbows on his thighs, and I was sitting on the floor nearby. To lighten the mood, I steered the conversation to an upcoming show in which we'd be supporting Billy Thorpe and the Aztecs. I told Mal, 'Wait till Billy hears how loud you guys are! He's gonna die!' Billy's band had the reputation of being the loudest in Australia, but that was about to change.

This incident changed our relationship further. We became closer, close enough to have sex. From that time on Mal would come to me whenever he wanted to talk, or just wanted a break. I had my own room, providing a quiet space for him. We would hang out on the bed at times, him at one end and me the other, sitting cross-legged, talking. I could be a sounding board of sorts, someone he felt safe with. Sometimes we wouldn't speak at all, just lay there until one or both of us fell asleep.

Angus had his girlfriend at the time, Heather, looking after him. Malcolm put up a strong front, but he also needed looking after, and he could talk to me. Were we an item? No. It would have got complicated if it was common knowledge that we'd slept together, and that would have changed how the rest of the band viewed me. My worst nightmare was any of the Boys thinking I'd only taken the gig so I could sleep with one of them. Try putting that genie back in the bottle. I'd like to think Mal was protecting me from the potential negative reactions of the rest of the band – or he may have just been acting like a typical guy. That was the AC/DC way: you just didn't talk about it. I'd never been in a relationship, so I had no idea what I was doing, and Mal was busy preparing to conquer the world. The last thing I wanted was for anything to jeopardise my job, my ticket out of the life I'd been trying so hard to leave behind.

What is it they say about your first crush? He will always have a place in my heart. We were just a couple of kids sharing a moment in time.

6

IT'S A LONG WAY TO THE TOP

NEVER A TRUER LINE has been written than 'It's a Long Way to the Top (If You Wanna Rock 'n' Roll)'. I travelled an incredibly long distance with the Boys in a relatively short time. What a band sets in stone at the earliest part of their journey guides and strengthens them throughout. With that, this band couldn't fail.

Now we had all positions filled, we were finally ready to get down to some serious gigging. The very first show with the complete line-up that would be the five members the world would get to know as AC/DC was at the Station Hotel in Melbourne. A gig that almost didn't happen. The owner of the hotel was refusing to let Mark in because he'd been barred for a bar fight on a previous occasion. I put my skills to work and sweet-talked the guy, promising that Mark would be on his best behaviour or he'd have to deal with me. The owner thought that was funny, and conceded. This was the moment we'd been waiting for, the moment of truth when we would hopefully see all our hard work come to fruition.

I was excited while setting up all the equipment, but also a bit nervous for the Boys; there was always a lot of industry types at this venue. When they arrived, I took them to a little backstage area and I could see they were nervous too. Phil was the calmest, as he'd been gigging around Melbourne for a while with Buster Brown. He told them, 'It's fine, we'll go out and kick some arse!' That became their mindset: no matter the size of the audience, the band would give their all and 'kick arse!'

The show went well, with no major disasters from my perspective. After they finished their set and were back in the dressing room, their excitement was mixed with the relief of getting that show – Mark's first – over with. Mark, like Phil, seemed to be a good fit. Angus was in the corner not moving, just trying to get his breath back while smoking a cigarette. They'd lost their AC/DC virginity, and the audience – who were a mix of music industry and punters – weren't sure what they'd just seen, but most would come back for more.

Browning had money to recoup, so our new schedule was brutal – still, we were up for it. The AC/DC work ethic was unwavering. Sadly, though, it brought to an end those nights at the house where Malcolm and Angus would sit around for hours, having deep and long conversations about their favourite musical influences, and playing new and old classic albums. Whenever I hear an acoustic guitar player slapping their instrument to the rhythm, I think of Malcolm sitting on the end of his bed just lost in playing music. That was a great time, and I'm happy to have been a part of it.

Once our new line-up started gigging around town, it became obvious that the house PA systems weren't loud enough to carry Bon's vocals over the volume of Angus's guitar. I was sent off to a company in Moorabbin called Nova Sound to get our own PA that would travel with us. Now, I really didn't know much about sound, being a backline person, but I remembered that gig at the Whisky a Go Go with Swampy – if you didn't pay attention, you could really fuck it up! The guys at Nova Sound listened carefully to the problems I said we were having with the overall sound but mostly Bon's vocals. After I told them the name of the band – word was out on AC/DC – they set up a system that they said would work for us. One of the guys, Wynn, knew Bon from his days in The Valentines as he'd played guitar in that band, so he knew Bon's voice, and that was a great help. As it turned out, Wynn was one of Australia's best sound engineers, and I'd have the pleasure of touring with him down the road a piece.

The sound guys warned me that I'd have to control Angus's amp volume. 'You'll have to keep it down,' they said. Right, no problem there – maybe I could just tell him to turn it down. Were they kidding me?

The first sound system I was given was woefully inadequate. I had to work within Browning's budget. It would work for the most part, but it wasn't large or strong enough to consistently rise above the growing guitar volume.

The console that came with the system was a big aluminium box that I christened the 'picnic basket'. It controlled the PA for the audience to hear, as well as the monitors for the band to hear each other onstage over their own equipment, all from the front-of-house position. This meant I couldn't hear the monitors during the show and had to rely on hand signals from the stage to make changes – not at all the set-up you'd hope for with a notoriously loud band.

The other change that came with the PA was that suddenly, without warning, I would no longer be doing backline: I would become the band's sound engineer. 'Does this new and unfamiliar equipment come with an instruction manual?' Apparently not – I would just have to figure it out as I went along. This was my crash course at doing front-of-house sound. The good news was that I wouldn't have to go onstage anymore while the band was playing to change Angus's broken strings while he was spinning around on his back playing as though I wasn't there. The bad news was that when they played 'She's Got Balls', audience members would turn to look at me. It's been said that the song was written for Bon's ex-wife, but where was she when the audience was pointing and giggling? Don't even get me started on 'She's Got the Jack'.

* * *

Around this time, Browning decided it would be great publicity if a newspaper published an article on me as a female roadie working for AC/DC. Oh … I didn't like the sound of this at all. 'Come on, Tana!' he said. 'It would be you doing your bit for the band.' Like ten to twelve shows a week wasn't enough. This sort of thing may have been on Browning's mind from when he'd first hired me.

I thought I might be able to wangle my way out of it if I spoke with the band. 'Come on, guys, don't make me do this,' I protested. 'Why would anybody want to know about me? They all come to see you. The article should be about you.' But they said I should do it – what was I to do? I think they just wanted to see me squirm. Very funny, Boys! So it went: if they wanted it, they got it. That's how I'd become their sound engineer.

Finally, a date was set for the photo to be taken while we were at the Hard Rock Cafe, Browning's club, doing a show. I thought maybe, just maybe, the camera person would snap me doing the load-in, or even at the sound desk during a sound check where I could save some face. Some way that I wouldn't notice the photo being taken.

But no. Browning took me out of the venue past the truck full of equipment, to an alley where a car sat with the rear passenger door open, and he said, 'Here, take this mic stand and put it on the back seat so we can get a photo.' How embarrassing! He could have got a shot of me carrying a Marshall cab on one shoulder and a Marshall amp in the other hand as I did at every load-in, or one of me flipping a PA base bin up onto the stage. But this was the call.

It got worse. When the article came out in the newspaper, the headline read: 'She Does It for the Band'. I was mortified. I never forgave Browning for that, and I swore it would be a cold day in hell before I'd ever agree to do anything in the press again. The band, by the way, thought it was hilarious.

This incident served as a reminder that what I was doing was unheard of for a woman. Until that time, I hadn't given it much thought.

* * *

With *High Voltage* working its way up the charts, we were scheduled to make our third appearance on *Countdown*, the weekly national pop show on ABC TV hosted by Ian 'Molly' Meldrum. A force to be reckoned with, Molly had the reputation of being able to make or break a band depending how much he pushed their songs on his show.

Now as the 'Molly' in his name would lead you to believe, he is gay, and Bon was nervous about appearing on *Countdown* in case Molly hit on him. I'm sure Bon wasn't Molly's type, and Bon knew Molly from when he'd played in The Valentines, but jokingly he wasn't taking any chances. The result was the much talked-about AC/DC appearance on *Countdown* in which Bon wore a memorable costume while performing 'Baby, Please Don't Go'.

As usual, I was busy setting up the backline equipment for the filming. Bon, on the other hand, was up to his tricks – you really couldn't leave him alone. When the band took their positions onstage to start filming, he wasn't with them. I headed over to the studio entrance, looking for him. Just as I got to the doorway, there he was, in all his glory.

Well, I almost died. Bon was in a schoolgirl uniform, not unlike the ones I'd worn during my boarding school days, only with torn stockings, the skirt hitched up, a blonde wig, and make-up that looked inspired by the film *What Ever Happened to Baby Jane?* I ran beside him towards the stage, and just as he stepped up to take his place, he leant over and whispered in my ear, 'This makes you and me the only safe ones in the studio,' then winked and jumped onto the stage. Being there that day, I witnessed Bon's true strength in the band, his ability to grab an audience.

Bon loved a good prank! Molly saw the joke in it and from that time on was a strong supporter of the band.

* * *

Early 1975 was great for AC/DC, with the single 'Baby, Please Don't Go' racing up the charts, and *High Voltage* becoming the second biggest selling album of the year, eventually staying in the charts for a record-setting twenty-five weeks. Life was good. Our home base, gig wise, was the Hard Rock Cafe; Browning was no fool by owning both the venue and the band. Whenever AC/DC played, the club would be packed, and he would clean up on the door while getting his manager's percentage and club share – I believe that adds up to 100 per cent. Of course, it was good for all of us too, with lots of friends coming by. Oh, and we got free food!

At one of those shows I was operating the front-of-house sound when I noticed this rather straight-looking guy standing to my left, just staring at me. He didn't look like an AC/DC fan and seemed barely aware of the band – which isn't an easy thing to do, as anyone knows who has ever attended an AC/DC concert.

When the set finished, he asked me if my name was Tana Douglas. I became nervous for some reason, and almost said no. I answered with a noncommittal, 'Why?'

He said, 'Because if you are, I am your brother.'

Wow! It took me a minute to register the word. Brother? I didn't know anything about a brother.

He introduced himself as Paul, and explained he was my father's son from his first marriage, and that there was another son named Mark. So I had two brothers! When I asked him how he'd found me, he smiled and said he'd read the newspaper article. He made a joke of it, as he could see I was uncomfortable. After that I decided he was okay.

It was a difficult time for me to try and build a new relationship of any type. We were working nonstop, and there were more and more out-of-town shows with long travel times. Paul came to the house on a couple of occasions, one of which was my birthday, but we didn't get to spend quality time together. I don't think getting him drunk on Jack Daniel's and watching him stagger off down the road into a cemetery is the stuff that true sibling bonds are made of.

Family has always been difficult for me. Although my personal family experiences have always been chaotic to say the least, I truly envy people who have that mythical (from my perspective) bond. I think that's one of the reasons I liked Malcolm and Angus so much. The Youngs had that, and to me it was amazing to watch and become a small part of it.

On our first trip to Sydney as a band since Mal and Angus had moved to Melbourne, there was much cause for celebration. They weren't only returning to their family home in Burwood to see everyone they'd been missing, but they also had a hit single and album – return the conquering heroes!

When we arrived in Sydney, Malcolm and Angus were to be dropped at their home while the rest of the band and crew went to the hotel in Bondi Beach; we were about to play four nights at the Bondi Lifesaver. Malcolm invited me to visit their home with them, a sweet gesture that I was happy to accept. I'd met Brother George on several occasions but only heard tell of the other family members, including sister Margaret who made all of Angus's costumes and whose now-infamous sewing machine was the source of the band's name.

The Youngs had an 'all for one and one for all' attitude. When we arrived at the house, the whole family had turned up to greet us. There were three brothers I hadn't previously met, along with Margaret, and I was introduced to all of them between the front door and the living room, where I met their dad. Their mum was upstairs in her room resting. It was what I would call a full house.

'How was the trip?' one of the brothers asked Angus, while Margaret asked me, 'Can I get you anything, dear? Do you want a wee drink of something?' While another of the brothers asked, 'Where's your bag? Give it here and I'll put it in your room.'

With that, my bag disappeared, I was ushered into the kitchen and a cold drink was placed into my grasp. So it was for the entire visit. Everyone went out of their way to make me feel welcome and included.

Now, when you get a bunch of Scots in a room together, especially family, the brogue gets stronger than ever. I felt a bit like a fly on the wall watching everyone interact. Preparing the family meal was almost like a dance, with items both hot and cold being passed from person to person, the odd crash of a bowl or piece of cutlery falling, all accompanied by a buzz of conversation. There I was, an Aussie girl whose father had spent a tidy sum to have her taught the Queen's English, catching maybe half of what was going on.

I hadn't, however, met the whole family unit until I'd had an audience with the matriarch, their beloved mum. That was when I got to hear an undiluted Scottish accent for the first time in my life, directed solely at me.

Margaret led me upstairs. 'Come and meet Mum. She wants to talk with you.' With that she brought me into a bedroom. It had that lived-in feeling with the big solid furniture of the time; there was a lot of stuff, but you could tell it all had a purpose. There in the bed, propped up and wearing a nightgown, was their mum. She waved me closer and into a chair positioned at her bedside, then smiled at me as she started to talk softly. I was amazed; could this possibly be the same language I was speaking? I hardly understood a word.

AC/DC with Vanda and Young, pre-Mark Evans days.
Paul Matters filled in briefly on bass when George Young
was unavailable. (PHILIP MORRIS)

She seemed like a very nice lady and was holding court from
her bed as she was in poor health. The whole family obviously
revered her; unlike the respect my mother tried to demand,
this kind came naturally. I was, however, struggling to answer
any of her questions for fear of making a total idiot of myself.
I could tell that I liked her, though. Finally, Margaret, who had
disappeared earlier, came to my rescue and brought me back
downstairs. As I turned to wave goodbye, I saw a calming
smile pass over the matriarch's lips.

It turned out she'd been confined to her bed for quite some time, which explained why the Aussie accent hadn't affected her brogue. Of course, in true Young family style, it never occurred to them to say, 'Oh, by the way, don't feel bad but you probably won't understand a word she says!' Another example of the Youngs' attitude: this is who we are, take it or leave it. They would test people to see if it was safe to trust them, and I'd passed the test. Being invited into their home, their private world, was a great experience for me, and I wouldn't have missed it for anything. I still love a good Scottish accent to this day. The good news is I can now understand what the hell they're all talking about!

* * *

I'd loved the reprieve at the Youngs' home, but now it was time to get straight back to work, with four nights and sixteen shows at the Bondi Lifesaver. This was a classic example of just how loud my life was gonna get.

The Bondi Lifesaver is one of those venues that's gone down in history due to its steady flow of both local and international talent. Back then it was a rite of passage. We were joining the company of Billy Thorpe, Lobby Loyde, Angry Anderson, all from notoriously loud bands. Thorpe would join us onstage for the last set that first night, and, much to the horror of the club management, the next day all the fish in the giant, well-established tank that was the centrepiece of the bar were dead. Hence, some people swear it was Thorpe that killed the fish, while others swear it was AC/DC. It was both, and from that night, it just kept getting louder.

There were always more shows to do in more locations. A seemingly endless list – twelve each week wasn't unheard of. From that point on, I had little time for anything apart from work.

By 1975, nobody could deny AC/DC had arrived, for better or for worse. We were getting booked for elite shows such as the Freedom from Hunger Concert at the Sidney Myer Music Bowl, playing to five thousand kids. That was when the Young Philosophy really kicked in: they came, they saw, they conquered. Step aside or get run over.

Now, when you're a member of or work for an up-and-coming band, all sorts of hangers-on come out of the woodwork. Some members are better than others at handling all the attention, but I'm yet to meet a single one who has managed to stay unaffected in some way by it all. Eventually, we all crack a little under pressure.

Bon was the first to show the signs. When we got back home from Sydney, the dark side of the industry raised its ugly head for the first time to us as a group.

Bon had been taking off every chance he had to hang with some girl from his past. She and her sister worked in a St Kilda massage parlour, and like most girls in that profession they had healthy drug habits. It seems Bon had rekindled not only their friendship, but also some old habits they'd shared in the past. These girls were personae non grata and rarely came to the house, so I never really got to know them.

Bon was having trouble with his voice, and his trusted cure of port and honey was no longer cutting it. People resort to strange behaviours when under pressure; Bon was under pressure vocally to keep up with our extreme workload. This was when I first noticed that he had real insecurities about his age difference from the other band members. He'd always joked about being older – it was the first thing he'd ever said to me – but now the jokes seemed darker. Bon, possibly out of fear of failing, had turned to a more serious remedy. In those early days, I was never present when anyone did anything apart from smoke pot and drink alcohol. Eventually, speed and cocaine made an appearance, but the boys were mostly drinkers – except Angus, who wanted nothing to do with any of it. Bon marched to his own drum and kept his doings very private. Let's not forget that he had a good ten years of this lifestyle under his belt while the rest of the band had still been living at home with their parents. Neither was it a regular thing.

The day it all hit the fan, I was woken up in the house by a girl's voice screaming that Bon wasn't breathing! It took a while for the rest of the house to wake up and realise that this was something serious – very serious. As I stuck my head out of my bedroom door, I recognised the skinny blonde wearing just undies and a tiny T-shirt standing outside Bon's room yelling hysterically. It was one of the sisters.

Malcolm looked at me. 'What's going on? Why is she here?'

'I don't know,' I said.

By this time, everyone was up. Angus and Heather came out of their room, while Phil was coming out of his, pulling on a pair of jeans. There was complete chaos. The guys took the blonde girl to the side to try and get some sense out of her. She wouldn't tell us what he'd taken, saying he'd made her promise not to tell, then she just kept sobbing, 'He isn't breathing! You have to help him.' No shit! Note to everyone out there: knowing what drugs are involved can save someone's life during an overdose.

Two of the Boys went into Bon's room, and I could see it was serious by the look on their faces as they came out. We needed to act fast. When we figured out that the girl was absolutely no help, we got her dressed and out of the house as quickly as possible. We had no choice – an ambulance had to be called. There was no phone in the house (seriously), so this meant running to a phone booth. While the band members were deciding who would make the call, I went rather tentatively back to Bon's room at the rear of the house.

I'd never spent any time in his room, having no reason to go in there, so it looked surreal to me. There was Bon just lying there calm and still in his bed surrounded by a clean and organised room with his ironing board set up in the corner, and with all the chaos happening right outside his door. How long had it been? I reached over the bed and shook him, then climbed up onto it, kneeling over him while trying to get him to respond. I felt embarrassed as I straddled him, in case he woke up and wanted to know what the hell I was doing.

I tried talking to him – rather, yelling and shaking him hard. 'Bon! Wake up! You can't fucking do this, Bon! Wake the fuck up! Breathe!'

Where the hell was the ambulance? I was panicking.

Heather came in and asked me what he was doing.

'Nothing,' I said. 'I don't think he's breathing.' I was freaking out and started CPR. After several attempts at mouth-to-mouth alternating with chest pumps, it clearly wasn't working, so I slammed him on his sternum – hard.

I looked up to see the medics arrive. *Thank God*, I thought; then, *Hopefully I haven't killed him.* But apparently it had been the right thing to do, keeping him there long enough for them to get him stabilised.

This was when we found out that Bon suffered from asthma and needed to be very careful when mixing or overindulging in substances.

We were all sworn to secrecy about this incident as the best thing for the band as a whole.

* * *

One night we totalled the equipment truck when the brakes failed as we were speeding to our third and last gig. We were lucky enough to hit a tram, which was barely affected, but it stopped us from travelling at a solid seventy kilometres to zero in two seconds flat. Shaken but not badly hurt, we managed to pick ourselves up, collect the equipment thrown from the truck onto the street, put it all back into the truck and limp to our last show for the night, using the truck's gears instead of the non-existent brakes to manoeuvre through the city traffic. We were a sad sight when we arrived at the venue, with the overhead storage area above the cab ripped out of the truck from the impact.

This incident heralded the arrival of the dreaded Blue Bus, touted as a solution to our transportation worries. It was a beast: an old Ansair Clipper with a Perkins diesel engine that was supposedly a selling point. This was a far cry from what springs to mind when you say 'tour bus' today. Our Blue Bus was just wrong in so many ways. Whoever – if anyone – gave it the thumbs up after a safety check had a pure-evil streak. The bus was divided in half by a wall that separated us passengers from the storage section where the stage equipment travelled so it could be loaded and unloaded through a rear side door. The front half consisted of regular bus seats: hard seats designed for short trips, not for comfort. The heater never worked. The air never worked. And the bus itself rarely worked. But the fans loved it! Meanwhile, us passengers spent all winter huddled in groups trying not to freeze to death – that was presuming we weren't pushing the piece of shit on one of its many breakdowns. Ralph was the designated driver.

As AC/DC's popularity grew, it was getting more difficult for us to have any privacy. Schoolgirls were turning up at the house with chocolate cakes they'd made for Angus. Others would do our laundry, and still others would clean or cook for us. This was great at first, but with many of the girls being underage or close to it, we were also often opening our front door to find an irate father looking to rescue his daughter and hoping to maim at least one of us in the process. I would run interference with these dads, telling them that their daughters were safe. But after a few brawls took place, with Bon usually bearing the brunt of them, the decision was made to move. To take some of the heat off the band, Browning decided to move us to the Freeway Gardens Hotel in the inner suburb of North Melbourne. His logic was we wouldn't really need a place to call home anymore, as we weren't going to be having any time off. The hotel instead became our port in a storm, and this had an impact on the band's dynamic. It was around this time that an old cohort of Bon's turned up to a show in Geelong. His name was Pat Pickett. He caught a ride back to Melbourne with us and never really left. From that time on Pat Pickett was hired to look after Bon and the band. He would room with Bon also.

Because we lived in separate rooms throughout the hotel, everyone was getting up to whatever they wanted to in their own space. Pat became the Master of R-rated Ceremonies. This was fair enough, as the boys needed to let off steam, but for me things were getting tougher. The more popular the band got, the more of a target I became. I felt isolated. I could no longer just wander into one of the other rooms like in the house, as now I was never sure what was going on behind closed doors. Frequently, I was getting sworn at by female fans, being called 'bitch' and worse. This was purely because

I was a girl in close contact with the band, and the Boys' new breed of rabid female fans weren't happy about that. If they'd known that Malcolm and I had been together, they probably would have hung, drawn and quartered me. Angus's girlfriend also left at this time. Management did not want any band members to appear to be in any sort of relationship.

AC/DC fans were a power to be reckoned with. These were the days before any security was supplied at venues for either band or crew, and I remember we were left to our own devices to get out of a venue surrounded by drunken punters. We were often fair game. To be clear, it wasn't only our band, and it could be worse if you were a pop band booked to play a show in an area frequented by skinheads. It became a bit of a sport there for a while; the local reprobates figured out that the road crew for bands playing their venues were there from early in the day until late at night. They saw us as a type of captive live game, as they knew we couldn't leave and were therefore easy targets for a random brawl.

And it wasn't limited to just the guys. A couple of instances stand out above the others.

We were playing a country gig in Gippsland, Victoria; the venue was a large room that looked like a community hall of some sort, probably more used to sock hops than rock bands. A group of locals were hanging around out front, looking like they wanted to cause some trouble and tell us out-of-towners that they were the shit. They heckled us with the likes of 'Look at this lot! They must have got lost. You guys are in the wrong town!' Meanwhile, we were dragging the equipment across the dusty carpark with no help, just to put on a show for these idiots.

That night I had trouble keeping the power to the stage turned on. Trouble turning the hall lights off. And more trouble at the front-of-house position from where I was operating the sound. No security anywhere in sight.

There was a girl in the audience who'd come with one of those guys from the carpark. But she'd taken a shine to a band member and kept asking me during the show if she could talk to him. I said, 'I don't know. I'm a little busy here. I don't go back there,' hoping that would get rid of her.

She and her guy friends stayed back after the show to heckle the crew as their late-night sport. She, of course, targeted me, and with her shaved head and rat's tail, tight, high-waisted, flared jeans and striped T-shirt – all fashionable for skinheads of the time – she just kept coming at me with insults. 'Slut! You've got no right to be here, you bitch.'

It took me a while to understand what the hell she was talking about. 'You want to step in, bitch, and load the bus? Go right ahead.' I wasn't quite sure where she imagined the glory to be in this roadie thing.

She swung at me, and I'd had enough. I knocked the bitch out. I then grabbed a pipe just in case her boyfriend, who'd been egging her on, decided to jump in.

That same night, on the way back to Melbourne, the Blue Bus broke down again! Where was she then? She'd wanted to be here so badly. I wasn't getting paid enough to fight my way in and out of venues.

On another of many occasions, I was rudely awoken one morning at the Freeway Gardens by some girl's foot in my face while she was climbing through my window looking for the band. I grabbed her ankle and pushed it away, toppling the girl from the window frame to the floor.

Unfazed, she picked herself up and asked, 'Where's Angus?'

'You're in the wrong bloody room!' I yelled. 'Piss off!'

When she realised there wasn't a band member in the room, she attacked me. Good morning, world! Want coffee with that?

I discovered I could hold my own in any brawl situation. Not necessarily the way to go, but good to know you've got it if you need it.

* * *

Now we were playing larger venues, we finally got the larger PA that we needed, but that meant more equipment to load. Then something else was added – something none of us were ready for, no matter how overdue: a lighting rig. True to form, nobody bothered to tell us, it just appeared.

We arrived at an out-of-town show to be met by a man who introduced himself as our ... lighting guy? This was news to us. To cope with our heavy schedule our crew had built a tight routine, and it wasn't a good move for this guy to turn up out of the blue and make demands about what power we could use and what areas were to be left clear for his lights. We spent the entire set-up battling with this guy, which isn't a great way to start any relationship.

During the show we had power problems, then we found out we were supposed to load his lights for him in the back of the Blue Bus and take them to the next show, where he'd turn up again to make our lives hell. The only saving grace was that he wasn't travelling with us.

I still don't know why I had such a bad reaction to the guy. Maybe it was because we were already stretched to capacity. Or maybe his lightshow just sucked. Who knows? But I knew one thing: I wasn't happy. Everything was changing so quickly, and I'd been dropped into the middle of what was becoming this huge machine. I was unprepared. Just a short time earlier, I'd been happily wandering around a rainforest where clothing was optional. Something needed to change – and just like that, we hit the next level.

The Blue Bus was history, after we finally managed to destroy it and leave the remains in Canberra. That was the only way we would ever be rid of the damn thing. Good riddance!

We had started headlining shows with other bands on the bill and full production supplied and air travel due to time restrictions. It turned out air travel wasn't all that great, as Australian pilots in the 1970s were a wild and woolly bunch. On one extremely turbulent flight, Angus was in the aisle talking to Mal when we hit an air pocket and the plane dropped dramatically. This caused Angus to become airborne. I grabbed him by the arm, and he was momentarily suspended as if flying. If I had let go, he would have hit the ceiling of the cabin. From that time on, Angus didn't like to catch planes.

* * *

There were good times still to be had. Things were just different.

One of my favourite memories of that time is from the morning after a party to celebrate not only the success of *High Voltage*, but also our first show at Festival Hall in Melbourne, in April 1975, which was followed by our first headlining, sold-out show two weeks later, at the Hordern Pavilion in Sydney.

At first it seemed room service had woken me up early before check-out. It turned out that Bon was delivering breakfast to all the crew as a thankyou. When we lifted the covers off the plates, we saw he'd arranged the eggs, bacon and potatoes into a smiley face with tomato sauce as the rosy cheeks. That was the kind of thoughtful thing Bon would do to let you know you were appreciated. Who knows how he talked the hotel staff into making smiley-face breakfasts for all the crew, or what he was doing up at that time of the morning? Must have been that Bon Scott charm.

But even with moments like that, I still felt I needed to take a step back.

When we returned to Melbourne after that run, Malcolm came to my room to talk. They needed to expand the production for the shows, he told me. This would mean bringing in a production company and lighting as a permanent part of the package. They also needed a real sound engineer.

No kidding! I'd done as much as I could without a single lesson or person to show me, so I was more than happy to let that one go.

Then Malcolm offered me the job of lighting designer. This took me by surprise, as I knew nothing about lighting. I didn't want to find myself in the same situation down the road as I was in now. Plus, I wasn't sure about the whole lighting thing after the mystery lighting guy had disrupted everything. Did I want to become that guy? The equipment was awkward to work with: heavy, sharp metal, and tons of cable.

Feeling very sad, I said, 'No, but thank you.'

This was August of 1975, and the Boys would be off the road while they recorded *Dirty Deeds Done Dirt Cheap*, so I felt it was the right time for me to leave.

If I was going to build a career as roadie, I'd have to find someone to teach me stuff. There's only so much that you can wing it before you risk being left behind or putting yourself in danger. We're talking a lot of electricity, people and equipment – everything needs to be treated with care. I was ready to start learning what it really takes to make things happen in the concert production world.

To this day, I thank the Boys for making me a part of their beginning and have nothing but the fondest memories of the band. Malcolm was once quoted as saying that his days in the house on Lansdowne Road were some of his happiest. I feel the same.

This was not goodbye.

Mal and Angus at Alberts – note the original AC/DC logo on the Marshall cabinet. (PHILIP MORRIS)

7

GIRL, YOU'LL BE A WOMAN SOON

WHAT TO DO NEXT? Finding myself in need of somewhere to stay and between jobs was somehow invigorating. It would also be a test to see if I'd really been accepted into this brotherhood of roadies. While I didn't know exactly where I was going from here, I did know my ability to continue on this path relied on how well I fitted in as a crew member, not how I stood out as a girl. I had always treated other crews well, and this had helped to solidify my good reputation. I was still getting grief from some of the guys, who would crack jokes or push me out of the way when there was a heavy lift. 'Step aside. Let a man do that! Don't want you hurting yourself.' This was a frequent reminder that there was a group who didn't want me there.

Heather, having recently split from Angus, pulled me aside when I was leaving AC/DC and said, 'Why don't you come over to Karen's place with me? I told her you need a place to stay.'

Karen Sullivan was the sort of person who walked in to a party and owned it. She was slight in build, with big eyes and a cheeky smile. Her hair was dark and, along with her make-up, always effortlessly perfect. She was twelve years older than me and was dating Shirl from Skyhooks. People gravitated to her. Forty years after their meeting, Keith Richards mentioned her in his memoir.

I hadn't seen her since she'd let me know that Phil Rudd had wanted to audition for AC/DC, so I was looking forward to catching up. My $60 a week salary from AC/DC hadn't allowed any savings to accrue, so I needed a new gig fast. When I turned up at her house in the quiet suburb of Moorabbin to take her up on her offer, she greeted me at the door.

'Hi, mate, come on in.'

She led me into one of the two large front rooms laid out as a flow-through double living room. *Great house for a party*, I thought.

My partner in crime, Karen Sullivan, who was mentioned in Keith Richards's memoir forty years after their encounter.

Karen explained, 'Your room will be at the back of the house, next to my son Shannon's. Shannon, come say hi to Tana!' In came the cutest little kid I'd ever seen, about six years old. He and I would become good buddies, and Karen and I good friends.

* * *

That afternoon I found out that Swampy was on his way to town with the Australian band Sherbet. Great! Maybe I could get some advice from him as to what my next move should be? I went down to the show to see him.

Afterwards, we all went back to the band's hotel. I was in Swampy's room, hashing out what I should do next. 'I don't even know how to go about looking for a gig. I've never had to. They've always come to me.' I knew that over everything, I wanted to be taken seriously in this industry. I also wanted my mother, on the rare occasions I saw her, to stop asking me when I was going to get a real job. Ugh, the only thing worse would be to tell her I had no job!

'You need to use the momentum you've gained from working with AC/DC and move quickly to your next gig,' Swampy advised. 'Don't hang about.'

I nodded. 'I'm leaning towards doing backline again – it seems a lot simpler than front-of-house sound. I think I need to learn more before I do that again.'

Swampy thought for a minute, then said, 'If you do backline, that means you'll be working directly for a band again.'

I hadn't really thought about that. I wasn't sure if I wanted that just yet. It could get all-consuming at times, and I felt as if I needed to regroup and take some time and distance for myself after AC/DC.

Swampy suggested, 'What about working for a production company that supplies all the equipment for the tours?'

Hmm, I thought. *That might be a good option.*

'Fuck this,' I said. 'Let's go join the party!'

Roadies copped a lot of flak back in those days; the public had no idea what we did apart from hump boxes and, sometimes, behave badly. There was a stigma attached to our position, but we revelled in it. Aside from 'roadie', the only other official title at the time was 'road manager', like Swampy, and you could instantly tell who that was: he would be the one with the briefcase. More titles were emerging as the size of the productions grew, but in those days we all did everything – it was always all hands on deck. So, although each of us specialised in different parts of the job, we were all just roadies.

I had built a reputation as being a hard worker who was easy to get on with (unless you pissed me off!) and someone who would do what it took to make the show happen. All in all, it was a good thing to be mostly accepted by this motley and diverse bunch who made up the core of the Australian music touring industry.

* * *

Still being reasonably new to all of this, I was totally unaware that there was such a thing as an international touring season in which the major Australian promoters ran a bunch of international bands through our nation each year. I knew these bands turned up to do shows in Australia, I just hadn't given all the logistics much thought.

The 1975–76 international touring season was about to get underway, and Paul Dainty was about to gear up as the number-one promoter in Australia. This was also going to be the year when everything changed from a production point of view in Australia for both national and international touring acts. A US sound company by the name of Clair Brothers had left one of their systems in Australia after a Blood, Sweat & Tears Tour and consigned it to Paul Dainty. There had been nothing like it to date in the country, and so this enticed a lot of the major international acts to the Paul Dainty stable.

Ron Blackmore, who was Dainty's main man and production manager (a title kept for international tours), would be put in charge of assembling a crew to look after the equipment. Ron decided they needed a lighting rig to accompany the sound system. Now, when I talk about lighting rigs in those days, don't get too excited – it was a far cry from what we have today. But it was absolutely the first evolutionary step. It consisted of four hydraulic light genie towers known as light trees, with sixteen steel par 64-type lamps on each tower, along with any other theatre-style lights we could clamp onto the frames or position on the floor as foot lighting. The front light was all from followspots, usually four but sometimes we'd get lucky and have more.

The dimmers were the first of their kind, built by Strand to tour. When I say built to tour, I use the term loosely: they travelled in giant wooden crate-like cases from which we would screw back on the protective front and back panels after every show, for transportation. They resembled large, double-wide, shallow coffins. I'm sure the only real difference between the so-called touring versions and the regular dimmer racks was that ours weren't bolted to the wall of a theatre somewhere.

All Ron needed now was someone on their touring crew to take care of the lighting system. With a nod from Swampy and a couple of others, I got the gig. Peter Wilson, their electrician, would become my mentor, with me becoming part of his crew. After turning down the lighting job for AC/DC, here I was, just a couple of weeks later, part of the primo road crew in Australia doing lighting. Life's funny, isn't it? Here, though, unlike with AC/DC, I would have a team to learn from.

* * *

I went out to Ron's farm, located near Sunbury, where the equipment was kept, to see what I would be working with and to meet the rest of our crew. His converted barn would be our workspace.

This was my first meeting with Ron Blackmore. He reminded me of the fathers of the outback girls I'd gone to school with – he had a down-to-earthness about him. He was older than the rest of the guys and definitely an authority figure, but he was still very approachable.

'Come over here, Tana,' he told me, 'I want you to meet Peter Wilson. He's your electrician and boss.'

I could quickly see that Peter had his doubts about whether a girl should be allowed to play with electricity, and I'd have to prove to him that I was serious about my career. I think his main concern was that I could possibly electrocute myself – then he'd be one crew member short, which would be a huge inconvenience.

Peter was a character, to say the least, and not your typical touring crew person. He didn't drink, didn't smoke, didn't do drugs, lived at home with his parents, usually travelled in the truck between shows, didn't attend parties, and always wore his electrician's boiler suit accessorised with his tin lunchbox. While he started each tour with an immaculately organised large rolling toolbox, rare for the time, by the end his tools would be in bags, the box jammed tight with contraband from venues and hotels. I was to find out later that the two-car garage at his parents' house was stacked floor to ceiling with his bounty, probably still there untouched to this day. We all have our quirks.

In music industry circles Peter had become notorious for an encounter with Mick Jagger on The Stones' Australian tour circa 1973, when there was much concern about an outdoor concert possibly being cancelled due to rain.

On his break Peter had gone under the stage, trying to find a quiet place to eat a sandwich from that tin lunchbox of his, when he was stumbled upon by a concerned – and a little high – Mick Jagger looking for somewhere to pee. Mick asked Peter if he thought it would rain.

Peter, not taking too kindly to the interruption, looked at Mick first, then looked out from under the stage at the sky, mumbled a bit, then settled back in to ceremoniously eat the rest of his sandwich. What Mick didn't know was that Peter had a severe stutter, especially if he didn't know you. Mick was surprised when Peter's stutter grew into a long, low 'mmmmmmm'. All the while, he continued eating his sandwich. Once he'd finished it, he said, 'Mmmight r-r-r-rain, mmmmmmm … mmm … mmmight n-n-n-not.'

Mick wasn't sure if he'd just met the wisest man on the tour, or if he'd been totally messed with. I'll let you decide.

That tour became known as the 'Mmmight Rain, Mmmight Not Tour' and each crew member was given a plaque with that inscribed on it.

The best pearl of wisdom Peter gave me was when he was explaining electricity to me. 'You can't see it. You can't taste it. You can't smell it. By the time you can, it's too late.'

Some of my early teachers. The Paul Dainty ACT crew: (left to right)
Wynn Milsom, D'Arcy (on cab), Peter Wilson, Bob Bancroft and
Russell Kidner. THE PHOTO WAS TAKEN BY NICK 'CURLEY' CAMPBELL, ANOTHER
CREW MEMBER.

I have passed that anecdote on to many a person, who was
silly enough to think it's no big deal to play with electricity.
It has always worked for me as a mantra, along with 'always
check your gear', inspired by the sound guy at my very first
show at the Whisky.

On Paul Dainty's crew, I'd found a great place to land.
Here I could learn – and learn I did – from the best Australia
had to offer. This is where my thirst for knowledge kicked
in to high gear. Our crew became the pipeline that received
the news first in Australia about what was going on with

production development in the rest of the world. It was truly an exciting time.

The crew's name was jokingly changed from the Paul Dainty Road Crew to the Very Dainty Road Crew, in honour of having a girl on board. The production company was Australian Concert Tours, known as ACT.

* * *

In late 1975, my first ACT tour started with Suzi Quatro. She was at the peak of her success as a hard-rocking, pint-sized and leather-clad bass player/lead vocalist. We were both unusual young women at the time, so I fit in well with her and her crew.

Suzi Q turned out to be a straight shooter with a great sense of humour. Oddly, this Detroit rocker chick introduced me to the very British comedy of *Monty Python and the Holy Grail*. She rented a theatre for us all to see a private screening, so we could all have a laugh together.

Before the movie started, Suzi stood up in the front row and turned to address us. She was tiny but easily commanded the room. Although she was clad in black leather, it somehow didn't make her look less feminine, and there was an ease to how she handled herself. I liked it, briefly wishing for that ease. 'We love this movie,' she said, 'and we wanted to share it with you guys, so let's have fun!' With that, the *Holy Grail* started.

Suzi and her group knew all the skits and were yelling and acting them out all through the film. It had been released earlier that year in both the UK and USA. One scene, the Dark Forest of Ewing, involves a photo of Mount Buffalo National Park in Victoria – a fact we learnt that night, which made us feel a part of it all.

This movie night set the mood for the tour. These guys just wanted to have fun!

When the film was over, someone yelled, 'Back to the hotel for a party!' from the front of the theatre, so off we went. This was my first out-of-control, multi-room tour party. AC/DC partied, but they were a more close-knit bunch, and although they were well on their way to being Australia's bad-boy 'teen' sweethearts, they weren't quite there ... yet.

Touring bands always stayed at certain hotels in major cities, so for the savvy fan it wasn't too difficult to figure out where the party was at. In this case, it was the Old Melbourne Hotel. Word had travelled like wildfire that night, and it was getting crazy.

Suzi liked the fact she had a girl on her crew, and she and her guitarist, Len Tuckey (and future husband), had come to my room to get away from all the punters who kept knocking on her door. I had a dozen or so people there, all crew except for my new roomie, Karen. There were more fans lining the hallways, so Suzi was able to relax with us.

The three of us went out on my balcony. It was a tight fit, as the balconies were more for show than use. 'Are you excited about the tour?' I asked her.

'Yes, it's going to be great. This is the second time we've been out here now. The last tour rocked! I love it here in Australia.'

I noticed her guitarist deferred to her – it was kind of endearing.

Suddenly, there was a loud banging on my door. I told them both to stay out on the balcony and closed the curtains after me as I went to see what all the commotion was about. The door opened just as I got to it, and a rather intense-looking guy with red hair started to come into the room accompanied by two large, gnarly-looking guys. The redhead asked, 'Where's Suzi?'

Now this guy looked like trouble, so I figured the best thing to do was to get him the hell out of my room as quickly as possible. That meant going into attack mode, so I started yelling, 'Get the fuck out of my room!'

The redhead said, 'I'm Bob, and I want to see Suzi now!'

Of course, my natural response was, 'I don't give a damn who you are. Get out of my room!' I think I was having a flashback to my AC/DC Freeway Gardens days. At this point I pushed him. The men retreated, and I slammed the door after them.

Then I realised the room had gone really – I mean, *really* – quiet. *What the hell is going on?* I wondered.

Karen grabbed me and said, 'Have you lost your mind?'

'Huh?'

'That was Bob Jones you just threw out of the room!'

'Hang on a minute – it's not *the* room, it's *my* room, and who the hell is Bob Jones?'

This would be the first of many instances in which people assumed I knew who the hell some high-profile or famous person was without ever being told. I guess it's assumed you're born with such knowledge.

I soon found out that Bob Jones wasn't only the new head of security for Paul Dainty, but he was also a highly accredited black belt (now tenth degree) martial arts teacher, and well respected in the industry. Not exactly the person you want to be yelling at in a confined space with alcohol involved.

After having this explained to me, I retrieved Suzi and Len from the balcony, and off we went to find Bob for her to explain that I wasn't only sorry but also young – too young to die, hopefully. Although I was working on the tour, I miraculously hadn't heard of Bob Jones, and therefore meant no disrespect. Apology accepted. Bob and I got on well from that time on; I think he got a bit of a kick out of the whole situation. So I started my first Dainty tour, thankfully in one piece.

The first show proved how much Australia loved this pint-sized rail of black leather and attitude. A constant stream of young male fans were being passed up onto the stage from the audience, and I soon realised they had fainted from her sheer presence.

One boy was totally out cold. Being a little concerned, we carried him down a hallway and laid him out. I was kneeling over him, trying to assess his condition, when he came to. 'Are you okay?' I asked. 'Can you get up?'

Well, he took one look at me in my black leather jacket, called out, '*Suuuzi!* I love you!' and passed out again. He was put outside as a lost cause. Somewhere in Australia is some guy who thinks he woke up to Suzi Quatro leaning over him, asking him if he was okay.

* * *

The Quatro tour was followed by one with David Essex, a pretty Englishman with a couple of hits, 'Rock On' and 'Gonna Make You a Star'. And then Gary Glitter hit town – only to be overshadowed by my next tour, for a UK band called Status Quo, and their tour manager was my old buddy Swampy. The first show was in Sydney, kicking off the On the Level Tour. I was excited we were finally going to get to tour together!

Swampy had a working relationship with Quo, as he'd done a previous Australian tour for them, so he put in a good word for me and I was welcomed. Right from the start, I liked these guys. There was an ease to both the band and crew. They also had a great sense of humour. I was noticing that British and American humour were very different – the Brits had much more of an irreverence and a cheekiness to them. They didn't take themselves too seriously. I liked it! Quo was a prime example of this.

Before the first show, the band came down to the venue early to check out the set-up and meet the crew. They each wandered onto the stage and started picking up their instruments and checking their equipment. I was onstage, focused the lighting rig, when Francis Rossi came to the front of the stage, turned and looked at the drum kit. He was gauging the size of the stage. He struck me as the leader of the band, as he commanded attention with his presence, and he walked around the stage as if staking a claim. When he spotted me, he said, 'Who put this girlie on my stage?', flashed a big smile, spun on one heel and headed towards his tech guy, strumming his guitar as he went. 'Just messin' about!' he called over his shoulder. Rick Parfitt, the other guitarist/vocalist, seemed a lighter personality and was joking around with an obviously playful nature. He would step up onto the drum riser to check his amp settings and have a joke with the drummer while he was there; it was nice to see. Alan 'Nuff' Lancaster played bass and also sang. While friendly and pleasant, he seemed a little quieter than the others, maybe a tad more reserved. That left the drummer, John 'Spud' Coghlan. Drummers are always a bit different. While he looked serious at first, when he smiled his whole face lit up. First impressions: an all-round good bunch.

The sound check gave me a clue about their music. It was tight with a good groove to it, a boogie feel, and it matched the personalities. Good-time rock. Straight ahead. To the point. Nothing fancy; what you see is what you get.

They were at a place in their careers where everything still seemed fresh to them. Although their band had been around since the 1960s, they'd managed to reinvent themselves, which had launched them to a whole new level of success as denim-clad working-class boys. This had given them a whole new lease on life. Whatever they were doing – playing a show, meeting the fans, or hanging out back in the hotel – they were all about having a good time.

There would always be a room set up in the hotel for after-show partying, and everyone on the tour was invited. This band didn't separate from their crew as some did. Blackie's Bar & Grill, as it became known, was a moveable feast of after-show revelry in every town and would over the years be manned by a crew member, Ian Black (hence the name). Ian had the unique talent of being able to drink 24/7 and still perform his job. Back then, alcohol and drug consumption wasn't a sackable offence.

When we arrived back at the hotel after that first show in Sydney, I got a call in my room from one of the Quo crew asking if I was going to the Bar & Grill. That being the normal entertainment for the night, I said yes! It was Mal, Quo's sound engineer, and he said he would come get me and take me to the bar. I said okay, although I let him know I could probably find it on my own, but he insisted. Off we went to this room that was like a conference hall in the hotel: too large, too bright, and really no atmosphere. It did have a bar, though. Maybe nobody had got the memo, as usually the room would be done up with mood lighting and staged to have lots of atmosphere. The other thing I found strange was that people kept disappearing, and then a different group would appear. When they returned, they would always come up to me and ask if I was having a good time. Now this was starting to get strange – these boys were up to something and failing miserably at being sneaky.

I gave my minder the slip and went to find out what they were up to. I soon discovered the other bar and peeked in from behind its floor-to-ceiling curtains. If they'd gone to all this trouble to keep me entertained elsewhere, I didn't want to spoil it for them. It turned out the promoter had put on some female entertainment for the band, and the girls, seemingly strippers, were doing a fine job. It made me smile, as it meant that they cared enough to think of me in this situation. Now, that was sweet, and it was especially sweet that they'd all taken turns in checking in with me. It must have been something they'd got together and decided to do, so the gesture wasn't wasted on me. That was when I knew I could really spend some time with this band. I snuck back to the other bar.

On the show side, I enjoyed working with their lighting designer, George Harvey. He had a natural way of showing you exactly what he wanted. This lighting rig was different again from what I'd seen so far, with a focus on wash combinations that would heighten the rhythms of the live music, its light patterns creating movements to match the song.

The audiences would line up for hours. I learnt that the Quo Army, as their fans called themselves, were very loyal, dressed in the denim of their band, and were mostly guys who would stand in the aisles and play air guitars along with every song. From the stage these fans looked like an ocean swaying to the music and building momentum with each song. The music made everyone want to get up and have a good time.

At the end of that tour, Quo offered Swampy a permanent gig overseas with them, looking after their backline and stage. This was huge! I was truly excited for him. He'd be leaving within a week, but I never doubted I would be seeing him again.

* * *

Paul McCartney with his new band, Wings, was coming to Australia as part of a world tour that would eventually be seen by a million people. The whole country was abuzz. A Beatle returning to Australia! There hadn't been a Beatle in Australia since they'd toured three cities in June 1964. The country had lost its collective mind, and so had all the local crew people. It was like Beatlemania all over again – they all wanted to do that tour.

It would have been a good one to add to the list of tours on my resumé, but I figured as the new kid I should probably sit this one out. Karen, not being one to miss a good opportunity, decided not to sit it out – she planned to throw a bash that neither the town nor our visitors would forget for a long time to come.

Wings would be on tour in Australia for two weeks, ending in Melbourne, after which they would go to their various homes for the Christmas break. This left band and crew in Melbourne with some extra time on their hands. The last show was on a Friday night, so that made the weekend perfect for a party.

When international bands and crews toured Australia, they were blown away by how good the local crews were, and how well they were taken care of. The international crews were basically on vacation, as the Australian crew would do everything for them. This meant that everyone got on well, and it helped forge long-lasting friendships across the oceans. What's not to love about an Australian roadie?!

Now that the tour was over, the least the Wings crew could do would be to turn up to a party being thrown in their honour. It was the perfect storm.

Karen and I had gone to see Wings at the Sidney Myer Music Bowl. It was another eye-opener for me, as I observed how production was changing so rapidly; it seemed that with every tour coming through there were new innovations, all truly wonderful to see. The sound and lighting for the show were excellent, and so was the music, with new songs like 'Venus and Mars', 'Jett', 'Magneto and Titanium Man' sprinkled with Beatles hits.

The tour had been a huge success, and now it was time to blow off a bit of steam. What started as a one-day event at our house would go for three. Saturday afternoon, people started turning up: the Australian crew, most of the Wings crew, pretty much what could be expected. By that evening we had the entire brass section, band members Joe English, Denny Laine and his wife at the time, Jo Jo, and half the Australian music industry – the likes of Shirl from Skyhooks, Angry Anderson and Lobby Loyde, to name a few. In the wee hours of Sunday morning, the rest of the Wings camp were now all present and accounted for: guitar player Jimmy McCulloch, McCartney's personal assistant Trevor Jones, all of the SHOWCO sound crew, and any remaining stragglers. Problem was, no one was leaving. This didn't go unnoticed by our neighbours, who decided they'd had enough and called the police.

As the sun was just starting to peek through the night shadows to announce Sunday's arrival, the cops turned up. They wanted to know what was going on and why we thought it was okay to have a two-day party. Of course, when we explained that we had Wings in the house, they were excited and impressed, and after meeting the band they dutifully set up a roadblock at the end of our street to stem the flow of traffic and keep the neighbours quiet. Nice!

After thanking the police for their help, and with the sun now up in full force, I wandered out into our large and lush backyard to find Jimmy McCulloch standing alone watching some dogs. We said hi, then just stood comfortably side by side, taking in the view. Keep in mind, everyone had been up for at least two days by this time.

It turned out Jimmy and I were both animal lovers, and the dogs had got our attention as they were acting rather strangely. It seemed that anyone who had a dog had brought it with them to the party, and the dogs had all ended up in our backyard. Neither Karen nor I had a dog. Arrow had been dognapped before I left Sydney.

Jimmy and I looked at each other and said, 'What is up with the dogs?' They appeared to be grazing like cattle. But once you've been up for more than forty-eight hours you see things a little differently. Add drugs and alcohol to the mix, and everything appears cotton-woolly to say the least.

We were thinking this was hilarious and pointing out individual dogs' antics, when I saw a glint in that early morning light. Then I saw it again in a different part of the yard. What? Then it hit me.

I wandered out to where the dogs grazed; Jimmy followed me. And there they were, the remains of a hundred Thai sticks that had been wrapped in aluminium foil. Oh, shit! I remembered someone saying on Saturday morning that they would hide the sticks in the backyard as they didn't want anyone stealing them. Jimmy and I started frantically salvaging what we could from a herd of very stoned dogs, while I was yelling for the person whose stash it was to come sort it out. Then Jimmy asked me, 'Are they any good?' meaning the Thai sticks.

'Of course they are,' I said.

'Great! Paul has been looking for some good Thai sticks. Can we send some to him?'

It turned out Paul had been stuck in the hotel room this whole time, as Linda didn't want to risk him coming to the party and getting busted for drug use in Australia. A shame, but I got it, even though our trusty policemen were guarding the block for us.

Jimmy took the sticks over to Paul, then came straight back. He and I bonded while we sat on my living-room floor, laughing about what had happened earlier and playing my collection of 78s that he was amazed contained the likes of Robert Johnson, Leadbelly, Bessie Smith and Jelly Roll Morton. The names fascinated me as much as the music. I'd bought a gramophone and had been collecting them since leaving AC/DC. It seems I had quite the collection. I was just curious about all types of music; Mal had taught me to look everywhere for it.

By Monday morning I knew I wanted to leave Australia to explore the places that all these new and exciting people were coming from. It'd been one hell of a party, but I needed sleep. Wasn't anyone ever going to leave? I eventually gave up and went to bed. I said my farewells, Jimmy and I promising to stay in touch. He was heading off to continue the Wings tour, so we weren't sure how we'd pull this off, but we knew we would. We hit it off as friends for a couple of reasons;

we'd both started in the industry when we were very young, and we were both excited at the prospect of what was to come. Whatever that might be didn't really matter to us then, as we had plenty of time. Or so we thought.

* * *

After meeting and working with so many people from outside of Australia, I was getting restless. I could now see there was a whole world full of fun and interesting people, and I was ready to discover more of what made this industry so unique.

My next tour was with Leo Sayer, who had broken box-office records on his previous tour and was repeating his success with two songs racing up the charts in Australia: 'You Make Me Feel Like Dancing' and 'When I Need You'. This tour was good for me, as two members of the British crew would play important parts in my life down the road.

The first was Chris 'Smoother' Smyth, who was doing sound on the tour. He was a tall Englishman with an afro similar to Leo's; he was also a funny and very likeable guy with a laid-back way about him. He's now an owner of a US production company, Delicate Productions, that was conceived from Supertramp's success with their *Breakfast in America* album.

The second crew member was Paul Newman (no, not the actor), who after this tour would start at TASCO London then became an owner/partner of TASCO USA, and is presently the vice-president of the aforementioned Clair Brothers audio, USA. But that was all in the future.

Back then, touring was all about the fun and games. Oh, yeah, and twenty-hour workdays, longer if we had to drive overnight to the next show. 'No sleep till Sydney!' You worked hard and you played hard and you tried to learn as

Leo Sayer and Paul Dainty, 1975. (PHILIP MORRIS)

much as you possibly could along the way. Here I was, at the beginning of my fourth back-to-back tour with no downtime. The schedule was tight. That was how you could tell a lower budget tour: no days off. Time was money, the new mantra for the industry.

But Leo was a very likeable chap. Kind of childlike in some ways. Didn't know how to drive a car, married his childhood sweetheart, no rock-star demands. And when the performer is likeable, so is the tour.

We finally had a night in an Adelaide hotel after the show. No overnight drive, a shower and a bed, and a second show to follow. This was clearly a cause to celebrate – God forbid we would sleep. It was always the same: we'd complain that we never got hotel rooms or sleep, then when we did get a room, we would stay up partying all night. Living from one hotel room to the next had become my new normal. I rarely got to see my bedroom back in Moorabbin, but it was nice to know it was there.

Now, the only perk to me being a girl was I got a single room. The downside, I was about to find out, could be thinking it was the best room in which to party.

We'd scored two very large plastic garbage bins packed with ice, and an assortment of beers, soft drinks and a few bottles of spirits that were lying around backstage, along with an assortment of party favours. The night was in full swing when I decided to sit on the rim of a plastic bin while deep in conversation, listening to ribald tails of the road. I'd sat in that exact spot earlier, so I thought nothing of it. However, ice has an uncanny knack of melting, and what had supported me just fine earlier now had a problem. The side of the bin buckled, then collapsed. I leapt up, falling backwards and taking the bin with me, which caused a chain reaction throughout the room.

In a matter of seconds what had been a regular hotel room now looked like the aftermath of a hurricane, with a couple of inches of water covering the floor. As each person had reacted, they'd caused more damage. Both huge garbage bins had gone over, along with anything that wasn't bolted down – chairs, glasses, bottles and ashtrays (yuck), and where had that pizza come from? But best of all, Smoother was standing in the corner with a 'What just happened?' look on his face and a lampshade on his head; he'd been lying on the chest of draws, his head resting on the bolted-down lamp stand. The hotel staff, however, were not amused.

The following day was a very sombre one for me, as I kept a low profile and awaited those dreaded words: 'You're outta here! You're fired!' But the words never came. Ron Blackmore had got to the bottom of what had happened and figured out he couldn't sack his whole crew, so with a strong warning that this behaviour wouldn't be tolerated, the matter was dropped.

At least until I got back from the show that night to find a bill on the table of my remarkably restored room (down to the new carpet and lampshade). The bill itemised each and every thing that had been replaced and/or repaired – including a section of hallway carpet? – and showed a total of $6872. That was a lot of money back in 1976. Is this how Keith Moon started?

The bill was sorted, and I am sure not for that amount. However, every time I stayed in that hotel, I always ended up in that room. I believe that was Ron's way of making a point – something he was very good at.

* * *

Life was starting to get a bit surreal. When you're constantly touring, it's like living in a bubble. Day-to-day life ceases to exist or even matter. You've no idea what's going on in the world outside that insular orb, and you tend not to care. You know that other bands are touring as you run into them from time to time on the road; they're your partners in crime, because they get it – they, at least, understand what you're doing out there, and how hard it can be. Slowly at first and without even noticing it, you become completely alienated from everyday people, and you lose the ability to communicate with them. When you do, they nearly always want something: 'Can you get an autograph? Can I come to the show? What, only tickets? No backstage pass?' This encourages you to isolate yourself more, to avoid the barrage of things that people want – not all people, but most. This leaves you vulnerable to dissociation. It's like a form of Stockholm syndrome: you become the hostage, and the tour is your captor. You find yourself loving your captor. It becomes your whole life, and you can't imagine doing any other sort of work.

For me it was perfect. I think it goes back to looking for that elusive family unit, somewhere I could fit in. I'd found it. By now being a roadie was more than a job: it was a lifestyle. Most of us were young and single, with no commitments outside of the next tour. This meant we worked together and played together both on and off the road. We were like a pack turning up at clubs or shows; everyone knew who you were, and in you went. No hassle.

You can get used to that quite easily – you take it for granted and no longer realise how special it all is. No matter how far from normal, it becomes the new normal. The disassociation can be extreme. I think that's why so many people in this job have such a difficult time once their touring days are over.

8

CALIFORNIA
DREAMIN'

SANTANA WOULD BE THE first American band and crew I'd get
to work with, and I was curious to see the differences. Carlos
was back as a force to be reckoned with, and his new album
Amigos was flying up the charts. Included in his performance
each night was his hit song 'Black Magic Woman'.

Bill Graham was also back at the controls as the band's
manager. He wasn't only a manager, he was also a major
promoter in America. He was very passionate and committed
to both the bands and crews in his stable, and among others
he'd worked closely with was my girl Janis Joplin ... Respect!
How could I not want to learn from this influential man?
Bill had served in Vietnam and used that training to run a
tight ship. He also kept close a lot of his service buddies by
employing them in his productions. When he spoke, people
shut up and listened. He was genuinely warm and friendly
with a great sense of humour. Not everyone got to see the
light-hearted side of Bill – thankfully, I did.

Bill's union with Carlos Santana had started rather unconventionally when he had caught a very young, and as yet unheard-of, Carlos sneaking in to one of his venues. From this chance meeting, he would become a strong supporter of the musician and when Bill was asked to help out with the logistics of the Woodstock Festival, he agreed on the condition that Santana was added to the bill. Bill was not like other promoters; he was a strong advocate for what he considered his 'people'.

This tour was a return to the style of Latin funk that had made Santana famous. His trusty sidekick, Tom Coster, was leading the band, with a new vocalist, Greg Walker. The musicians and fans alike were happy with the results. This music was nothing like anything you would find in Australia at the time, nor were the musicians. Carlos Santana is one of few front men who can hold the audience's attention throughout a performance while never singing a note – he leads through his guitar.

In the mid to late 1970s, Australia was still coming to terms with the recent dissolution of the White Australia Policy, and there was frequent discourse in the papers about the impending influx of refugees from the Vietnam War. Anglo-Australians tended to view other ethnic groups and races as either a curiosity or a problem. But the music of Santana seemed to breach those boundaries and give us a reprieve from our social problems, as only music can.

This was the first time I'd experienced anything to do with South American culture. I kept having to stop myself from staring, as I didn't want to appear rude. Among the nine band members and several crew, I was fascinated to see so many skin tones; I soon learnt that different countries in South America had completely different ethnicities – I'd had no idea. But when there's a common denominator such as music, there are no ethnic or cultural boundaries; those walls come down. As we slid into the routine of the tour, our diversified bunch became one. I was privileged to experience firsthand the differences in my daily ways of thinking to that of this group of people from faraway lands.

On this tour, I learnt that along with music, humour is also a great unifier. There was always one joke or another going on with these guys, part of the camaraderie that forms from working so closely together. Nobody was spared the pranks, including Carlos.

At the start of the tour's second show, I was stage right checking that all was good with the equipment. The keyboard tech had taken up position next to me, and I asked him if I should move. He said, 'No, you're good,' then, 'but you might want to see this,' and he pointed to Carlos onstage. About halfway through the first song, Carlos came to the front of the stage for the first time. He looked down towards the ground where his monitor wedge sat – and, after doing a double take, he totally cracked up with laughter. I couldn't figure out what was going on. A couple of the other band members moved to the area where Carlos had lost it, and they also started laughing. At this point the whole band had caught on to what their crew had done.

Carlos, a very spiritual man, followed the guru Sri Chinmoy at the time. He had taken on the name of Devadip and was in the habit of sticking a photo of his guru on his monitor wedge. On this night, however, the crew had replaced it with the latest *Playboy* centrefold – Miss January, I believe.

But the jokes weren't only played on the musicians. By the time we got to Adelaide, everyone was fair game. This time it was the turn of the Australian promoter's tour coordinator, Michael Chugg.

I'd first met Michael back in Mushroom House, when he worked for Michael Gudinski. I knew that while he was a good person, he could be a hard person if things weren't going to plan. He was notorious for swearing a blue streak which was rumoured to have ended his career as a horseracing caller. Another strong character in an industry of alpha males, who went on to become one of Australia's most successful promoters. On this tour, however, he would not be spared becoming the brunt of one of their jokes.

Michael was in the habit of making pre-show announcements from the side of the stage, where he wouldn't be seen but would be heard everywhere through the PA system. The American front-of-house sound guy decided it would be funny to cut Michael's microphone on and off while he was trying to make his announcement. Now, Michael wasn't amused by this and started a tirade of fuck this and fuck that, which ended with 'Youse are all fucking cunts!' being blasted through the venue when the mic was briefly turned back on.

When Michael calmed down and saw the funny side of it all, he was patted on the back and thanked for being a good sport as he headed to check the box office at the front of the building. While patting him, we'd stuck a sign on his back quoting what had just blasted through the PA system. When returning to the stage he walked down the centre aisle of the venue with all the house lights still on; the entire seated audience could read the sign on his back and started cracking up as they figured out he was the guy from the earlier announcement. Luckily, Michael is a good sport!

These are the things we did to pass the time. The hours were long, the job was hard, you had to find a way to relieve the pressure or you'd end up killing each other. Always better to make a joke.

These jokes didn't take away from the intensity of the performance every night. This was a big band compared to the others I'd worked with so far. When all nine band members were playing and moving about onstage, they kept everyone enthralled, including me and the rest of the crew. There was a different type of energy to this music – it was primal. It had a crisp sound that alternated between frantic and sensual. Every night the audience was up and dancing in the aisles. The dancing would continue back to the hotel, where we would find wall-to-wall women wanting to get closer to the men who made that sound.

* * *

Carlos was curious about the lone girl on his crew. He would seek me out to talk, and he'd tease me because of the things his crew told him about me. According to him, they said that they wouldn't mess with me, as they were certain I could hold up to the best of them. He also had been told I had an admirer in Carlos's crew, which was true. *This* I wasn't sure how to deal with, but I let it happen to see where it would go. We had got together on one of our nights off and continued a romance for the tour, which was nice as I could let down my defensive wall with him and be more like a girl, more like me.

I was having breakfast in the hotel one morning with this crew member when Carlos walked in and sat with us. I'd been about to dig into plate of steak and eggs, which all of a sudden I wished I hadn't ordered – I felt strange eating it in front of Carlos, as I'd heard he was a vegetarian and I didn't want to offend him.

He saw what was happening and casually asked, 'Can I try your steak?'

This threw me. 'I thought you were a vegetarian?'

His response went something like, 'You can do or be anything you want as long as you respect the other being,' as he cut off a piece of steak and popped it in his mouth; he looked like he was enjoying it. As he got up from the table, still smiling, he said, 'It's nice to see the two of you together.'

I found Carlos to be both an intense character and a calming one for someone who was quiet in word and quiet in nature. I think it was the religious influence on him. When he looked at me and smiled, I felt as though he could read my innermost thoughts. At first it was a little unnerving, but once I understood that he wasn't going to judge me, I felt safe and could relax and just enjoy his company. I never asked him about it in case he admitted that he could in fact read my thoughts. I never asked his crew, as I knew they would have laughed at me and still not answered one way or another.

But I was always asking the crew about what working and living in America was like, and one day their tour manager asked me what my plans were.

'What do you mean?' I said.

'Well, what are you doing after this tour?'

'I don't know. Whatever tour comes next, I guess.'

'Well, how about this? Neil Diamond is coming here a couple of weeks after we finish. I could hook you up with that tour if you want?'

I jumped at it – I didn't even ask what the job would be. I didn't care, so long as it meant I kept working and met more industry people. 'That would be great, thank you!'

I was also happy because I'd worried that my being with one of their crew members would make them look at me differently, but it seemed not to have changed anything. Not that I was going to make a habit of it, I told myself.

A few days later, I got word that I had a job working directly for Neil Diamond's crew. I'd be in charge of setting up something called a Mobius, apparently – whatever that was.

* * *

Right after the Santana tour, I had a short break at home. Karen had called me a couple of times saying that we had a peeping Tom. Now I was back, I promised to help sort it out. Karen's son Shannon's room was at the back of the house off mine, and his mum and I were concerned for his safety. The sprawling backyard provided plenty of shadowy spots for this creep to hide.

I came up with a plan: I would wire the entire house below each window with pyrotechnic flash pods. I figured that if I strung them into a daisy chain, it wouldn't matter which window the guy came to, as they'd all go off at the same time. What could possibly go wrong?

After calling in some favours from one of the bands that used pyro on their show, I got my hands on the necessary explosives. I spent the morning rigging my trap. There weren't pre-set, safely packaged flash pods back then; as with lots of equipment I handled on the road, it was trial and error. I used all of the explosive material, as I didn't want to leave any lying around the house – that stuff can be dangerous!

Two nights later, in the wee hours of the morning, I saw him. It was very creepy, his silhouette leaning through my open window. I slowly stretched my arm to the wall socket and hit the switch.

BOOM!!!

He jumped back in pain, while I jumped up in shock. Had I just blown up the house?

I may have overdone it a tad. A large explosion has a vacuum effect. All the curtains had blown out of the windows, while the whole house had lit up and momentarily felt like it had lifted off its foundations – which certainly was possible. Then there was the smoke and the tell-tale smell of gunpowder.

From where I was now standing, I could see the whites of his eyes. Then he yelped, fell backwards, screamed and took off over the high picket (ouch!) fence at the end of the yard. Mission accomplished!

Karen and I were soon sitting at the kitchen table, laughing hysterically and toasting my success, when there was a loud and official-sounding knock at the front door. Karen peeked out the window to see two policemen looking very serious indeed and demanding we open up.

We quickly hid our drinks and pretended to be sleepy-faced before we obliged. They were the two officers who'd turned up to the Wings party. On this occasion, however, they were not amused. They came straight to the point. 'What the hell went on here this time?'

'I don't know what you mean, officer,' I replied.

That didn't fly at all. 'Yours is the only household in a four-block radius that has not called in a bomb going off. And we are holding this conversation through a cloud of thick smoke that smells like gunpowder.'

The second officer chimed in. 'Time for an explanation, or we can take you down to the station.'

I told the officers that we'd called in a prowler on several occasions but no one had ever followed up. Being two defenceless girls with a young child, we'd decided to protect ourselves. 'It's no big deal,' I added. 'I read the instructions.'

They were a little intrigued at our ingenuity, but after explaining the dangers of what we'd done, and checking to make sure we were no longer in possession of explosives – and that the house wasn't on fire – they gave me a serious dressing-down!

As they were leaving, one of the officers complained, 'Now we'll never find this guy.'

I suggested they go to the nearest hospital. 'He'll be the one with the crotch burnt out of his pants.' And that was exactly where our policemen found him.

With the home front under control, it was time for me to go back out on the road.

* * *

I made my way to the Southern Cross Hotel where a welcome party was being held for Neil Diamond, his band and crew. I was finally going to meet the people I'd been hearing so much about from the Santana crew. Neil's tour manager, Patrick Stansfield, who also worked for Bill Graham back in the States, was highly regarded in the industry. I was excited by the possibilities that lay before me.

When I walked in to the reception room, the party was in full swing. I took a long, hard look around the room and wondered what on earth I was doing there. It was an older crowd – well, through my eyes – and they all looked very respectable and shiny, even the crew. Most in the room were wearing satin. Ugh! This wasn't my scene. But Santana's crew had thought it would be a good move for me, and they'd vouched for me on both a personal and a professional level and for the first time I would be working directly for an international band.

I really didn't know anything about Neil Diamond, and I was never really into choosing tours by the performers. I would choose a tour by the crew. If it's a good crew, it is going to be a good tour; good crew don't work for bad artists. But these guys all looked kind of straight, the opposite of those on the tour I'd just completed. How could they be friends? Out of curiosity, and not being one to look a gift-horse in the mouth, I decided to stay and give it a chance, so I started to mingle with the few faces I knew.

I'd had a couple of drinks and done my civic duty, and was making my way to the door for a quick exit, when this guy came up to me and said, 'Leaving so soon? Where are you going?'

'Out of here – anywhere.'

He laughed, grabbed a bottle of champagne and said, 'Can I come too?'

I was outside the main entrance, deciding which direction to take, when he caught up to me and said, 'I have a car. If you show me Melbourne, I can give you a lift anywhere you want to go.' Why not? There wasn't much to see after midnight in Melbourne in the mid 1970s, but a lift home would be great!

The car was a limousine and when he saw the look on my face when it pulled up, he smiled and introduced himself as Neil Diamond.

We ended up on Albert Park Beach drinking champagne out of the bottle, and this was where I discovered looks can be deceiving. After Neil laid his satin jacket down for me to sit on, we talked about how he liked being onstage playing his own music. He'd spent a lot of time writing songs for other people. As the conversation continued, I found out he also smoked pot and rode Harleys – not the impression you got at first look.

The tour started two days later, and I was happy to be on board. Not only was Neil one of the most prolific songwriters of his time, but he was also a very cool guy and respected by musicians from all walks of life. This was to be his first Australian tour on the success of his *Hot August Nights* album, which had spent an unprecedented 239 weeks on the Aussie charts. Its record sales translated to one in every three Australian households owning a copy. He also had a very talented road crew, not to mention a new hit album about a bloody seagull, of all things! Go figure.

* * *

The Sydney show was going to be filmed live. With this in mind, and the fact that several of the shows were outdoors, Neil – well, Patrick Stansfield, his tour manager – had brought over a structure to support his lightshow called the Mighty Mobius. Patrick was also the tour manager for The Stones, who had just used this system for their American tour, and he had adapted it for Neil's tour. It had become common practice to re-use set pieces and lighting effects/trussing configurations on multiple tours, as they were expensive to build. If you were careful to use them in a different musical genre, then each audience would see them for the first time and be wowed.

The concept of the Mobius was a new one. It was a circular trussing configuration that covered the width and depth of the stage. Its main support tower came up through the rear centre of the stage behind the backline. It resembled a large sombrero covered in a yellow-and-white striped tarpaulin that floated above the stage and was perfect for the outdoor arena shows. This meant there were no sightline impediments, and that transferred into more ticket sales. Music was becoming big business. Ticket sales were starting to dominate the evolution of production and concert touring.

The Mobius became my baby/responsibility. I soon learnt that no matter how innovative a structure it may have been, it was a cumbersome beast. The overall shape made the trussing sections difficult to put together, and nobody wanted to have to deal with it on a daily basis. It would be mine for the next two months, the length of the Australian tour. I didn't care: I was impressed that it could support a real lighting system, with front lighting out over the stage in an outdoor environment. This was huge for the time and changed how lights were used for live performances. I was happy to wrestle with it each day, as each challenge meant I was learning something new.

At the first load-in, I'd started to walk away after my truck was unloaded, only to be called back by one of the American crew. 'Where are you going, Tana?'

'My truck is done.'

'Not so soon. There's more.'

What? I was already starting to see why nobody wanted this job, even if it meant a free trip to Australia. There were another two-thirds of a truck of screens and dressing still to come.

This was when I first figured out the best way to deal with something BIG. I would mentally break it down into manageable sections – that way you don't waste time running backwards and forwards doing a bit here and a bit there, and holding up the stage area so no one else is able to start their jobs. Nothing worse for a crew at a load-in than waiting on someone while they get their shit together; I didn't want to be that person.

Neil Diamond's tour, 1976, in Adelaide with the Mighty Mobius. Looks like a giant Sombreo. (NEWS LTD/NEWSPIX)

Our first outdoor show of the tour was at the WACA sports stadium in Perth. We had a tech day before the show, which was standard whenever a road crew started putting up this much equipment – especially equipment they'd never seen before.

Patrick was checking in with me through the different stages of the set-up and was happy with the results, or so I thought. 'I have to tell you, T, I've got to make some changes here,' were the first words out of his mouth when we stopped for dinner. Uh-oh! That didn't sound good. 'I'm changing your nickname from T to Tenacious T, because you've mastered the Mobius.' That was a huge compliment coming from such an experienced person. I was only once given a derogatory name on a tour and that was Useless (pretty bad and just because I was a girl), but it was quickly changed to Ace, and that was pretty good! That was compliments of a SHOWCO crew.

The Mighty Mobius never did catch on: it was the ugly stepmother, a stepping-stone to the outdoor staging roofs you see today, with motor-driven roofs that climb up trussing to reach their nesting places high above the stage. It was also another stepping-stone for me in my career.

* * *

The lighting rigs had been getting bigger and more complex since the start of ACT. Everything I was being taught was new, not only for me, but the industry. This levelled the playing field and I found this exciting, which confirmed for me that I'd chosen the right job. We could do a lot conceptually with front-suspended, side and back lighting, and free-floating screens that were retractable for projection. It was all about the challenge for me.

It also made me more involved in the performance as there were now cues for screens and other equipment moving under my guidance. Plus, I could climb over these structures, which helped reduce the time I spent focusing the lights or making repairs once everything was up in the air. Now, for the first time, I got to look down on the stage from that bird's-eye view. It was a rush.

Taking my new nickname to heart, I took control of the crew assigned to me for the show calls. For the first time I was in charge and giving clear directions to the people working under me. The American crew would call, 'Look out, she's coming through!' from the bottom of the ramp off the stage. This was a compliment. Under my direction, we matched The Stones crew's time for the Mobius load-outs and by the end of the tour we had it beaten on both set-up and tear-down by over an hour each. I was on a roll and loving it. A world record, yeah! These things were important because of the new mantra going around: 'Time is money!' By the time we hit Sydney, my crew was a well-oiled machine with me at the controls.

Having been hired by Neil's production team meant I was socialising a lot more with the American crew, and I was now being included in production meetings and logistics – more for me to learn. This was also the tour that opened the door for me to leave Australia.

The general public tends to look at roadies as a bunch of wild, tough, and not necessarily talented, yobs. At least that was the impression in the days before you could go to school to get a degree on how to be a roadie. (Oops! Sorry – 'technician'.) This impression, I can assure you, was inaccurate. Under those gruff exteriors lurked innovators who knew no fear or boundaries for change while creating the new face of the music industry. That's what inspired me to keep at it – this innovative thinking was what made the loading of endless trucks seem worthwhile. It was the time of 'If you can imagine it, we will find a way to make it happen!' Usually on a shoestring budget, with zero engineering or technical assistance, just a whole lot of ingenuity. Some experiments yielded better results than others, but it was all a learning curve.

This next show would be at the Sydney Sports Ground and was to be televised nationwide. Huge by Australian standards, it was a first for its time – a feat never before attempted.

Two years had passed since I'd fled the Cross and started my life as a roadie, and here I was back, a totally different person. Working on becoming all grown up! I made no direct contact with anyone from the old days, but I did anonymously drop a pair of tickets to the show for Carl at the pool hall, my private way of saying thank you.

The load-in call was for early the following day, and for now we were hanging out in one of the hotel rooms. Sam Cole, who worked for Neil both on tour and in his recording studio, Arch Angel, mentioned that Larry Williams, Neil's guitar guy had written a song. Did I want to hear it? Well, shit yeah! I hadn't been a part of listening to new material since my AC/DC days, so I was excited. Larry was a quiet guy, a nice guy, and seemed a little shy about playing his song to a stranger. The song was good, catchy, and called 'Let Your Love Flow'.

When it won a Grammy after being recorded by the Bellamy Brothers, Larry couldn't attend the awards show – he was on tour doing Neil's guitars. So goes the lot of a roadie.

Oh yes, and the next time I saw Santana's monitor engineer, he was playing drums for Bob Dylan on his US/European tour. He also became a highly regarded cinematographer.

The list of these unpretentious roadies' aspirations and accomplishments is unending. These years laid the foundations of production that would evolve and explode onto the stages of touring bands worldwide, with milestone after milestone being achieved by crews that just wanted to see if they could make it happen.

* * *

The televised show was a huge success, and we were all invited to an end-of-tour party to celebrate. This turned out to be quite the event, attended by a recent prime minister and his wife; ABBA, who were also in Australia on tour; and some guy called The Fonz.

The party was in full swing when Neil came over to me and said, 'Tana, come with me. There's somebody I want you to meet.'

I was like, 'Ahh … okay?'

Neil put his hand on the small of my back and led me away from my group to the bar area. There was a short guy dressed in jeans and a black leather biker jacket. He looked very 1950s, with his dark hair combed back in a quiff. As Neil and I approached, the guy turned to us, put his hands out to his side and did this very animated 'Heyyy!'

Everyone around us turned to look at me with big smiles. But I was just confused. What did this mean? I looked to Neil, hoping for some clue as to what I was supposed to do.

Before I could say anything, the guy did it again. 'Heyyy!'

This time everyone laughed. Neil looked at me and said, 'The Fonz.' I had no idea what he was talking about.

The guy then said, 'Can I get you a drink? What do you want?'

I said, 'No. Thank you. I, uh, have to go back over there.' I pointed in the direction from which I'd come, then I beat a hasty retreat, back to my group who were all excited that I'd just met The Fonz. It took the next fifteen minutes for them to explain to me who the hell The Fonz was, that he was a character on a popular TV show, *Happy Days*. When someone told Neil later, he thought it was funny – luckily so did a young Henry Winkler, aka The Fonz.

* * *

Patrick Stansfield and I had got on well throughout the tour. He reminded me of my father in a strange way. His next tour, when he returned to the States, was to be the second leg of Bob Dylan's Rolling Thunder Revue due to start mid April. By the end of Neil's tour, he offered me a job on that one. I was noticing a more unilateral level of acceptance with these international crews. Was it that they were more secure in their own positions, each being established in their own fields and not having to fight for the next tour?

Wow! Could I possibly be accepted internationally? These visitors also confirmed what I was beginning to know. There were no other women out there touring.

The tour was a couple of months away, so I had time to decide. Dylan had a hit with the song about Hurricane Carter that I'd heard on the radio, and it would mean going to America. The season was coming to an end here, so the timing seemed right.

I'd enjoyed my time with Neil, his band and his crew, and had learnt that first impressions could be deceiving. What I'd first seen as a sea of satin had turned out to be so much more. I'd got to learn about both lighting and production. I'd also got to know Neil, and our paths would cross again, each time being a pleasure. Patrick would become another friend and mentor.

But I still could have lived without all that satin. I hastily gave my tour jacket away.

Not all tours go to plan, and Dylan's second leg of the Rolling Thunder Revue was one. I was warned off, and then the tour collapsed a couple of weeks in with less-than-acceptable ticket sales. I'd have to come up with an exit plan B. I was glad I hadn't mentioned Patrick's offer to anyone.

9

LONDON CALLING

DEEP DOWN IT WAS every Aussie roadie's goal to get a job with one of the international bands, giving you access to the rest of the world. Most of the crew people I was now working with had been doing this a lot longer than me and the competition was fierce. I felt some trepidation about how soon another offer might come my way.

It was the end of March 1976, six months since I'd left AC/DC, and in that short time I'd worked on seven international tours. Neil Diamond would be my last tour in Australia. It had been a hectic couple of years since I'd moved to Melbourne, but I'd used the time well to learn as much as I could about the equipment and its operators. I'd learnt to pick my battles and stay away from those who didn't want me there. Discretion was the better part of valour.

With my mind made up to leave Australia, I kept to the departure schedule I'd had for Dylan in April. I was eighteen, but my father had to sign off on my passport application, as I didn't have any ID or a birth certificate. I filled the time it took, working odd shows with local bands like The Dingoes, who were good musicians and always had a good-time feel to their shows, and Dragon, a hot mess with their talented but very wasted lead singer. I focused on doing backline, but not committing to any band. I was sticking close to Melbourne, so most of these shows were at pubs. This left me open to getting hassled by drunken punters. The general public just didn't get what I was doing there. Many assumed I was some sort of groupie, and that really bothered me. This solidified that I had made the right decision to leave.

* * *

I felt the shift in pressure when the plane reduced speed, accompanied by the rising pitch of the engines. Could this be us at last descending into Amsterdam? As if in response to my thoughts, a loud crackling came over the inflight intercom, accompanied by the cabin lighting being turned on. 'Ladies and gentlemen, we would ask at this time that you all remain in your seats. The captain would like to make an announcement.'

As a group, we passengers were not happy. This had become the flight from hell.

'Good morning, passengers! This is your captain speaking. Due to unforeseen circumstances, we will be making an unscheduled stop at Dubai Airport to refuel, allowing us to continue to our destination of Amsterdam. All window blinds are to remain closed.'

We finally landed at Schiphol Airport thirty-seven hours after we'd left Melbourne. An airport had never looked so good to me. Amsterdam! The Leidseplein, the Café Black & White, Vondelpark and, of course, Club Paradiso. This would be my first home away from home.

I hadn't planned on company for my trip, but Karen and Shannon were with me. Her reason for wanting to come could have had something to do with still needing to pay for the hundred dog-devoured Thai sticks. As for me, I was just happy to be on my way to touring with bands in countries I'd only heard of.

I quickly discovered I liked living in a foreign country. Everything was different: the way things smelt and tasted, even the daylight. It was like being thrust back into childhood and having to learn things all over again – but this time it was fun. I spent my days at the many art galleries in the city, seeing up close the works I'd loved and studied in school, by artists such as Rembrandt and Van Gogh, while sitting for hours with my sketchpad replicating these masterpieces. The images in books hadn't prepared me for the real thing. How rich and textured these amazing pieces were, how they smelt of a time that had passed but somehow lingered in the room. As if all those who had stopped to view these pieces left a small part of themselves behind. Finally, one part of my boarding school education was making sense.

Then, one day, I saw it! Status Quo was to tour in Austria, just a train ride away. I'd be able to catch up with the band and crew, but mostly Swampy.

Quo had just completed a six-week tour of the States supporting the likes of Robin Trower, Wishbone Ash, Peter Frampton and even Fleetwood Mac, and I wanted to know what it was really like in America. Unfortunately, Quo's time over there had been rough, and to this day they've never cracked the American market (for a band that has sold over 18 million albums, this seems very strange). It was important that the first gigs back on their regular turf went well, to get them back on track with sold-out shows, performing for fans who loved them.

I reached out to the management company in London, and they asked me to take three hundred glow sticks, which would be delivered to me in Amsterdam, over to Austria where they would be sold as part of the merch. I said yes.

Each glow stick resembled a small stick of dynamite in size and shape: about fifteen centimetres long, two centimetres in diameter. They were a sci-fi green-ooze colour with a glass capsule inside that when cracked caused the glow reaction. This was a new thing, with very few people knowing what they were or what made them work, including Karen and myself. If this got us to Austria, though, who cared? Shannon would get to stay in Amsterdam with his Auntie Nene.

Where we crossed into Austria was a small railway station with a shed on the platform that acted as a customs office. We hadn't expected to have our bags inspected, and when the two guards found the mysterious-looking packets, and hundreds of them, there was a big fuss. Not only did we not have any paperwork, but we didn't speak Austrian. I was still trying to figure out how to say 'hold the mayonnaise on French fries' in Dutch, for Christ's sake!

We decided to pantomime a demonstration of the glow sticks.

'How do you want to do this?' Karen asked.

'I don't know. Just act it out for them.'

She took one and I took another. 'Sir, look,' we each said to our chosen guard, speaking slower and louder than necessary like all anglophone tourists do, somehow thinking this can magically translate our comments. Karen and I each peeled open a packet to expose the stick, then waved them back and forth in imitation of a concertgoer. 'It's for fun!' I said.

The guards still weren't getting it. One said, '*Was ist das?*' suspiciously pointing and shrugging.

One last-ditch effort: we turned the lights off and at the same time cracked the sticks, while waving them and yelling, 'Wheee!'

All hell broke loose! There was a huge crash, then lots of yelling and barking of orders. By the time the lights came back on, one guard had dived over the desk to get away from us, while the other had drawn his gun and had it pointed right at us. This wasn't good.

Fortunately, when a third guard arrived on the scene, the misunderstanding was cleared up, but only after he'd yelled at us, '*Bist du deppert?*' which I believe means 'Are you an idiot?' We just thanked them for not shooting us and ran for our train.

We arrived at the venue thinking we'd have a great story to tell, but everyone was panicking and in no mood for frivolity. The band had also had a problem upon their arrival. At the Austrian airport, a fight had broken out when a customs officer placed his hands on Nuff, the bass player. After the resulting scuffle, three band members had spent the night in jail.

Some of the crew weren't having any better luck: the lighting system had been loaded on the truck without being patched for the tour, which meant there was no way of controlling the lights from the desk or anywhere else. This was something George, the lighting designer, had only found out after it had been set up. (There's that 'check your equipment' thing again!) Now he was running out of time.

My training in Australia kicked in. You never sit back and watch someone struggle; you always find a way to make it work.

I asked George, 'What's the problem?'

He was irritated at first. 'You're wasting my time. I don't have time to explain it to you. You're not familiar with this system.'

He was right, I didn't know that system – but it was just really mathematics.

'Try me!'

After he said it out loud, we came up with a solution. 'What if I hot-patch the lights, and you focus each one and call a channel for me to send it to?' We salvaged about two-thirds of the system. The rest would have to wait; the show had to start. Karen and I stayed on for the next two shows, as I worked with George to get the rig on track.

Now I'd had a taste of working again, I needed to get back into it, plus we were running out of money. I'd been paid for the shows in Austria, and Karen and I sold merch at the Rotterdam show – we figured the merch guys owed us, what with us almost getting shot 'n all.

We earned just enough to get us to London. Karen decided to send Shannon back to Australia to stay with family. We were heading into uncharted waters, and I had a feeling it was going to get rough.

* * *

What you want isn't always what you get. Nor do you always get what you need. No matter what Mick Jagger says! I've never been good at asking for help, so I probably made this time in my life harder than it had to be. My father had bailed us out a couple of times, but now I'd moved to London he was worried for me, and rightly so. After my third request for money, he sent me a return air ticket only. I said thanks but no thanks! I wasn't going to give up without a fight.

As I found my way around London, I ran into people I'd met on different tours, but I never let any of them know how desperate I was. No one will hire a desperate person, and I needed a job before the winter snows came and the touring season started.

The summer festivals were becoming big moneymakers, but people would work them for free in some cases just so they could say they were there. I was invited to Knebworth to see The Stones and Lynyrd Skynyrd that year, and Reading Festival to see the mud! Oh, I mean to see Pat Travers Band (who I had landed a paying job with) on the Saturday and AC/DC on the Sunday. Work was finally coming in. Karen returned to Australia, while I went out on a package tour – Route '77 Tour for Doctors of Madness. I was hired to do backline for the band Tyla Gang.

On that tour, we were being held up each day by the guy whose job it was to set up and operate the lighting rig. As I knew lighting, I was asked whether I'd help him out. This I did, and once he saw I could do it, he suddenly started arriving each day with the band, just to operate the show, leaving me to do his job and mine. On the last show I let him know what I thought of him taking advantage and being a lazy bastard. When he tried to leave without helping to load the truck, I snapped and chased him around the venue with a scaffolding pipe. I cornered him in the back of the truck, the one place he'd been avoiding all tour. I allowed myself to be talked down from inflicting bodily harm, on the condition he load the truck. I've never minded hard work, I just could never stand a crew member not carrying their weight.

This wasn't a glorious start to my UK career, but from that tour I gained an introduction to two men who became my lifelong friends, Steve Sunderland and Tony Selinger. I was now officially up and running: that tour was followed by a Pat Travers tour, where I once again did backline (at this point I still didn't care what the job was; I would do whatever it took). Nicko McBrain was the drummer on that tour, shortly before he joined Iron Maiden.

It became obvious to me I needed to get in with a production company for a steady income. I had nowhere to live. I even spent the night on a park bench once, as I was uncomfortable asking people if I could stay on their couches. I'd been at the Speakeasy earlier that night, where I could get free drinks and was hanging with the likes of Ginger Baker, and members of both The Stones and The Who, but I didn't want to let anyone know I was homeless.

I toured with Nicko McBrain for the Pat Travers Band before he got the gig with Iron Maiden. This photo was taken at Download Festival in Donington Park, UK, in 2003. (DANNY CLIFFORD)

It was a surreal time, as the following night I was house-sitting David Essex's new mansion, located at the infamous crosswalk for Abbey Road. I even stayed on Richard Branson's canal boat near Maida Vale, which he'd converted to a recording studio. It was cold and damp on the water, and I knew I couldn't continue like this. Even for me this uncertainty was too much, and having to keep moving from place to place was nerve-racking.

I'd grown up without the help of others. This meant now when I really needed it, I was unable to ask. I didn't know how. I couldn't break the habit of coming in through the bathroom window even though the front door was wide open. The front door scared me. I constantly felt, as the only girl out there, that someone would realise and decide it was a mistake and shut me down. I also didn't want to go home with people who would probably expect me to sleep with them, and then be branded a slut – that in, my book, was worse than desperate. And it wasn't an unrealistic fear for a young woman in the male-orientated music industry of the 1970s.

Around this time, I reconnected with Paul Newman from the Leo Sayer tour back in Australia. Paul's position had changed since I'd last seen him: he was now running a department of one of the major production companies in London called TASCO. He started showing me around town; he introduced me to The Who crew, and his business partner, Terry Price.

Terry and I hit it off straightaway. Terry, Paul and I had met up in The Ship pub on Wardour Street for a drink. After a couple of rounds, Paul suggested we go to The Speakeasy club, which was the place to be. All the top musicians and their crew hung out there, and on its small stage the likes of

Marc Bolan, Ginger Baker, Jimi Hendrix and Elton John had all performed.

But I had to confess that I was barred from the venue.

'What?' Terry said. 'You've just arrived in town.'

Although I felt a little hesitant, I went on to tell the story. 'This guy was being a dick! I was sitting there, minding my own business in the restaurant area, when this guy I don't know comes over, sits down and orders a plate of spaghetti. Then he started mouthing off!'

'And ...' Terry said.

'Well, he said something really shitty about my friend Karen. So I took his plate of food when it arrived at the table and cracked it over his head.'

Terry didn't say anything, just stood there looking at me.

'I may have overreacted,' I said, to try and get out of the moment.

'Who was he?' Terry asked.

'The tour manager for some band called Savoy Brown?'

Terry just broke out laughing, and from that night on he took great delight in sneaking me into The Speak under different disguises as his guest. His opinion on the matter was, 'Fuck him, Savoy Brown isn't a client anyway.' That was when our friendship started, along with a long working relationship.

* * *

Swampy was briefly back in town, having finished the European leg of the Quo tour. Soon he'd be on his way to France for a tour with Véronique Sanson, a French megastar and the soon-to-be ex-wife of Stephen Stills – a very jealous

Stephen Stills. Swampy said I could stay in his flat while he was away on tour. Saved!

I got a call one night at the flat from Swampy, who was in Paris. He said, 'Mate, I gotta tell you. These crazy fucking Yanks!'

'What?' I said. 'I thought Véronique was French?'

'Yeah! Not her – Stephen Stills.'

'What's going on, Swampy?'

'Well, mate, I gotta tell you. He's figured out that Véronique and I are close, and he keeps turning up. We played Paris tonight, and the French president was there, right in the front row. What do you think this crazy fucker does? He's standing across from me on the other side of the stage, just staring at me, then he pulls what looks like a gun out of his jacket pocket.' He was laughing nervously. 'Yeah! *Faaark!* Right there while the show is going on.'

'Jesus, Swampy! You need to stay away from her. Well, from him. Well, hell, from both of them.'

'It's okay. Security hustled him out of there before anyone knew what had happened. Mate, really, with the president right there!'

'What are you going to do? Are you coming home?'

'What? No. Uh! I gotta go.'

'Are you okay?'

'Yeah, no, everything's fine. Véronique just walked in.'

'Véronique?' I said. 'Wane Jarvis, some woman is going to be the death of you!'

And with that, the line went dead. You can't make this shit up! It can get rough out there, folks. As for me, I was just happy to have a roof over my head.

* * *

It all started falling into place when I got the call to help build a lighting rig for Status Quo. The band had purchased their own sound and lighting systems, and both were being built from scratch. Swampy was back in town doing pre-production for the tour, and I was busy working at the Showlites warehouse soldering multicores and circuit boards, assembling dimmer racks, and doing whatever else it took to build the lighting rig from scratch. Finally, I was on my feet workwise, when tragedy struck: Swampy had a serious heart attack.

In true Swampy form, he called me from ICU sounding a little more subdued than normal. 'Hey, T. Can you bring my briefcase and files for the tour to the hospital for me?'

What? He'd only just regained consciousness.

'What do you mean?' I asked.

'Just bring them, I don't have time to argue. There's still a lot that has to be done for the tour.'

There I was smuggling in all the paperwork under the guise of being his sister, as only family was permitted to visit due to the seriousness of his condition – well, I did have the right accent. All of this so he could finish putting the tour together from his hospital bed. 'Swampy, let someone else finish this,' I pleaded. 'This is silly.' But he was too proud. He knew only too well he might not be able to tour ever again, but he wouldn't leave something half-arsed. Like a true professional, he never let his condition stop him from completing the job at hand. What should have been a truly happy time for me was bittersweet.

While the Quo family that I was now a part of headed out on the next leg of the Blue for You Tour that would eventually evolve into the Rockin' All Over the World Tour, we were missing a key figure and my best friend. Swampy flew back to Australia to get the extended care he needed.

He became a much-loved and respected tour manager, father and husband, and my lifelong friend.

As the story goes, the show must go on! And on it does, sometimes at great cost, with participants falling by the wayside. Everyone, it seems, is replaceable – something we would be wise not to forget in this job, where the lines are blurred so easily.

10

ROCKIN' ALL OVER THE WORLD

SOME TOURS ARE UNEVENTFUL, while others can be extreme. The Rockin' All Over the World Tour had started in Ireland in June 1977 and continued through to the European leg that followed, starting 6 January 1978 in Rouen, France. The entire tour would run for sixteen months, sold out!

This leg would be rough. There was severe weather, with many tours cancelling. We ended up being the only ones out that season who went the distance without cancelling any shows. But the weather wasn't to be our only problem out there.

We'd graduated to real tour buses – no more vans, or even driving the band's Range Rovers between shows. The new normal was a driver and bunks to sleep on. It's amazing how quickly we adapt to change, makes me wonder why we fight it so vehemently at times. Maybe because with change we don't automatically become smarter.

We had a day off to get from the show in Essen on

12 February to our next show date in West Berlin on 14 February. This required us to drive through the border checkpoint at Helmstedt–Marienborn and along the stretch of autobahn that allowed access to West Berlin. The checkpoint was heavily patrolled by both the East German and Soviet Armies. You didn't want to mess with those boys.

Stopping was *Verboten* on the autobahn and there was a maximum four hours allowed to travel the distance. That was, unless for some reason your trusted bus driver was running out of fuel. Seriously? Yep, there we were, looking for a gas station in the corridor, as the only thing worse than being low on gas would be to run out of gas. On our third attempt to stop, we were approached by a military patrol and eventually given an armed escort to a filling station.

A small supply shop was attached to the station and being both bored and curious as we waited for the driver to sort himself out, we went in for a look. Just as you aren't meant to stop, you are definitely not meant to shop, but the temptation of Western currency was too much for the beleaguered shopkeeper; he unlocked his cages to release a bounty of alcohol previously unheard of to us from the West.

Upon resuming our trip, we tasted several of these concoctions. Jägermeister was the hands-down winner – in fact, we decided we needed more. We convinced the driver to stop again so we could purchase more of this herbal elixir. We wouldn't back down, convincing him it was his fault in the first place: if we hadn't run out of petrol, then we wouldn't have found Jägermeister. The next stop went smoothly, and the one after that. Then we spotted a shop just off the road a bit and feeling full of Dutch courage we barrelled towards it.

The East Germans decided they'd had enough of our antics. They'd been monitoring our movements and, without notice, opened fire on our bus. Just like that! Well, holy shit! In all fairness, if they'd asked us nicely at that point we probably wouldn't have listened. We were all completely shit-faced from our first and very in-depth encounter with Jägermeister.

After the soldiers rousted us off the bus and confiscated our caseloads of the evil brew, we were sent on our way with severe warnings of what would become of us if we stopped again. My German isn't great, but I swear I heard some reference to us, travel and Siberia.

Upon finally arriving in West Berlin, we all decided we needed a decent meal. We chose an Italian restaurant, feeling good about our escape from the corridor. But the staff at the restaurant were not feeling good about us. It was awkward from the start and went downhill rapidly. Kind of like *Fawlty Towers* on steroids. As the arguing continued, one of the waiters came at us swinging a bottle of wine, and the next thing I knew I had a broken nose. I still to this day do not know exactly what happened, or how I ended up being the one koshed. The government later closed down the restaurant and deported the Turkish staff – it seems we weren't their only victims.

We turned up at the show the next day with Bob Young, Quo's tour manager, holding the West Berlin newspaper that relayed what we'd gotten up to on our day off. In great detail, I might add. It was 14 February. Happy Valentine's Day to me!

* * *

We set our course for the next stop on the tour. Back in West Germany and feeling safe away from East Germany, we pulled over at one of the service stations off the autobahn to refuel. Two military tanks were sitting just off to the side of the entrance; they were US World War II vehicles that the army paraded up and down as a show of power. We'd witnessed these displays: the Americans would travel in one direction on the autobahn in a tank and truck convoy, and the West Germans would travel in the opposite direction with a similar convoy. How strange to find these tanks abandoned.

I had to brave the blisteringly cold night to use the service station restrooms. Staff directed me down a wide set of stairs to a long, tiled hallway that resembled the access tunnels to the London Underground, clearly much older than the building above. Halfway along this hallway, I came across a group of American soldiers who looked homeless. When I asked them if they were alright, I thought they were going to cry. They jumped up, ecstatic that someone was speaking English to them and not swearing at them in German.

It turned out they'd been part of one of those silly exercises, when two of the tanks had broken down. Army law decreed they had to stay with their equipment until it was repaired or removed. What was meant to be a one-day exercise had turned into a five-day ordeal. They'd run out of money after day two, which was when the staff had stopped them from sitting in the heated restaurant area. They'd been designated to the tunnel, as it was dry and slightly warmer than their tanks.

I felt sorry for them and brought them back to the bus with me. We fed them and gave them each a blanket along with Status Quo merch swag that would help them keep warm: sweatshirts, T-shirts, scarfs, beanies. We also gave

Cable, cable and more cable. Me onstage during set-up for Status Quo.
(ALAIN LE GARSMEUR)

Setting up with George Harvey, my fearless leader during my Quo days.
(ALAIN LE GARSMEUR)

them a couple of shots from our recently restocked bar, to stave off the cold.

I had to ask, 'So, what's it like inside a tank?'

One of the soldiers answered, 'Why don't you come with us? We can show you.'

All of us spent the next hour or so playing inside a tank. What was it like? Uncomfortable, tight and cramped. The fun bit was playing with the gun that the soldiers explained could hit a target from an extremely long range, making the discomfort worthwhile. I tried to convince them to let me shoot off just one round, to which they obviously said no. They did, however, confess two things. Firstly, that these Sherman tanks broke down here all the time; they'd been configured for the North African desert, so they rattled apart on the hard road surfaces. Secondly, they never carried live ammo – so, all those pissing contests were just that.

We left our soldiers at the truck stop with their clean, warm clothes – branded for the Quo Army rather than the US Army – and what cash we had on us to see them through until someone came to get them from their base. A week later, they turned up at our gig and volunteered to help us with the load-out as a thankyou.

* * *

Over the next few years, as I worked with Quo under George Harvey, I underwent a growth spurt in my career. George was a strict teacher: intelligent, generally clear with directions as to what he expected from me, a hard but fair taskmaster. He also had a good sense of humour. He wanted to try his hand in the US market and was training me to take over from him. However, at the time he never discussed this plan with me, or the band as far as I know. Occasionally, and out of character, he would test me. He once walked away from the lighting console during a show, leaving me to jump in totally unprepared and not knowing when or even if he was coming back. I wasn't sure if I was supposed to copy him exactly so the band didn't notice his absence, or do my own thing. Another time, he gave me the 380-instrument lighting blueprint for the Rockin' All Over the World Tour – hand-drawn on a pub napkin – and said, 'You don't need this; you know what to do.' I kept that napkin a long time as a reminder to myself: whatever curveball was thrown at me, I could look at the napkin and think, *I got this!*

Every successful band experiences what I call a 'sweet spot'. The happiest time in their careers. Not only are they making a shitload of money, but at the same time they're truly happy with each other and their music. There's serendipity at play, and it feels magical. This was another part of what drew me to touring and held me there, as had happened with both AC/DC and Quo during the years I spent with them. In multiple books, articles and interviews, the original members of Quo have confirmed that the 1970s holds a special place in their hearts. That was their sweet spot.

We were having fun! None of us took ourselves too seriously. The band members were happy to be in control of their own destiny. They'd found the manager they needed to take them to the next level, in the form of Colin Johnson. They were able to choose their team, from merchandising to a professional crew that consisted of not only backline but also full production of sound and lights to run the custom-built PA and lighting rigs they now owned. And all of this was being overseen by the ever-present Bob Young. Bob has been referred to as the 'other member of Quo': he appeared onstage and wrote multiple hit songs with them, and, as tour manager, he was the bridge between the band's world and that of the crew, caring for both. And on many occasions, his was a voice of reason, often giving me advice that afterwards I wished I had taken.

What did we all have in common? A sense of humour. This thing called humour played an important part in the Quo inner circle. If you couldn't have a good laugh, usually at your own expense, then you wouldn't last.

Francis Rossi was a total jokester. During sound check he'd play little ditties to me about my interactions with stagehands; for example, 'Tana Douglas beats up humpers', to the tune of 'Deck the Halls'. He also thought it would be funny to get me one night during the show, making his guitar tech Mal Craggs complicit this time.

We were all wearing blue jumpsuits with the tour logo on the back and slits for ventilation in our side pockets. For parts of the show my position was stage right, the same side Mal worked from. I was there monitoring the performance when Fran started making head movements as though he needed something. I looked to Mal, and weirdly he was holding a guitar in each hand while signalling to me that something was wrong.

The show was in full swing, and between the lights from the rig and the truss followspots in my eyes, I found it hard to see everything that was going on. I went over to take one of the guitars from Mal, thinking that was what he wanted, but he shook his head. Then he signalled with a jerking motion of his head to his right-side pants pocket. Now I was really confused.

Fran swung back around towards me, looked right at me and flicked his pick into the crowd. Then I got it: he wanted

Quo member Rick Parfitt, always time for a good word. (ALAIN LE GARSMEUR)

me to get a pick out of Mal's pocket. I reached inside, only to discover that not only was there no pick in there, but his pocket was taped shut – so my hand had gone into the side vent, and he wasn't wearing underwear. *Eeeuuuwwwh!*

Scarred for life? No. Rather it didn't happen? Yes! Was it done as a sexual thing? No, I don't think so. I took it as: 'Let's mess with Tana. What will really get her?' Well, yep, that was it! Everyone joked about it during the show and the load-out, then it was over. On to the next victim. That incident wasn't as bad as some of the things the boys did to each other, and social norms were different back then.

Over the course of my career I did encounter a lot of sexual and sexually charged situations. I wasn't always able to read the signals and put a stop to them early on; sometimes a band or crew member would make unwanted advances, and keep making advances after I told him I wasn't interested. It was always tricky. Sometimes I misread it. If I decided that I was interested in a fellow roadie, and the feeling was mutual, I had to keep two factors in mind. First and foremost, I was there to do a job. Secondly, once I was in a position of authority as the crew boss, I knew that if I decided to go for it and it didn't work out, I would be stuck in close proximity to that person in some cases for up to a year. That could get uncomfortable.

The main rule I implemented was that the band members, for me, were off limits. However, my male colleagues didn't abide by that rule – if there was a female artist or band member on tour, most of the crew members would find a way to see if she was up for it. They would do the same with me. Test the water. At this level of my career, it would be

Quo in holding pattern waiting to go onstage. (ALAIN LE GARSMEUR)

frowned upon if I hooked up with a muso. Another blazing sign of the double standards. I had earned the respect of a lot of people, so I felt I needed to be careful not to jeopardise all that hard work.

Egos could get in the way, so I had to keep mine in check. Joking around and winding each other up was a good way to do that – it all came down to letting off steam. And on the Quo tours, the crew were more than capable of giving as good as we got.

One night shortly after Andy Bown had been promoted to a permanent position playing keyboards stage left, as part of his initiation a can of dog food attached to a piece of string was put up in the truss to be lowered on cue while he was doing his solo for 'Rockin' All Over the World'. The joke pertained to the number of women he'd befriended, 'give a dog a bone', and his name was Bone/Bown. While we'd been

Status Quo on stage. Together, we can rock'n'roll! (ALAIN LE GARSMEUR)

Fran Rossi and Mal Craggs, possibly scheming on how to get me to fall for the old 'pick in the pocket' trick. (ALAIN LE GARSMEUR)

plotting this prank, it had been suggested that one of the truss spot operators should be in charge of that task, but it was decided that his roadie would do it from the stage level. Well, sure enough, the can got stuck in the truss; when it was finally freed up, it fell hard and fast, clocking Andy on the head and almost knocking him unconscious. It drew blood. Welcome to the group, Andy! I'm sure that night he wished he was still playing from offstage behind the PA.

* * *

Joking aside, each member of Quo had very different personalities. Rick Parfitt, I always felt, had a lot of layers to him, besides his reputation for being a chick magnet. He could be a jokester like Fran, and he wasn't one to have an early night – a bit of an Energizer Bunny like the AC/DC Boys – but he also had a gentle side that I liked.

One night, while on tour in Europe, in the quiet time after dinner and before the doors opened to let in the audience, Rick called me back to the dressing room. I was surprised when he asked me if I would try on a dress for him; he explained that he was thinking of giving it to his wife but first wanted to see what it looked like on. This seemed like a strange request, especially as I wasn't sure if his wife and I were the same size. I told him I was too dirty from the load-in and set-up. He said, 'Would you just try it on for me? Please.' It could have been a creepy request coming from some guys, but from Rick it wasn't. The steel-blue dress was pretty, not too flash with a flattering cut, so I tried it on. I emerged from the adjoining room somewhat self-consciously, as this would be the first time anyone had ever seen me in a dress – or in anything apart from jeans and T-shirts, really.

The rest of the band had come into the dressing room. As I looked at myself in the full-length mirror, the general consensus from the room was that it looked great, and I should wear dresses more often. I said, 'Do you not see the problems that would cause, if I started looking like a girl?' Food for thought.

Fran was one of the guys present, and he and Rick mentioned to me that the band was going to fly out the crew's significant others for our upcoming four days off – and if I wanted to invite someone, it didn't have to be a guy. I took from this that they thought I might be gay. 'Thanks, guys!' I said. 'But I won't be bringing anyone.' I think a lot of people on tour assumed I was gay, but I wasn't going to fuel that rumour one way or the other. I think this was Rick and Fran's way of saying they didn't care, which was nice.

Nuff the bass player was a cheeky one, but I found him easy to chat with. The only time I saw him really upset was after the whole fiasco with the puppet. We'd just finished an Australian tour where Nuff had met an Aussie girl, the woman of his dreams, and when the tour finished he decided to stay in Australia for a while. The newly released single 'Rockin' All Over the World' was flying up the charts, and the band needed a video for the British TV show *Top of the Pops*. This was unscheduled, and Nuff was still AWOL in Australia. A decision was made to film it without him, but with a life-size puppet holding a bass guitar. Although the video looked funny, it was hurtful to Nuff at the time, with far-reaching repercussions. But it worked out in the long run, as he's been happily married to that Aussie girl, Dale, for forty years.

The drummer John Coughlan, nicknamed Spud, was also good fun to hang out with. He could look a lot meaner than he really was. I was lucky enough to get invited over to his place on the Isle of Man to watch the annual TT (Tourist Trophy) motorcycle race, which happened to coincide with a break on our tour. Spud was a gearhead who loved playing with cars, trucks and old military vehicles. He was generous to invite me, and his girlfriend at the time (now wife of forty years), Gillie, was also very sweet, so off I went.

Before asking me over to watch the race with him, Spud had originally invited his drum tech, Hot Dog, who'd had to cancel at the last minute. Word had got around the Isle that a roadie was coming, and this news had been met with a mixed response – as I found out on our first night there, when Gillie hosted a formal dinner for friends and neighbours. My luggage had been lost on the flight over, so graciously Gillie had lent me something to wear. I was seated next to a woman who confided in me she was so glad 'that roadie person' hadn't come and that I was there in his stead. I didn't have the heart to tell her I was that roadie!

* * *

With that short break over, the Quo touring regime had taken on a life of its own. Before I knew it, I returned to Australia the conquering hero as a fulltime member of the Quo crew. That felt good, and it was great to catch up with all the roadies who'd shown me the ropes – guys I'd grown up with, in a way.

Over two years had passed since I'd left Australia. I planned to visit my father when we hit Brisbane, just to let him know it had all worked out in the end. When the band found out about this, they made the kind gesture of organising for me to skip rehearsals in Sydney and fly up to Brisbane to spend a couple of days with him. I was looking forward to surprising him. So much had happened since we'd last spoken.

I arrived at the family home in Brisbane and knocked on the door, only to be greeted by my grandmother, who curtly responded that my father didn't live there anymore. When I pushed her for his whereabouts, she coldly replied, 'He is dead. Why are you here?' Her opinion of me obviously hadn't changed.

My father had been buried only a matter of days earlier, she told me. She added that just prior to his death, he'd started saying that I was on my way, and he was going to see me soon. This, in Suze's mind, somehow indicated that it was my fault he'd died. I went to his local RSL to try and make some sense of what she was saying. His friends had all

Happy Days! (PHOTOS BY DANNY CLIFFORD)

thought he'd lost his mind when he'd insisted I was coming home, so at my sudden appearance they were surprised and even a little guilty for not believing him. No, he hadn't lost his mind – I guess I was just late.

How had he known I was coming? We hadn't spoken in over 18 months. He'd died in his sleep, supposedly of heart failure. In my soul, I believe he died of disappointment. In me? Partly, but also with his life in general – having lived, but only just. Such wasted potential. He'd had such great untapped abilities and desires. That wasn't going to happen to me.

This was yet another tough family experience for me. I'd fantasised about a reunion of some sort, with the slim possibility of a parent finally saying they were proud of me. Or even just, 'Good job!' Once again, I felt let down by, but also a sense of loss for, this strange man who I never really got to know. Sadly, I'm not sure anyone ever really did.

Quo was great to me during this time of loss. When I rejoined the first show of the tour in Newcastle, I had to tell them what had happened as they could see I'd been crying a lot. I was understandably still shaken and upset. I buried myself in work, as I couldn't have my personal problems affect the job at hand.

That would be the last contact I had with my father's family, and the experience strengthened my bond with Quo. I'm grateful for their kindness at that time in my life.

* * *

I would remain with Quo over a four-year period with my last shows being four nights at the Hammersmith Odeon for the If You Can't Stand the Heat Tour in June 1979. It was the right time to leave. The band would take 1980 off as a tax shelter and also to deal with internal problems among the members. One of my favourite memories while with Quo was when they recorded their live album at the Glasgow Apollo. Three sold-out shows! The balcony area resembled some massive mythical beast bouncing and writhing to the music, with thousands of tenacious members, the Quo Army hanging on for dear life. It was a beautiful thing to see, especially from the stage.

After forty years, I still haven't come across another crowd that matches the sweaty joy of a Quo audience. They're different from other rock/metal fans – while not taking themselves too seriously, they are loyal to the grave. It's refreshing.

The fans couldn't, however, help with what went on with the band members. Maybe they were starting to take themselves a little too seriously. If video killed the radio star, then drugs killed the fun. We were all guilty! Not to make excuses, but that was just how it was. Fractures appeared that went beyond the puppet dig to tear the band apart. Rick and Fran were both doing a lot of drugs while pulling away from Spud and Nuff. Spud, in particular, got tired of Rick's drug use, which he couldn't relate to.

Trashed seats post-show at the Hammersmith Oden, where I did my last shows with Status Quo. The end of an era. (DANNY CLIFFORD)

Tragedy struck Rick in 1980 when his two-year-old daughter fell into the home swimming pool and drowned. You can never recover from that.

When Quo imploded it happened quickly, and the ripples spread throughout the crew. When the dust settled, there would be only two band members standing, Rick Parfitt and Francis Rossi. So it goes in the music industry.

George had left to pursue his career in the States, so I'd become manager of the lighting rig. It was leased to the British production company TASCO, run by my friends Paul Newman and Terry Price. With George gone and Quo not touring, I was left in control. A deal was done with Paul and Terry at TASCO and I would head up lighting crews for TASCO using Quo's rig. Up till then TASCO had been solely a sound company, so this was a big move for them. It was also a big move for me, as now I was in charge: Yep, a girl! If TASCO toured, I toured. And TASCO did a lot of touring.

11

LUST FOR LIFE

IT WAS 28 APRIL 1978 when Iggy Pop wandered into my life, and when the clock struck midnight I would officially be twenty-one. As only someone like Iggy could, he turned my three-week break between Status Quo tours upside down.

It felt strange to be able to say officially, 'I am an adult!', like I'd reached a milestone of sorts. Otherwise I didn't feel any different. I'd never envisioned making it to such a ripe old age. That desperate need to keep moving I'd had since I was a kid was by now a thread in my fabric. As long as I stayed in the present and didn't look closely at myself, I could stave off feeling the lack of self-worth and depression that always lurked just below the surface. The difference between what I showed the world and what was really going on would have shocked most. I expected nothing and had even lower expectations of something lasting long enough to be enjoyed, really taken in, to become a real part of. Always teetering on the edge. I was living one day at a time, and each day like it might be my last, as if I was a passenger being hurtled down my very own Highway to

Hell – but I didn't care, that was just how it was. I was rudderless.

At the time I was living in a flat just off the Kings Road in the World's End district of London. I shared this place with the landlord, Jack, his brother and a friend named Val. It was in one of those massive old U-shaped apartment buildings with a courtyard in the middle, built around the beginning of the twentieth century, with a marble entrance and sweeping staircase that wrapped around the open metal cage lift. The building had the grand name of Ashburnham Mansions, and the flat was just as grand. On the rare occasions I had time off between tours, it was a great place to try to call home.

I'd just started a three-week break between Quo tours and was already bored. I could never sit still for long. I'd been in a funk all day, and I was half-heartedly thinking I should go out somewhere. I had never made a big fuss about my birthday, but this time I was feeling as though I should do something about turning twenty-one and being legally able to do all the things I'd been doing for years. I wasn't sure how this whole adult thing was supposed to work, so maybe it was better not to draw attention to it, just in case I was supposed to start acting responsibly all of a sudden. The fact I was still here, still standing, would be enough for now.

As I hadn't bothered to tell anyone about this milestone, I felt it might be a bit late to start planning anything, although in London you could get a party together on a moment's notice and easily keep it going for twenty-four hours. I didn't lack options – I just wasn't feeling it.

The Marquee Club had become my stomping ground, my usual place to start off a night's entertainment, as it was right across from Status Quo's offices. Jack Barrie, the manager, let me in for free and would slip me drinks, while denying the likes of Billy Idol alcohol as he was 'too young'. The funny thing was, Billy is two years older than me, so I'd be the one slipping him the odd drink.

Richard Branson had opened a new club, The Venue, that was hot at the time and I had a standing place on every guest list in town. I could go to Dingwalls, The Rainbow, Hammersmith Odeon, or the punk rock Vortex Club if I wanted rough around the edges.

The phone in the apartment had been ringing all day for Jack, my roommate, who'd just signed on as tour manager for Iggy Pop's upcoming TV Eye Tour. It seemed the band were having some problems in the rehearsal room, and Jack couldn't be found. I'd answered the house phone a couple of times, and each call got a little more desperate and a little less polite. There was a bad buzzing sound through the PA that nobody could figure out how to get rid of. After yet another angry call, as there was still no sign of Jack I offered to go over to try to sort it out. I was really doing it for Jack, as they were threatening to sack him on sight.

Off I went to the rehearsal room, hoping I could stall them long enough for Jack to turn up. I walked into the midst of a rather unhappy bunch, consisting of both band and crew. I didn't recognise anyone, and I didn't know anything about Iggy or the band backing him. While the rest of the band were huddled on the stage area, and the crew acted busy trying to fix the problem, Iggy came towards me to introduce himself.

Straightaway, I knew there was something dynamic about this guy. While Quo were all-round nice guys, with a clean-cut, denim-clad, approachable working-class image, here was something completely different. This was a raw energy I hadn't seen before. This was the other side of the working class: the unemployed, the disenfranchised, the anti-establishment. All rolled up in a 'five foot one' snarling package. As he swaggered over to me, he resembled a sleek feline predator; he was bare-chested, wore silver leather pants and had piercing eyes – the perfect combination of good looks, trouble, and what turned out to be a great and exciting talent.

I suddenly felt happy to be there. This was just what I needed – a change, something that embodied the feelings I'd had my whole life of living for the moment. And here it was, crossing the room to talk to me. I was soon to discover there were a lot of layers beneath that punk exterior.

I had no idea who Iggy thought I was, this girl who'd come in out of a dark, rainy London night to fix his problems. I guess he was just desperate to get on with rehearsing. He introduced me to the sound engineer, and I asked this guy what his crew had done so far to find the problem. The engineer gave me a somewhat cold response and a 'how dare you' glare. Remember, these guys had taken a ration of shit from Iggy, they had no idea who the hell I was, and if I fixed the problem this would make them look bad. The whole crew seemed sceptical of me – to put it nicely. I could see on the sound guy's face that he didn't think I could help at all, but maybe I could make his crew a nice cup of tea while they got on with 'men's work'. As I was under no obligation to be there, I was again wondering why on earth I'd bothered to volunteer.

I took a deep breath and explained that he had nothing to lose. And if I didn't fix it, at least the pressure would be off him; he could blame me, and I could disappear back into the dark and rainy night, never to be heard from again. I'd found over the years that if I had to deal with a man who was resistant to a woman taking charge, the words 'what if *we* try it this way' got me a lot further than '*I* think *you* should try this'. Simple, but it worked every time. It worked so well that I would use the 'I' version when I wanted to piss someone off.

When the engineer agreed that he and his crew had nothing to lose, we all went to work. This wasn't an easy task, as the room was a big mess. We had to contend with the poor condition of the equipment, the dodgy-at-best power supply, the cable runs all over the place, and a new crew just learning the equipment set-up – and Iggy, of course, wanting to keep rehearsing while we were troubleshooting.

After several tries, we found the only way to get rid of the loud buzz was to ground-lift the sound system. Not the ideal solution, but as Iggy wasn't prepared to stop rehearsing while we fixed it, this would just have to do. It was a very punk rock solution, though, and as long as nobody touched a plugged-in instrument while touching a live mic, it would work. Hopefully, no one would die. The crew and I made this clear to the band and said that we didn't want them running the risk of getting shocked (or worse), although a couple of the crew might have felt differently by this time. Our solution wasn't permanent, but someone from the production company could come out the next day to fix the problem, which was probably in the wiring of the building.

Everyone agreed, and I prepared to make a speedy exit, not wanting to be around if it all went south. Now, a speedy exit from a rainy South London rehearsal room in the wee hours of the morning wasn't going to be easy. Not the best neighbourhood, I might add. And at this point any birthday plans were out the window, as it had taken a couple of hours

DRESSING ROOMS

15a.   The Management will ensure that there will be no
       'no smoking'or other petty restrictions in the
       dressing rooms area, if necessary by negotiation with
       the local fire chief or other authority.

16.   It is agreed and understood that the Management
       shall provide and pay for the following refreshments
       for the group and their personnel.

       a. IGGY POP'S DRESSING ROOM

       1 bottle Jack Daniels
       12 bottles Coke
       12 bottles of beer
       Wheresoever possible Hot Saki and Sushi for two
       people. If this is not possible please advise
       well before the day of the concert.
       2 bottles of mineral water
       6 clean towels. .

       b. THE BAND'S DRESSING ROOM

       1 bottle of Tequilla
       1 bottle Jack Daniels
       1 bottle of dark rum
       24 bottles of Schweppes Dry Ginger Ale
       12 bottles of Coke
       24 bottles of beer
       4 bottles of mineral water
       Salad and cold cuts of meat and general snacks
       sufficient for eight (8) people.
       1 hairdryer
       10 towels

       c. ROAD CREW DRESSING ROOM

       . (on arrival)

       Tea, coffee, sugar, milk and a selection of .
       pastries, sandwiches etc. sufficient for nine (9)
       people. (Please note: These people are usually
       hearty eaters.)

       (at 6p.m.)

       A three-course hot meal, the main course of which is

       These meals should be sufficient for seven (7)
       people. Plus one (1) vegetarian meal and three(3)
       dozen pints of lager.

       It is absolutely essential at the conclusion
       of the show that there is a nurse in attendance
       with two (2) cylinders of oxygen,with masks, and
       that he or she is qualified to administer the
       oxygen.

       PLEASE NOTE: THIS REQUIREMENT. ABOVE IS ABSOLUTELY
       ESSENTIAL.

An extract from the Iggy Pop rider from the TV Eye Tour, 1978. Either
dressing room was fun to hang in.

between songs to make tea and fix the problem. Now it was one in the morning. (Yes, I had made tea and brought it to the Doubting Thomas sound guy – my sarcasm wasn't lost on the room.)

The good news was that I really liked the music I'd heard. Finally, something down and dirty with both talent and substance, a sound from Detroit very different from what was being passed off as punk in most of the London scene at the time.

The rehearsals had started up again, but I chose to wait outside for my taxi. I always felt a bit self-conscious just hanging around musicians if I didn't have a work reason to be there. I'd done my bit. It was a long wait; if the rain hadn't still been coming down, I would have started walking back to the flat.

Then Iggy appeared. 'Come inside,' he said. 'Hang out with us; we're taking a break.'

Sure, now they're taking a break! Typical.

I'd had just about enough by this point. My birthday night had been spent with a roomful of grumpy strangers – not exactly how I'd envisaged it.

'No, thank you!' I said. 'I really have somewhere else to be.' This was a lie, as it was after 2 a.m. and swinging London had been safely tucked away for the night.

It was probably the first time anyone had said no to an invitation to watch this group of musicians rehearse. Somewhat bewildered, Iggy asked, 'What are you heading off to that's so important?'

Just at that moment my taxi finally arrived. 'My twenty-first birthday,' was my response, and I jumped into my cab and waved goodbye as I left.

* * *

The next morning, Jack was a little standoffish, to say the least. I figured he'd got yelled at and it would all blow over. Later that day, he told me the band wanted to see me, and I should go meet Iggy at RCA, his record label in London. I thought it strange that Jack didn't thank me for jumping in and helping him out, but no big deal. Curiosity got the better of me, so off I went.

It seems all wasn't well between the band and their label, and this get-together at RCA was meant to be an icebreaker for both sides. Iggy would be introduced to all his label people in London, and they would hang out together in an attempt to bond with him and pacify him. For a little guy, he really could be a force to be reckoned with.

Iggy had completed his obligations to the label with his *TV Eye* album, and he wanted out. As record labels and Brits do, they pretended everything was just fine; there were no problems at all, and it was going to be a great tour. To seal the deal, after much fanfare the label presented Iggy with a life-size Nipper. Now, you might recognise Nipper as the dog on the HMV logo, the company that had become RCA. This was a rare honour – in fact, a life-size Nipper had never been bestowed before. Having said that, what the godfather of punk was meant to do with a large plastic dog on the eve of a balls-to-the-wall European tour, I don't know.

Well, Iggy didn't know either. Immediately after the handing-off ceremony, he presented Nipper to me in front of everyone. 'Happy birthday, Tana!'

I was ecstatic. The RCA label personnel, not so much. I'd wanted a dog for ages, and this one would do just fine for the moment. At least it wouldn't miss me when I went on tour.

I was happy, Iggy was happy, and the record label people were gobsmacked. Iggy, his band and I all made a quick exit together, laughing and mumbling something about having to rehearse.

But wait, there was more good news! Iggy wanted me on the tour – Nipper was just a bonus thrown in to piss off his label. I thought this was great, as I was starting to really like this strange, intense but funny little guy, with a nervous energy that transferred to his performances. And this tour would fit in to my time off from working with Quo. Nice! My job description hadn't been clarified yet, but I was to go to the production company the very next day and help get all the equipment ready for the tour.

I was looking forward to touring with Jack. We'd always got on well but never worked together, so I thought it would be fun. In the days before we were to leave on the ferry to Europe, I didn't see him, but I wasn't bothered as I figured we had time to catch up on the road.

When I arrived at the dock, I still couldn't see Jack. As tour manager he should have been an obvious presence, and he was six foot seven, but nowhere to be found. I presumed he was already on the ferry with the band. Finally, I asked after him. Iggy's manager told me that Jack wouldn't be with us: he'd been fired, and Iggy wanted me to take his place.

This wasn't good. Not good at all. I wasn't a tour manager, and Jack was my friend and landlord. Shit! *Tell me this isn't happening*, I thought. *I like where I'm living.*

After I'd declined, they still wanted me on the tour. So what was my job to be? I don't believe in giving someone a title only to justify their existence on a tour. Everyone in a crew depends on the others to do their jobs to their utmost capacity. In difficult situations, resilience and teamwork can be what holds it all together.

What I'd thought would be a three-week bonding experience for me and Jack was now something totally different. It wasn't going to be easy – there was still going to be a lot expected of me. I was to work closely with Iggy while making sure everything was good on the production side. I would also work on the lighting crew and stage-manage; that way, keeping tabs on both sides. There's no point keeping the star happy if it goes to shit every time he walks onstage.

The new tour manager probably saw me as a bit of a challenge, with me and Iggy getting on so well. This was never my intention, but I've learnt over the years that people either take you as you are or have some preconceived notion of you that can be difficult to change.

The crew filled me in initially on who the band members were, as I had no knowledge of the early US punk scene or the importance of these individuals in that milieu. Only by getting to know the band members personally did I truly understand their dynamics. I was about to be educated on this part of US music history.

* * *

The first show was 10 May in Vitrolles, southern France. The musicians needed some time and room to breathe with all the dynamics involved, but now I could see this band was something special, an awesome machine.

Fred 'Sonic' Smith, Scott Asheton and Gary Rasmussen had come to the tour from Detroit as members of Sonic's Rendezvous Band. The three had previously been in successful Detroit punk bands and had a history with Iggy way back to his musical beginnings. Now they'd been hired as his backing band. The problem was that Fred had been under the impression they would share the bill with Iggy, but that never happened.

Scotty Thurston, who had started with Iggy in 1973, had been hired to lead the band. His history as one of the Stooges and having spent the prior year with Iggy and Bowie together on the Lust for Life Tour made for another tricky situation as now Fred was not only not getting co-headline, but Scotty had been hired to lead Sonic's Rendezvous Band. All of this for a singer who felt jilted by his friend David Bowie so soon after having released two successful albums directed by him – Bowie, was currently MIA due to 'personal differences' (to put it nicely) with Iggy. It all made for a chaotic beginning.

Lesser things have sunk bigger ships.

The itinerary was unusual, with many obscure and out-of-the-way venues. We did the first two shows in France, then set off to Barcelona. The band members were still getting their legs.

There was a show in Brussels, before we headed to a familiar venue, the Paradiso in Amsterdam, my old stomping ground. I invited a couple of local friends to the show, enjoying a rare opportunity to hang out with people I knew outside the industry. The Paradiso was a unique venue: there weren't too many places, at that time, where you could play a show then wander into the lobby and legally buy pot. God bless the Dutch! This gave everyone a chance to chill.

Next stop, Helsinki. I hadn't been to Finland, so this was a new experience for me – in more ways than I bargained for. Our old ferry took seventeen hours to cross the Baltic Sea from Stockholm to Helsinki, and it groaned loudly as if complaining about each movement of the water. We were travelling in the off-season, and the crossing was overnight with predicted rough seas and temperatures that would likely plummet below zero. The ancient vessel was in for a battle against the elements, and it wouldn't be a world title fight but a back-alley brawl.

As the crew didn't know each other very well, instead of using this time to sleep before the show, we had a crash course in who would lead and who would follow for the remainder of this punk rock adventure. As total strangers, we'd been thrust inside each other's pockets by the confines of a low-budget tour, and we needed to work closely together. The usual way to get camaraderie flowing was to play a couple of games that always included alcohol and usually included drugs. We were young, we worked hard and play harder, so this was how we did team building.

Step one: We opened our duty-free purchases. Step two: We each did a shot. Step three: the Dare.

We were out on the deck to not draw attention to the fact that we were drinking our duty-free. We'd been at sea for an hour, the lights from the port had faded into oblivion, and we were being jostled by the swirling black currents beneath us. The old girl was putting up a good fight – my money was on her.

Then it came to me: the Dare. We would take turns climbing over the rail to see who lasted the longest, who didn't chicken out. We'd already been coated in the salty smell and taste of these black waters: time to get up close and personal. It's an Iggy Pop tour, and I'm Bored.

I was on my third challenge when we were rushed by some of the ferry staff. It seems a fellow traveller had reported that a bunch of crazy Brits were throwing themselves over the

ABOVE We loved them. And YES! the world would love AC/DC too. (Philip Morris)

BELOW Wane 'Swampy' Jarvis, the person who first answered my question 'What's a roadie?' On stage at Diamond Head, Hawaii, with Little River Band, 1978. (Michael Wickow)

Me, backstage at a Leon Russell show in Melbourne, before it all began.

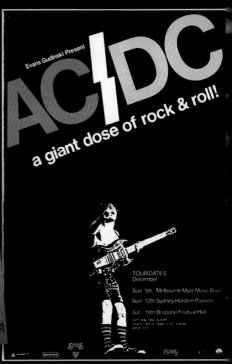

E LEFT The poster for the 1975 Sunbury Festival, reflecting the aesthetic of the time. Just as well idn't put the bands appearing that year on the poster as it didn't quite go to plan.

E RIGHT Following the lead of 'The Jack', 'She's Got Balls' and 'Soul Stripper', of course there was to be a giant dose of this band …The tour poster also had a giant dose of the colour scheme ted with AC/DC.

LEFT Me (on right) with Vicki Marks, a life-long fan and friend to the AC/DC camp. (Vicki Marks)

RIGHT Bon Scott's 29th birthday bash at the home of the Marks family, 1975. I'm the one in the background. (Vicki Marks)

TOP The bigger the venue, the bigger the rig. Setting up for Status Quo at Wembley Arena. (Alain le Garsmeur)

BOTTOM An important part of my job is to keep everyone on track and on schedule. Time is money. Here I am at *Rockpalast*. (Manfred Becker)

LEFT Angus Young being Angus Young, with Bon Scott, on stage at Nuremberg, 1979. (Alan Perry)

MIDDLE Carlos Santana, a true talent across the ages. (Philip Morris)

RIGHT Suzi Quatro was my first international tour and also my first female artist. (Alan Perry)

ABOVE The Quo family: Status Quo band members, crew and management. I'm in the middle of the back row, trying out blonde for a change. The lighting console on the right was the one I took on a flight as carry-on luggage. (Archive of Bob Young)

RIGHT 'Here, Tana, hang on to this truss that is 44' x 36' and keep it steady!' Whatever it takes. (Alain le Garsmeur)

LEFT Welcome Alain! The Quo initiation for a photographer new to our group, Alain le Garsmeur. Meanwhile, I'm trying to call the show. (Alain le Garsmeur)

LEFT Status Quo's band members in their civvies during soundcheck, before changing into their trademark denim for the show. (Alain le Garsmeur)

MIDDLE The reason we do what we do. The Quo Army loving Status Quo on stage, 1979. (Alain le Garsmeur)

BOTTOM What starts as a pile of metal in three 40-foot trucks ends up looking like this. (Alain le Garsmeur)

TOP Status Quo – in a bunch; just how they liked it. Fran Rossi, Rick Parfitt and Alan Lancaster. (Danny Clifford)

BOTTOM We lit the audience so Status Quo could see their fans. (Danny Clifford)

LEFT Rigger Ian Hill who shortly after this photo fell from the roof of Wembley Arena. Skill sometimes isn't enough and now there are strict health and safety guidelines. (Alain le Garsmeur)

BELOW LEFT David Bowie and Iggy Pop boarding a train in Copenhagen during the Lust for Life Tour, 1976. (Jan Persson/Getty Images)

BELOW RIGHT Iggy Pop onstage at The Music Machine, London, 1978. Could he possibly be looking so despairing because he just lost my leather jacket in the audience? I think not. (Denis O'Regan/Getty Images)

TOP The Who were given a place in the *Guinness Book of Records* for being the Loudest Band in the World after this concert at Charlton Football Stadium in 1976. (Danny Clifford)

BOTTOM My old band AC/DC supporting my new band The Who at Wembley Stadium, 1979. (Alan Perry)

TOP Zac Starkey getting a few pointers from Keith Moon. It must have worked because Zac is now the drummer for The Who. (Danny Clifford)

BOTTOM Jack McCullough, Pete Townsend, Jimmy McCullough and John Entwistle backstage at Wembley Stadium before the show, 1979. (Robert Ellis)

TOP Bon Scott and Cliff Williams of AC/DC fame backstage after their set for The Who & Friends Roar In. (Robert Ellis)

BOTTOM *Blizzard of Ozz* band members for the European leg of the 1980 tour: (left to right) Bob Daisley, Ozzy Osbourne and Randy Rhoads, with Lee Kerslake on drums. (Alan Perry)

TOP Three-quarters of Deep Purple back together. Whitesnake band members for the Lovehunter Tour: David Coverdale, Mickey Moody, Neil Murray, Bernie Marsden, Jon Lord and Ian Paice. (Alan Perry)

BOTTOM When Elton's having a good night, everybody's having a good night! (Danny Clifford)

TOP Last minute adjustments before The Police start their soundcheck at *Rockpalast*, 1980. (Manfred Becker)

BOTTOM This was my baby: the biggest lighting rig ever built! It was for Johnny Hallyday's six-month residency at Le Zenith in Paris, 1984.

TOP Red Hot Chili Peppers perform at Lollapalooza, Waterloo, New Jersey, 1 August 1991. They found that fire on your head kept you warmer than socks on your cocks. (Steve Eichner/Getty Images)

BOTTOM Members of Pearl Jam: Stone Gossard and Eddie Vedder. One of the many bands that reaped the benefits of touring Lollapalooza in the '90s. (Ebet Roberts/Getty Images)

ABOVE It was always fun to see different bands performing together in the Lollapalooza Festival atmosphere. Ice T & Henry Rollins (both my clients) at Lollapalooza, 14 August 1991. (Ebet Roberts/Getty Images)

LEFT I was able to get Chris Thomas to produce INXS for what would be their breakout album, *Listen Like Thieves* – and here is Michael Hutchence hanging out with another client, Lenny Kravitz, at Michael's villa in France. (private collection of Tina Hutchence)

BELOW It's been a long day. Did someone say they were getting me a pint? Me at the Golden Lion pub, London. (Lynne Cox) side of the ship – I guess they didn't hang around to see us come back up somewhat wetter and worse for wear. After we explained it was only a game, which didn't go down well, and were chastised for drinking our duty-free before leaving the vessel, we spent the remainder of the crossing locked in shoeboxes that passed as cabins (apparently for our own safety). We all arrived somewhat hungover but closer as a crew. Danger brings people together.

Through our hazy vision, we first glimpsed the venue: outdoors with a barebones stage in the middle of what appeared to be a community park, set on the edge of a large artificial lake. The further north you go, the longer it takes for that whole 'joy of spring' thing to kick in, and it hadn't arrived in Helsinki for this show. A lot of punters were there, but the vibe was strange. Iggy felt it straightaway when he hit the stage and wasn't giving any breaks to the crowd; he could be tough on an audience.

My first clue that it had all gone to hell was something weird thrown up onstage. What was that? And why was it moving? Well, it seems the audience could give as good as they got: it was a live fish, approximately five inches long, fresh from the nearby lake.

Within what seemed like seconds, the stage was being bombarded with live fish. How the hell were they catching them and throwing them so quickly? And what the hell did it mean?

Of course, Iggy lost his shit and stormed offstage, and we crew members packed up and got the hell out of there before the audience decided they were bored with fish and started throwing us around.

Back at the ferry for our escape from Helsinki, we were only allowed to board after many solemn promises to behave. We were returning to Stockholm for our next show that hopefully didn't come with fish.

* * *

We had four more shows until we got to West Berlin. These went much better, and the band was sounding tight as if they'd played together forever. Fred sang backing vocals, while Scotty was changing it up from keyboards to guitar and harmonica on 'Lust for Life'. The only audio recordings to surface from this tour are from Helsinki (where you hear Iggy yelling at the audience) and Copenhagen.

West Berlin was Iggy's home at the time, where he and Bowie had each taken up residence. With the chance that Bowie was still there, Iggy was excited to be back. We had two shows at the notorious Kino Club coming up, and a week to do them in. Luxury! But first we had to make yet another ferry crossing.

This was when I got to know Fred better. Onstage he was an unstoppable force with his low-slung guitar; offstage he spoke quietly with a deep drawl that was intense but calming, and his eyes would bring home the point. He wasn't only a musician but also a poet, and someone I enjoyed spending time with. I was always interested in learning from people older and mostly wiser than myself. Sex was never a thing between us; we would just hang out and talk for hours, until it was time for him to call the States. This was a regular thing that, even with our tour schedule, Fred tried never to miss. The love of his life was Patti Smith, a punk rock icon in her own right. He told me their relationship was new, and he would talk to her long distance for hours. She was his driving force. Witnessing their bond, which seemed to complete him, made me feel like there was hope for me yet. From those late-night calls came Patti's hit single 'Because the Night'; she had been in an adjacent studio in New York to Bruce Springsteen when he was working on a new song, which he then decided to give to her. She adapted the lyrics to relate to one night when Fred called late and she had been kept waiting by the phone for hours.

Scotty was the other band member I befriended, and he was the total opposite of Fred. He was bubbly, his eyes sparkled when he talked, and there was something almost childlike about him. I'm sure he was an easier person for Iggy to take direction from, as there was a lightness about Scotty, but Iggy needed both of these individuals to balance himself out.

Some musicians you don't have to worry about; others will give you a nervous breakdown if you let them. Which brings me to Iggy: he was obviously extremely talented, tortured (mostly by himself), mischievous, and very dark at times. He had his own childlike quality that was both endearing and troublesome, a scrappy kind of kid. It became my job to try to wrangle him and keep him on track.

In 1978, West Berlin was electric, full of nervous energy fed by the fact it was surrounded by what was considered enemy territory. Out of a very sad situation had emerged a population that seemed to live purely for the moment, something I could relate to. From the red-light district in the underground train stations to the wall that divided east from west, there were constant reminders of life's frailty. Because residents of West Berlin were excused from military service, the city attracted young people. A relatively high percentage of the population was under twenty-five, and this had caused an explosion in pop culture. Then there were older residents who had lost loved ones on the other side of the wall and wanted to stay close just in case, through some miracle, they were reunited. All of this melded together to create a city on the edge. In some parts of Germany the war seemed almost forgotten, but Berlin was different; you could still feel it there. Having said that, the city was one of my favourite places to visit.

Iggy and Bowie had solidified their friendship in 1976 by entering into a writing/recording partnership for the album *The Idiot*, followed by *Lust for Life*. It was never fifty-fifty, even though some of Bowie's biggest hits came from this creative union; 'China Girl' had come from Iggy's infatuation with a Vietnamese woman. Iggy released the song first, but Bowie and Nile Rogers made it a hit. Iggy always appeared the underdog, always trying to prove his worth to his master. Now they were out of touch, Iggy kept me close those days in Berlin. We visited the Hansa studios where those two collaboration albums had been made. I couldn't help but feel sorry for him as he pined for his friend, seemingly not knowing why he'd been exiled from the House of Bowie. It was the first time I'd seen a musician with a broken heart. I related to his situation, as it reminded me of when I'd attempted a relationship with a lighting guy, thinking he really liked me – turned out he was just using me to further his career.

Iggy and I had lunch with Wolfgang Flür, a member of the German band Kraftwerk. He was friends with both Iggy and Bowie (probably the reason) and has since credited their meetings around that time as being inspirational to his songwriting. At this luncheon, Iggy decided I should come back to Berlin after the tour and work for Tangerine Dream. Our ensuing discussion happened in front of Wolfgang and was a little awkward to say the least – I was able to bow out gracefully, as I was booked to rejoin Status Quo right after Iggy's tour.

Iggy's behaviour in Berlin seemed a little forced, and maybe he was trying to prove to himself that he belonged. His nervous energy was like that of the city, but there was still no sign of Bowie – would they just kiss and make up already?! Iggy was like a cat on a hot tin roof.

When it came time for him to perform his shows in West Berlin, he hit a whole new level. It was like he had something to prove; he was desperate to rule, and rule he did. I know he was hoping Bowie was somewhere in the audience, approving from the shadows, although to my knowledge he was a no-show.

* * *

I left Berlin two pairs of jeans lighter after a clandestine visit to East Berlin. We were then in Nuremberg, only one show away from London: three sold-out shows over four days, at the Music Machine in Camden Town. Home sweet home!

The Music Machine was the go-to venue in London. It officially held two thousand people at capacity, but as all the hot bands were playing there, staff would jam in the audience way over the limit. This kind of crowd was exactly what was needed to boost everybody's moral. What could possibly go wrong?

We arrived in London on 10 June, two days before the first show. I wanted to let Jack know what had really happened – the last thing you need after a rough tour is to come home to aggravation. The only thing worse is to find out you no longer have a home. I didn't end up seeing Jack until I got back to our flat after the first Camden show, and straightaway he announced that I should find somewhere else to live; he was convinced I'd had something to do with him getting sacked. Jack had been doing this a long time, so he really should have known better and that musicians aren't the most logical beings, and nonsense is par for the course – add a large amount of drug and alcohol use to the mix, and it really is quite amazing that any tours happened from the early 1970s through the mid '90s. There was no point arguing, nor did I have the energy, so I sucked it up and went to work at the second Iggy show.

Something felt off, but I was a little distracted by trying to figure out where the fuck I was going to live the following day. The stage was fine, the house was fine, and everyone was ready. Not being in the mood for small talk, I headed to the front of house where the lighting and sound consoles were located, my usual position for the start of the show. There were close to 2500 punters in the jam-packed venue, and they were intent on giving it heavy punk. I prepped the followspot operators, then on cue called the house lights to black. The crowd went wild!

The only problem was that there was no band. No Iggy. What the hell was going on? I'd been given the cue for house to black; now the band was meant to appear as if by magic.

I got one of those requests/demands over the intercom that nobody ever wants to get when they've just called the house to black. 'Tana, come backstage now! Iggy wants you in the dressing room.' *What, are you nuts?* There was no way to get backstage at the Music Machine without battling your way through more than a thousand of the most rabid punk fans in the world. This wasn't going to be pretty. It took me a few minutes of desperate pushing, shoving and literal fighting to get there, then I was hustled upstairs to the dressing room.

Now this was a sight I couldn't have anticipated: the hallway outside his dressing room was jammed with management, record label execs, curious hangers-on, security and crew.

The band was smart enough to wait on the side of the stage – which was probably how someone mistakenly gave the cue for the houselights; they were in the home stretch, so best to keep out of it. I should have been so lucky! It seems Iggy had locked himself in his dressing room and wasn't coming out until I came in. This made absolutely no sense to me; we were supposed to be heading to the stage, not away from it. We were now at about four minutes with the houselights out. This could get ugly at any moment. *Think fast!* I knocked on the dressing-room door and asked Iggy to come out.

His response was, 'Who is it?'

Was this some strange joke? 'Who the fuck do you think it is? Unless you know another Australian girl who works for you!'

'Oh, great, T! Quick, come in.' He opened the door just enough to drag me through, and locked it from the inside. 'That got them.'

'Them? I *am* one of them, have you gone mad?'

'No! No! Wait! I want you to meet someone, a really good friend of mine; it's important.'

Call me crazy, but I couldn't think of any good friend who would let him pull this shit. I looked over at the only other person in the room, a tall, slender guy in a coat and a fedora. I couldn't see his face, not that it really mattered at that moment: to me, he was a problem.

Iggy shoved a mirror in my face and said, 'Let's all do a line then go do the show.' He did one, then passed it to me – that meant there were two left. I did both, thinking whoever the arsehole was he didn't deserve one for putting me through this hell. Just when it was too late for me to stop, Iggy dragged the guy forward and said, 'Tana, I want you to meet David ... Bowie.'

Damn! Well, too late. 'James Osterberg, get your arse on stage before we have a riot on our hands!'

I dragged him out of the dressing room, leaving David Bowie holding an empty mirror and feeling somewhat shocked, I'm sure. But he wasn't my problem – the show was my problem. We ran to the stage with Iggy thinking it was a great laugh. I can't begin to tell you how pissed off I was, and worst of all I had to fight my way back to the front of house. As I left, I noticed Bowie tucked away behind Fred's speaker cabinets so he could watch the show from up close.

Think it can't get any worse? Of course it can!

I'd spent the best part of two years wearing in a black leather jacket – the real, heavy-duty biker type that all self-respecting punks would kill for. Iggy had his own leather, but he'd taken a shine to mine, and for the entire tour he'd been asking if he could wear my jacket on stage. 'Hell NO!' was always my response.

Iggy started each show on that tour in the same way: he came on stage bare-chested in his own leather jacket, and during the first number he took it off, smacked it on the floor in circular motions, then threw it into the wings. His little striptease never missed a beat, never lost the jacket.

The night in question, I left my jacket in what I thought was a safe space behind the monitor desk, on the side of the stage, as there was no way I was going to fight my way back through the now rabid crowd in leather – I would probably have passed out. I dived into the crowd to get back to my position at the front of house, then gave the followspot operators the run-down as the first song started.

Everyone was excited, and there was a lot of talk on the intercom. I hated that, because that's when people make mistakes, so I called for all mics to be turned off. But one guy kept talking. I told him it had best be important, or he was going to be out of there. He said it was a shame Iggy had lost his leather jacket, which was getting ripped off the front of the stage.

I looked up just in time to see *my* jacket, not his, disappearing into the pit. The bastard!

This made for a very long and miserable show. As soon as it finished, I went to the head of security – a friend of mine – and told him my jacket had been nicked off the stage. He saw how upset I was and remembered my jacket as I always wore it. No one from the audience seemed willing to leave straightaway, which gave him time to get the word out that anyone with a real biker leather jacket should be questioned by security. Yeah, that limited it to about half the audience; bless him, he tried the impossible. We ended up with about a hundred confused punters against the wall at various points throughout the venue, to no avail.

I went backstage to give Iggy a piece of my mind. He said he was sorry. Right! His manager thought I was overreacting and offered me a fifty quid to let it go. I told him what he could do with his fifty quid – and picked up a crate of beer and threw it in their direction before I stormed out.

We had a day off before the third and final show. I spent the time feeling sorry for myself, as now not only had I lost my place to stay but I'd also lost my trademark leather.

That last show was a little icy to say the least. Afterwards, I said my goodbyes to the band but not to Iggy. I was still pissed off. But I'm sure it had gone from his mind – to him, the only important thing was that he had his friend David back.

12

WHO ARE YOU

THE WHO HAD BEEN named the loudest band in the world by *The Guinness Book of Records* following their 1976 concert at the Charlton Athletic Football Grounds in London.

It was now 18 August 1979, one of those rare warm, sunny summer days in London town. The entire demeanour of the Brits changes when you add a little sunshine to the mix – it's a glorious thing to behold. And for my part, life was looking up! 'I Don't Like Mondays' by a new band, the Boomtown Rats, was making its way up the charts, and I could just feel there was change a-coming. The music industry was metamorphosing, growing up, coming of age, and me right along with it.

I was standing on the stage of the largest venue in London, Wembley Stadium, looking out over a vast, empty floor that fourteen hours from now would be covered by about eighty thousand fans there to see four bands: Nils Lofgren, AC/DC, The Stranglers and, last but not least, The Who. I'd recently completed my final tour with Status Quo, and was now with TASCO as head of lighting. Around a hundred road crew and stagehands were working together to make this massive concert happen. There would be just one female roadie: me, the expat Aussie girl.

Wembley, a goliath of a structure, was to stand proud for decades and earn its place in history as an iconic London landmark. Its main entrance was straddled by imposing white twin towers that could be seen from far and wide. The stadium had been built to usher in an era of change back in April 1924. On that occasion, King George V himself had MC'd the opening ceremony for the *British Empire Exhibition*, which would eventually grant access to twenty-seven million attendees over eighteen months. The whole extravaganza had been organised for the masses as a much-needed shot of British pride, with the Empire flexing her muscles to the world by bringing together, under one roof, all her colonised and annexed lands, comprising 25 per cent of the planet. World War I had brought a global shift in power, but Britain wouldn't concede to hardships. As only the Brits can do, they had picked themselves up, dusted themselves off and put on a brave front. Nothing wrong here! Move along.

On this day, some fifty years later, the venue was serving as the site for a very different type of gathering: a massive and much-anticipated rock concert promoted as The Who and Friends Roar In, part of what was intended to become the Who Are You Tour. Wembley resembled the arenas of ancient Rome, and the band would be faced with a type of gladiator battle to win over their fans. It was The Who's turn to pick themselves up, dust themselves off and put on a brave front. This concert marked the return of the band as a rock icon that less than a year earlier had survived the loss of its drummer, Keith Moon. The shot in the arm the surviving members needed was to match the success of their 1976

Charlton Athletic Football Club concert. This was a make-or-break situation. While the fans seemed willing, could they pull it off? Would this be their swansong, or would there be a tour to follow?

Keith, a little guy with a larger-than-life personality, had spun out of control only to crash and burn. He'd been the loveable and sometimes annoying court jester who would dress up in disguises and do outrageous things to get attention. Whether he was somersaulting onto the stage, blowing up his drum kit, or doing vast amounts of cocaine during the show, there was no off button. His death, following those of such talented young musicians as Hendrix and Joplin, acted as a wake-up call to an industry discovering the true monetary worth of these gifted but highly unpredictable individuals who had become the faces of popular music. The industry could no longer tolerate musicians acting like petulant children with all the idiosyncrasies and tantrums that entailed; no matter how cute or funny the child might be at times – there was too much at stake.

At Wembley, Kenney Jones would be playing drums for The Who, along with the addition of a keyboard player, John 'Rabbit' Bundrick, and a string section. Kenney hadn't been picked randomly: he'd worked with Pete Townshend on his solo album with Ronnie Lane the previous year, so he wasn't a total stranger. I'd met him a few months earlier – out one night with friends at Dingwalls, a popular London club – and I was glad to see he'd landed the job. We'd managed to talk during rehearsals, and, as you can imagine, his excitement at the possibility of becoming the new Who drummer was conflicting with his sadness for the circumstances that had brought him there. Keith and Kenney had been friends, and they'd hung out on what unwittingly became Keith's last evening, so it all hit very close to home. But each band member had to be ready and on the same page for this monumental show.

The pressure was on that day at Wembley, and we the crew were also feeling it. A good production crew takes on that pressure and goes above and beyond to make everything perfect so the band can focus on the show. They nail the performance; we get the rest! My job at this larger-than-life concert was to monitor the upkeep and operation of the front of house in relation to the onstage part of the show. Once the load-in was done and I'd directed the hanging of the lights on the trussing, I left the stage while the rest of the hands continued with the cabling and trimming of the lamps. I moved to the front-of-house area to oversee the installation and operation of the six followspots, and the miles of power and intercom cable that had to span this huge arena to enable us to communicate with each other.

Last but not least, I needed to set up the front-of-house lighting console area. This was the heart of the lighting production, where the lighting designer stood to make the magic happen. I was excited that the band's lighting designer had requested I work with him for this show, enabling me to become part of this milestone for the band. I needed to make sure everything was done properly while covering such a vast area, as correcting problems once an audience is in place and a show has started can be time-consuming and very noticeable to those who matter.

I would also remain front of house for the focusing of the rig. The followspots were no ordinary followspots: they were Gladiators and Super-troopers. Yes, those were their names! We're talking old-school here. Monster pieces of lighting equipment with carbon-rod feeds that to this day only a handful of people know how to control. At the time you wouldn't have seen a more pure light source. They were also good for assisting in bringing down enemy aircraft during World War II, which gives an idea of the strength they projected. I loved working with them; in the days before moving lights on stage, they were the way to keep performers constantly illuminated from the front of house.

Shepperton Studios was the home of The Who's production crew. Over the years the band and crew had cleverly come up with a way to cover operating costs for the maintenance of both crew and equipment when the band wasn't either touring or recording. The crew had turned it into a business by making the band's customised sound equipment and special-effects racks available for rental by other bands when The Who weren't using them. The crew had taken it one step further by doing a deal with Volvo trucks in Sweden and starting a trucking company for the transportation of the ever-growing amount of production equipment that was becoming the norm for not only The Who but all major touring bands. It just kept getting bigger – we were creating a monster. These two branches of the company became collectively known as ML Executives, and it was the place to go for specialty audio equipment and equipment transportation.

Other bands wanted to reproduce that loud, clean sound, so they too could aspire to great heights in the industry. I'd come across this before; when I'd stopped doing AC/DC's front-of-house sound back in Australia, I'd been approached by a bunch of bands wanting me to do their sound 'just like AC/DC's'. It's almost a superstition: it worked for them, so it will work for us. Not how it works, unfortunately. That 'it' factor must be there from the beginning, or nothing else matters. There's a common saying among crew members: 'You can't polish a turd.' ML Executives had that 'it' factor from a crew perspective and that was why I was there. I'd become part of their circle, so they were willing to teach me the production skills needed for a show of this size, knowledge I could take with me.

Building a large rock show is like performing a ballet. Each crew member has their own job to do (the routine), and how they complete that directly affects each other part of the production (the performance). Like the show that follows, production crews run to a strict schedule that must be adhered to at all costs. Irrelevant of which part of the production you are working on, you must all come together as a team. Yes, there's teasing and bickering, but that's just to keep you on your toes. When it comes together it's like *Swan Lake* – a big, messy, loud *Swan Lake*, but a thing of beauty nonetheless.

* * *

Wembley was yet another large venue annexed to put on these ever-growing productions that hadn't been designed with live music in mind. This added a degree of difficulty to our jobs and could make a simple task daunting and time-consuming, especially once you were working in the front-of-house area. And, as with any large one-off show, something always happened at the last minute.

I ended up being called on to operate Pete Townshend's followspot, one of the Gladiators. Everyone was getting a little nervous as the time drew near for The Who to hit the stage, and Kieran Healy, the lighting designer, was unsure whether anyone except me could keep up with him. There's an art to operating a followspot, especially from such a distance. Everything had to be perfect! No problem – it was a great opportunity for me, and it showed that Kieran trusted me. My

The Who onstage for The Who & Friends Roar In Tour at Wembley Stadium.
(ALAN PERRY)

And backstage at Wembley after their set: (left to right) John Entwistle,
Kenney Jones, Pete Townsend and Roger Daltrey. (ROBERT ELLIS)

position at the followspot also gave me a perfect view of the show's lights and lasers. As lighting was my specialty over the past few years, I was in heaven. The upper-tier seating areas of venues are nicknamed 'The Gods' due to their height and distance from the stage, and on this perfect summer evening it felt like Mount Olympus. As I gazed down at the sheer size of both the audience and the venue, I was on top of the world.

Finally, it was time: the moment we'd all been waiting for. The lights went out, and The Who exploded onto the stage. Like the true professionals they were, the band members instantly came into their own. Pete Townshend and Roger Daltrey took control of the audience and never let go – Pete with his erratic presence and teenage wasteland angst, alongside Roger the consummate performer. AC/DC's set had a raw energy to it; this was different. There was an ease to it, that showed through all the frantic movements, something that's only possible after many years of performing together and getting to know one another intimately.

It was a terrific set, especially considering the restrictions that the Greater London Council had put on the show, both sound and lighting wise. The GLC had pulled the plug on the special-effects laser pyramid that was to be a main part of the show. The time, money and effort put in by John Wolff, the band's laser designer and tech, had been unceremoniously canned by the GLC out of sheer ignorance. The council had a fear of lasers among just about everything else they couldn't wrap their heads around; they wouldn't take the chance of the entire audience being blinded, or – like in an early sci-fi movie – the stadium being demolished by malfunctioning lasers. Anything the GLC couldn't understand wasn't permitted, and this would be the case for a long time to come. But you have to remember that the people who worked for this council were basically public servants: they had no interest in music or evolving technology, or especially in pushing boundaries. Rock'n'roll was a barely tolerated inconvenience that would be resisted at all cost. How on earth could they sit back and have a nice cup of tea with all this silliness going on? But go on it did; we were not going to be stopped. Nor have I come across any instance in which the audience was blinded by a laser show. Go figure – any surviving former members of the GLC, which was dissolved in the mid 1980s, probably still think that's due to their restrictions.

The Who started their set with 'Substitute', and I'm still not sure if it was directed at Kenney or Keith. Kenney, in my humble opinion, was the only logical substitute at the time. He was never to become a real member of the band, though, which he found difficult, and Zak Starkey has since stepped in and found a home among his older peers away from the pressures of being the child of a Beatle. Keith Moon, coincidentally, had taught Zak to play the drums when he was a small child.

But on that day in 1979, after we'd all busted our arses for weeks on end, there was nothing more gratifying than to see The Who get up there and make their magic. On that day, the band let everyone know, without a doubt, exactly why they were known as rock gods.

I can't imagine how each of the original members must have felt hearing the drums while knowing it wasn't Keith. What that concert established was that their machine was more than the sum of its parts. Keith would be missed, but the show would go on. The Who had returned.

This experience was part of a pattern throughout my career: I participated in many firsts for musicians. The enormity of it all was lost on me at the time, as I was just doing my job.

* * *

After The Who's set, my job at Wembley was over – for once, I didn't have to do the load-out. Thank God! That would have taken another several hours and lots of heavy lifting. Some of us, me included, had been up for two days getting last-minute programming resolved. The equipment was all going back to the production company, so I could deal with it tomorrow.

For now, I had some catching up to do. I was keen to see the Boys of AC/DC again. It had been almost three years and as many continents since I'd been present for the start of their phenomenon, and it seemed a lot longer – so much had happened.

I battled my way through eighty thousand incredibly inebriated punters to get to the sanctuary of backstage. There I came across Bon Scott, just the man I was looking for. I had always really enjoyed his company. It was good to see he was still doing his 'lone wolf thing', as I called it; he'd always been the one to just take off, no explanation. This time he'd obviously been sneaking a look at the other bands, and he'd scored a bottle of Jack Daniel's, my poison of choice at the time, for me. He'd heard that I was working the show. Earlier in the day I had wound up the Boys' new crew a tad, just for the hell of it, and word must have got back – probably in the form of 'Who the fuck is this Australian chick giving us shit?' That would have been enough for Bon to know he had an ally in the camp. He didn't miss much.

After setting up camp on a couple of road cases, we had a chat and a couple of shots – well, *swigs* from the bottle, to be more exact. We talked about the sound problems AC/DC had during their set – my clue not to go back to their dressing room to see the others. As I'd been working for The Who that day and it had been their production, I figured best steer clear of Angus and Mal backstage, as they always took any technical problems very personally, with a hint of sabotage in the air. I would catch up with them over dinner down the road a bit, on neutral turf.

Bon and I then moved on to more pleasant topics, such as what we'd each been up to since working together. This was fun, but before long the tone of the conversation changed. 'I'm having trouble keeping up with the Boys,' Bon said. 'Our plans keep falling short, tours cancelling, people dying and we still haven't made it in the States. Maybe I'm too old for this shit.' He sat with his hands in his jean waistband, hunched over against the road case, looking a little dejected. It saddened me to see him with such self-doubt. Bon had just celebrated his thirty-third birthday, which may have had something to do with it.

I gave Bon a reassuring look and shook my head. 'After this show,' I said, 'nothing will get in your way. You just whacked eighty thousand Brits over the head with a severe shot of Aussie rock. There's no turning back now.'

Bon thought this over for a second, taking an extra-long drink of Jack Daniel's, then wiped his mouth with the back of his hand as if trying to wipe away his doubts. I could see he was still bothered. 'Yeah, fuck 'em!' he replied with one of his wicked sideways grins.

I don't think Bon truly believed in what I'd said, and I had a feeling that something else was on his mind. Probably a woman in the mix, causing him to be conflicted; his concerns weren't strictly about AC/DC, as he'd always needed more than just the band. Maybe that was because he was older, or maybe because he'd been to the brink of success with The

Valentines, only to see it slip away – I can't imagine how hard that must be for a musician. And one sure thing about Bon was that he truly loved and even relied on women. He was always happiest when he thought he was in love, even if it wasn't the real thing. The rest of the band, well … not so much. Bon's search for contentment outside the band nucleus was always considered a distraction by Mal and Angus from the cause that was AC/DC.

When he said I should come by his flat to meet his girlfriend, I knew that meant he felt she was special. I said I looked forward to it.

I've always thought it strange that a talent such as Bon Scott, the perfect fit for AC/DC, could be so unaware of his strengths within the band. Insecurities have been a recurring theme among some of the most talented people I've had the pleasure of knowing and working for.

Bon Scott onstage in Nuremburg supporting The Who, 1979. (PETER BURKE)

Another gig with The Who, filming tracks for 'The Kids Are Alright' at Kilburn.
(DANNY CLIFFORD)

Still, Bon and I shared a lot of laughs that day. We reminisced about where it all started for us with AC/DC, back in the now-infamous house on Lansdowne Road. That seemed like a million years ago, a time when our views had been so much simpler. Just a bunch of kids and Bon living in a house together, not doubting for a minute that it was going to happen for all of us. Nothing distracting us from the goal at hand. There would be no stopping us. That way of thinking is contagious, and I carried it with me long after I'd left the AC/DC camp.

'Hey, where did you go?' Bon snapped me back to our conversation.

We started talking about how Angus had come of age, so to speak. He'd now evolved into the spitfire that had started to form when he'd first scaled a rickety PA stack in Melbourne to get the audience's attention.

As Bon and I hugged goodbye, he pretended to stick his tooth in my ear – his preferred form of torture for me. He had a front tooth on a plate that he would flick out to gross me out. Or maybe he did it because we were pals who'd shared so much, and he felt safe and uninhibited with me. The tooth torture had started one hot summer day when he wanted some of the ice-cream I was eating; when I said no, he came at me with his tooth popped out and chased me around the room (he got the ice-cream). It became something he would do as a parting gesture.

When you say goodbye to those you care about, you have the silly thought that it's definitely just 'see you later'. If I'd known that was to be the last time I would ever see Bon, would I have changed anything? He and I never spoke of that morning in Lansdowne Road when he could have died from an overdose. It was a taboo topic in the AC/DC camp. Yet another sign that the machine rolls on.

Just before Bon and I parted, I told him I was soon to start a sold-out tour with David Coverdale of Whitesnake, ex-frontman for Deep Purple. Yes, the same Deep Purple we'd come to blows with. Bon thought this was hilarious. 'Let me know if they give you any shit! I'll come and give 'em a kicking!' was his parting comment.

* * *

That night, I also ran into my friend Jimmy McCulloch backstage, he of the Thai sticks incident. He was caught up in all the after-show clamouring with the band and said, 'Come have a drink! Hang out!' But I couldn't – I was knackered, not to mention covered in the day's work grime. So I made my exit and headed home to my bed. No good comes from staying up for three days, plus I was always a bit self-conscious in my jeans and T-shirt surrounded by everyone dressed to the nines.

My friendship with Jimmy had grown since shortly after my arrival in London. When he didn't have a model in tow we would hang out, although there was a special model, a girl from Texas, who he was really keen on.

He'd changed from when we'd first met, but our casual comfort with each other remained. I thought he was a bit lost after leaving Wings, hurt in a way, as if he'd been disowned. He was looking for a new place to belong, a band that he could become a part of, and I was on a similar search for acceptance and belonging. The feelings ran deep.

Jimmy's brother, Jack McCulloch, was his minder through these few years, and no matter how endearing Jimmy could be, he was a handful. I think Jack was relieved when he knew Jimmy was with me; he trusted me to look out for him. I would frequently stay over at his flat in Maida Vale. The flat came with a room decorated for a child, and that was where I slept. But why had Jimmy kept it like that? 'I want to have kids and a family. This room reminds me of that. Sometimes it's easy to forget.' Whenever I slept over, we had a morning ritual: we'd meet up in the bathroom and brush our teeth together while we rehashed the prior night's events. Jimmy taught me to brush my tongue back then, to get rid of that something-crawled-into-my-mouth-and-died taste. We'd see who could brush their tongue the longest without gagging, a silly game – after a long night, you just know you're going to gag. To this day, every morning when I brush my teeth and get to my tongue, I think of him. Funny the things that trigger memories.

In Jimmy's quest for a new band, no matter who he was with, he always introduced me to its members. When we met up with Stevie Marriott from the Small Faces that Jimmy did a short stint with at Dingwalls Club one night, Stevie said, 'Tana, come with me for a minute.' So off I went to the men's loo, not too uncommon in those days. I thought it was to do a line, which it was, but Stevie then said, 'Stand here while I pee, would you?' I found myself standing at the urinal with him, stopping people from coming up to talk to him while he tried to take a piss. He told me that he couldn't go if a stranger was watching, so I reminded him I was a stranger; we'd just met. 'No, you're good! You're with Jimmy.'

I was also with Jimmy early on the evening that turned out to be his last. I left him when he said he was going to hang out with the Thin Lizzy boys – I'd always got a weird vibe from Phil and Scott, so I bowed out. From my early days in Sydney, I'd never liked heroin or people who used it. And a couple of guys on Phil's crew didn't like the fact I was a female roadie.

When Jack called me the next morning asking if Jimmy was with me or if I knew where he was, my blood ran cold. I told Jack he was home and to 'break the door down if you have to'.

Jack found Jimmy in his apartment. He was dead from an overdose. I'd never known of Jimmy doing heroin before that day.

I felt I had let both Jimmy and Jack down. I didn't go to the funeral, and I never saw Jack again. I'm still sorry for that. Some things don't go away. That was a time of many losses in the music industry, and it's hard to be so young and know so many dead people. Jimmy was only twenty-six. He died just nine days after The Who's show at Wembley.

13

WHAT IS LIFE

HEAVY METAL HAD ARRIVED! It was spreading across England and Europe faster than an STD in a brothel. From the early heavy groups like Zeppelin, Purple and Sabbath, solo artists had emerged such as Robert Plant, Ritchie Blackmore and David Coverdale. Even Ozzy Osbourne was rumoured to be coherent enough to put a band together. Add to this the new kids Judas Priest, Michael Schenker Group and Iron Maiden, and there were more than enough to keep our production company very busy.

Within months of me coming on board, the lighting division of TASCO had outgrown their fledgling Quo rig. Even the audio side was given a complete overhaul with new speaker cabinets being designed to address the volume needed for the growing popularity of larger venues. Money was no object. TASCO had a reputation: if it was loud, we did it!

While live sound was being rethought, lighting was being born. The audience would pay more money to see a spectacular lightshow, so everything changed.

Our humble par cans now came in aluminium and several shapes and sizes, even in a block to almost totally blind an audience.

One light could suddenly have a rolling colour changer, making it sixteen different colours.

The bulbs for all this came from the aviation and automobile industries – that's bright enough!

We needed to lift the new size and weight of the sound and lighting equipment from above, so we adapted motors built for moving heavy items in factories to run upside down.

Aluminium trussing was great, and what if we put the lighting inside for transportation? It would save space and money.

Followspots were great, and what if we put them up the truss and told the operators to 'just be careful'?

Wait a minute! We could move the trusses during the show? Holy shit!

We built multicore cables so we only needed one instead of six, eight or even sixteen.

Those dimmers were big and heavy. What if we followed the same principle as the sound guys, building modular racks that could be configured to suit our needs?

Oh, I was liking where all this was going – and it absolutely felt that quick! 'Bigger! Brighter! Louder! Faster! More!' soon became the mantra of the 1980s.

On stage that first year of the Monsters of Rock Festival on 12 August 1980, I looked out in awe over a denim-clad sea of testosterone with the arc of the motor-racing track off to the right. I then found myself putting a microphone to the exhaust pipes of Rob Halford's Harley-Davidson, which he rode onto the stage to start Judas Priest's set.

LOUD! had arrived, with heavy metal spilling out of every disenfranchised kid's bedroom. These previously ignored kids hit the streets like hordes of the walking dead, finding their tribe. Donington was the first festival to answer the call of these fans, and both AC/DC and Whitesnake were quick to sign up the following year, 1981.

* * *

For me, the first heavy metal tour out of the gate was Whitesnake on the Lovehunter Tour. It was October 1979. The line-up was David Coverdale, Jon Lord, Bernie Marsden, Mickey Moody and Neil Murray, with Ian Paice who had replaced their original drummer. Luckily none of the original Deep Purple members put together that I was the Australian girl from the brawl with AC/DC.

Around this time I added rigger to the list of things I was paid to do. George Harvey, Quo's lighting designer, had taught me a lot of different tasks, usually by throwing me in the deep end. For example: one night after three sold-out Status Quo shows at Wembley Empire Pool, George and I were left to de-rig the points for the lighting system after our rigger had fallen from the roof. I hadn't see it happen, but I'd heard a thud and felt a gust of air as if a door had suddenly been opened. There was our rigger lying on the ground as if he'd appeared out of thin air. Which he had.

That left me and George to finish the job. 'Come on, we're going up,' he called to me. 'We need those steel cables for the show tomorrow. If you don't help me, there'll be no show.'

I looked up into the cavernous roof with the treasured steel cables dangling there, taunting us to just come and get them. *Don't stop and think, just do it!* That meant climbing into the roof and then onto the catwalk that swayed and creaked beneath my feet. When I looked down through the worn metal-lattice floor, I could see the stage thirty metres below where our rigger still lay, waiting for an ambulance. That's how it was back then: you stepped into the shoes of the crew member who had fallen.

George and I pulled the rigging that was needed for the show with every bit of strength we had, all the while feeling that catwalk groan under the stress of the added strain. We stayed up there as long as it took to remove enough steel cables and hardware for us to rig the show the next day at the Birmingham NEC, and left the rest hanging there for a more experienced team of riggers to remove. We had what we needed to keep going.

The two of us rigged that show the next day without hesitation, as it was both a sold-out concert and the grand opening of the venue, so there could be no excuses for it not happening. This was what you did – you kept working, and from that you learnt. A lot! There was no stopping to see how the crew who'd just witnessed their workmate's fall were feeling, to see if we were okay. None of that. There was no department to handle these incidents.

Do roadies suffer from PTSD after an accumulation of these events over the years? Trusses falling, stages collapsing, bus and plane disasters, audience members dying. More than anyone will let on. Back then, stopping or taking a day to get yourself together would have been seen as a sign of weakness. No one wanted to take responsibility, so they just kept us moving.

From then on, I found myself spending time in the roofs of many venues. It turned out I liked it up there. Nobody messes with the rigger. Plus, if I rigged it, I knew it was good.

Classic David Coverdale pose. (ALAN PERRY)

There are two things you never want to hear from a rigger above you: 'Oops!' and 'Heads up!' There's always that split second where you have to decide if you'll stand dead still ... or run! When I wasn't rigging, I always kept one eye on the rigger's whereabouts for that reason.

But rigging was just one of my growing list of jobs. Between being crew chief, dimmer city (the nerve centre of the lighting system), electrician and designer, I was keeping busy. We all were – we all did multiple jobs.

* * *

Although the musicians in a successful band blend into a unit onstage, they tend to have totally different personalities offstage. Out of the Whitesnake guys, my go-to in the long run was Jon. He wasn't only the creator of 'Smoke on the Water', arguably Deep Purple's anthem, but he was also classically trained and what I call a thinker. I always gravitated towards intelligence over looks. Jon's keyboard set-up was stage right, and so were my dimmers. He would arrive before sound check and frequently have his *Times* Sunday crossword in hand; although he was the intellectual type, he also liked to play, but we bonded over doing this crossword.

David was also intelligent, but he revelled in his good looks, and that combination fed into a large personality. When he wasn't surrounded by models I would be his wingman for practical jokes. I'd choose Jon to hang out with in the quieter moments, and David in the bar after the show. Mickey and Bernie were more laid-back, while Neil seemed to be the new kid – I knew that feeling.

Picture this! I was at the bar with David and some of the crew, while the rest of the band were scattered throughout the room. David spotted Neil, from across the room, with his arm around some girl. That was all David needed; we waited. Eventually, Neil excused himself to go to the bathroom, and this was David's signal to swoop in, dragging me in tow. If he had a girl with him, he'd told me, it gave him credibility. He introduced himself to the girl who'd been chatting with Neil, and she swooned. Really, that was all he needed to do – the girls just loved David. But no, he then said to her, 'So, I see you've met our bag guy, Ron.'

Now, this confused the girl, as she'd thought she was talking to Neil the Bass Player. She said, 'No, I'm with Neil.'

This was when David did his thing. He turned to me, shrugged and said, 'Ron's at it again. Telling this lovely young lady he's in the band.'

I just shook my head as if it happened all the time.

David smiled and said, 'Just thought I'd give you a heads up, my darling.'

Before Neil's return we headed back to the bar, to watch the chaos from a safe distance. This scenario happened a few times, and the pranks never ended well for Neil: usually with a few harsh words and a sudden departure by a girl who only moments earlier had thought she'd landed her rock star. These girls were obviously new to all this, or they would have known who he was. Neil was obviously new to this also, or he would have known better than to leave girls unattended around David.

* * *

At the end of that tour, Jon threw a party for the crew at his country estate, Burntwood Hall in Henley-on-Thames. It was adjacent to George Harrison's Friar Park with a strip of land in between that was turned into a cricket pitch for those days when a quick game was in order.

At the end-of-tour party we were having a great old time, shooting pool and blowing off steam. You do need to shake off a tour once it's done – it's like scuba diving; you have to decompress. Jon's dog was due to drop a litter of pups in the middle of all this and had commandeered the upstairs bathroom. It was also George Harrison's birthday, and he wandered about having a chat before settling into a comfy armchair by the pool table where I was playing.

The doorbell rang and in came a stripper to the tune of 'She Loves You!' That was my cue to head for the kitchen, but I popped my head back in for a moment. Poor George looked like a cornered animal as the girl straddled the arms of his chair, pinning him with her breasts. She was the first of two strippers booked for that evening.

I was sitting cross-legged on the kitchen counter when suddenly George was standing in front of me. He looked a little in need of rescuing.

I didn't know what to say, so I just said, 'Happy birthday!' and lit a cigarette.

George smiled, then said with a somewhat pensive expression, 'Can I hang out here for a bit? I don't want to go back into the other room just yet.'

'Sure,' I said, 'why not?' After I'd introduced myself, I asked him, 'How did you end up here, it being your birthday and all?'

'I took a walk through my garden earlier – I do that a lot – and Jon had mentioned he was having a party with you guys, and so I just kept walking. I wanted to get away from the house for a bit, and here is hassle-free.'

Our conversation flowed freely. He was curious about Australia, mentioning that his one time there was rather rushed; The Beatles had performed three concerts in Australia in the 1960s. I said we now had hot and cold running water and everything! He laughed. I told him about my favourite beaches in the rainforest areas of northern Queensland, and he said he'd like to spend some time there. Then he asked how I liked touring. He was very easy to talk to.

I lit another cigarette, and, as I took a hit, out of the blue he said, 'I'd marry you tomorrow if you stopped smoking.'

I had no idea how to respond to that and was a little embarrassed. Just when I'd been coming to like this George Harrison guy, here he was making demands.

I mumbled something about wanting to check on the dog, leapt off the kitchen counter and took off up the staircase two steps at a time. Sure enough, she was giving birth, so I ran to tell Jon. As I passed back through the kitchen, I said to George, 'Guess what? You and the puppies have the same birthday!' I continued into the main room to play pool and avoid my new friend the birthday boy.

Well, you'd think it would have ended there, but no! I received multiple messages, through Jon's personal assistant, that George wanted to see me again. I was told on good authority that he was serious about wanting to spend time with me. I'd since found out about Olivia, his wife and the mother of his son; I'd also found out that he could be quite the philanderer. I wasn't going to encourage anything with him – I had no plans to become his May Pang, even though he'd seemed quite endearing.

The relationships of these talented and successful musicians are never simple. Some of them want to find a companion on the road who 'gets it' – who knows how it all works and can both contribute and be a sounding board. Some also have trust issues, and they figure if you're already in the music scene, you're safe. I think George was one of those, and I guess that's why he wanted to 'see' more of me.

Olivia stood by him, they made a family, and sadly we all lost him way too soon. He was lucky to have her, and she him. And no scarlet letter for me.

How did I deal with all this? I ran away! I'd learnt the hard way not to trust guys like George. I was starting to learn the language of touring – although a little late. When a roadie or musician says he's not with his wife or significant other, it can mean he's not with her because she's at home and he's there on the road. Gotta watch those boys! It can get very confusing, especially if you meet someone who you really want to believe.

The Whitesnake tour finished 8 November 1979. I was booked to continue on the second leg through 1980 but I bowed out, saying I hadn't had any proper time off since the start of 1977. I told TASCO I'd be returning home to Australia for a well-deserved break. I was lying.

* * *

The truth was, I was pregnant, and nobody had noticed. I was scared, and I was in denial. I'd found out the week before the Whitesnake tour had started, and I hadn't known how to deal with it. I wasn't prepared to tell anyone, least of all the father. I couldn't see how this could happen to me – God knows I rarely had sex. But contraception was spotty at best, not to mention trying to get the pill in the middle of a tour somewhere. There was no allowance for any of the things a woman might need out on the road.

Before the tour started, I'd found a doctor who would see me on short notice, but only if I paid for the visit as I wasn't British. That should have been my first clue. I arrived at his office thinking it was a shame the building hadn't been bombed during the war, as it was tired, old and bleak. The mood didn't change when I told him why I was making this visit. 'Doctor, I'm in a very bad situation here. I'm too young with no family in the UK. I work to support myself, and I can't do my job in this condition. What choices do I have?'

He peered over his rimless glasses with a look of distaste on his sallow face. Then he rose up, holding each edge of his impressive leather desktop, and announced, 'You brought this on yourself! There is nothing that can be done for you. You will need to accept the consequences of your promiscuous lifestyle.' With that, he turned his back on me.

'You don't understand—'

'No, young lady, *you* don't understand. You will get no help! You deserve no help!' He pointed to the door. I'd just paid to be berated, as he hadn't even bothered to do an exam.

Terrified, I ran out of that sad office not stopping until I reached the safety of my flat. As I came through the door, the phone rang. It was TASCO. 'You need to come in now, we have to get the equipment ready for this tour!' I hung up the phone and went to work.

I'd read that England was very pro-choice, but I guess that depended on the doctor. I felt I had nowhere to turn. Was I being selfish? Probably, but I was spurred on by my fear of being judged for having sex – 'See what happens when you hire a girl!' – and the thought of losing everything I'd worked so hard for after I'd survived everything that had been thrown at me. *I can't fail*, I thought, *I can't throw it all away, I can't lose control!* More importantly, I couldn't become my mother. That was my biggest fear: resenting my own child.

Not knowing what else to do, I continued touring while I tried to figure it all out. I couldn't just sit down with a bunch of male roadies and ask them for advice after the reaction I'd received from a medical professional. No matter how good I was at my job, it would be like I'd contracted the plague. A double standard? Absolutely! One of many – but this was the big one.

I worked as usual, climbing trusses, loading trucks, and nobody noticed. Maybe because of my tough schedule, I didn't put on any weight. I didn't show at all. Did I drink alcohol, smoke cigarettes and do cocaine? YES. Did I know any better? NO. Did anyone back then? NO.

Only once did anyone say anything. We were in the production office at the end of the tour and one of the guys said. 'You know, Tana, you've put on a couple of pounds. You might want to watch that. If I didn't know better, I'd think you might be pregnant.' And everyone in the room laughed.

I looked at him as though he was crazy. 'Well, that shows how much you know, now doesn't it.'

To the men I worked with, my pregnancy was probably up there with seeing a pig fly. *No, can't be! Must be imagining it.* Funny, I thought that for a while too, until I couldn't deny it any longer. I needed to make yet another life-changing decision alone.

After closing out all my commitments with work and a month after my encounter with George Harrison, I got on a plane to Australia. I still had no real plan in place, but I would be far enough away that hopefully I could think straight.

This was where I fell apart, questioning all I'd been doing with my life. Was it all wrong? Had I wasted my life?

Should I have left the battle of women being accepted in this industry to someone easier to deal with, someone with a better education, someone better looking? Someone with self-worth? I was tired of it all. I felt I should have been happy by now, or at ease to some extent. But here I was back in Australia, staying at my mother's place. Hadn't I earned a bit of happiness in my life? I wanted a partner, but it's hard to find love when you don't know what it looks like. You see a diamond where there's just a piece of glass. If nobody ever took the time to show you the difference, how do you know what you're seeing? They both shine in the beginning.

I had always struggled with matters of the heart. I was never sure how to interpret sexual advances. I would usually laugh them off; my go-to when I get nervous is to make a joke. I'd been touring the world on my own as a single woman since I hadn't been much more than a child, and I was living in close contact 24/7 with up to a hundred guys. If I wasn't careful – very, very careful – I was bound to get hurt. Some saw me as a therapist, some as a pal or buddy, some as a conquest: how could I tell which ones honestly saw me as a long-term partner as opposed to a tour romance?

And there were the old double standards at work. A male roadie could get laid every night, and that was funny; if he scored with a female band member, he was a hero! If a female crew member got laid, everyone got involved with an opinion – and, to some, she was a floosy. If a female crew member slept with a band member, she was a gold-digger, groupie or both!

I was yet to come across another woman independently touring in this field, so there was no comparing of notes or asking for advice. I'd met a girl who was dating a production manager while helping in his office, but that wasn't the same – I saw that as a bit of a free pass. Women were coming on board for catering, and a woman was working for Supermick Lights in London with her boyfriend but she focused on small, local shows. The only other woman I knew of worked at the Rainbow Theatre in Finsbury Park and when that had closed down in December 1981 the lighting equipment was taken from the venue to establish a company, Rainbow Lights. She also didn't like to tour. Change takes time, and the hands of time can move ever so slowly.

* * *

In Australia, I finally had to tell my mother what was going on with me, as she hadn't noticed either. I guess this is an example of why eyewitness reports are so unreliable: we see what we want to see. Once I'd told her, she set me up to see her doctor. He did an examination and told me I had possibly one month to go, based on the fact I was barely showing. I left his office in the Melbourne CBD and as I got on a tram, my waters broke, right there as I stood on that tram.

By the time I got back to my mother's flat two kilometres away, I was in labour. So much for that doctor; he obviously knew nothing.

In the hospital after giving birth, my mother gave me some news. True to form, she put it like this: 'That friend of yours, Bon, from that band you used to work for, is dead,' quickly followed by 'and you have a baby boy'. I went into some type of shock. I couldn't comprehend anything clearly. There was a baby. There were nurses, a doctor and my mother, and they were all asking me questions, but I couldn't hear them. All I could hear was my mother saying again, 'Your friend Bon Scott is dead! It's the drugs that got him! It's in all the papers.' All I could do was cry. I didn't know if I was crying for Bon, my son, or myself. Now I know it was for all three. It was 19 February 1980. I'd lost another friend, and I was a mother. How was this going to work?

Over the next several months, my mother and I came up with a plan. She was no longer drinking alcohol and had settled into a quiet existence but was still working full-time. She suggested she could quit her job, stay at home and look after my son, while I continued to work as usual. TASCO was expanding to America and Terry Price had asked me to transfer to the LA office. If I agreed, they would sponsor me for a resident green card. When I moved to the States, my mother and son could join me, and we'd be one big happy family. Until that time, I'd visit them for a minimum of two months each year around his birthday, which would be more time off than I usually took, and I would be in a financial position to support them both. Men did this all the time in the music industry. Why couldn't I?

With this plan in place, I reached out to TASCO London and put in for the next tour out the door. I needed the money – I now had a family to support. My first tour once back in England was mid August 1980 and the tour they put me on would start rehearsals end of August with shows from 3 September to 8 November. I would be working with another heavy metal icon. The tour would be Ozzy Osbourne's Blizzard of Ozz Tour, his first as a solo artist since the demise of Black Sabbath.

I was back! I was working! Unbeknown to me, I was about to board the 'Crazy Train'.

14

CRAZY TRAIN

I HAD RETURNED TO London in time to catch the rehearsals for Ozzy and his Blizzard of Ozz Tour. The band was tight and consisted of Ozzy, Randy Rhoads, Bob Daisley and Lee Kerslake. Each of these men had a strong pedigree in metal/ rock music, and the line-up was a stroke of genius. I didn't know Ozzy's reputation or anything of the recently-on-the-scene Sharon Arden. I did surmise she knew exactly what she wanted and wasn't afraid to get it.

Sharon came from a stable of music management. I'd met her dad, Don Arden, two years earlier when working on ELO's rehearsals for the Out of the Blue Tour: the tour with the spaceship – the very expensive spaceship, that was rumoured to have been paid for with Mafia money. Don had a reputation for being dodgy, so who really knows?

There we were, doing the first technical run-through. This entailed the inaugural opening of the top of the flying saucer to reveal the stage set within. Slight problem – there's always one – the piano didn't completely fit inside, so the top section of the saucer couldn't close all the way down to the stage level. The decision was made to put a packing blanket over the brown piano, so it didn't get all scratched up, when the saucer lid was in the closed position. The randomly selected packing blanket just happened to be green.

This was the first time everyone got to stand out front of the stage and admire their handiwork and see the full reveal, including the band alongside the management that had outlaid a lot of money for this beast. It should have been a moment of sheer joy at seeing the concept of the flying saucer finally fulfilled.

All of a sudden, someone on the crew said, 'It looks like a big hamburger – look, the blanket is a lettuce leaf, and the piano is the beef patty!'

Pause for a moment to take that in. After several months of research and development and a rumoured $300,000 price tag, some things can't be unseen.

From that point on among the crew, the spaceship was known as the Flying Hamburger. It wowed audiences all over England and the States, breaking attendance records. All the while, the band couldn't hear what the hell was going on due to the weird acoustics it created, so there was a heavy reliance on tapes for the shows. When Don threatened to sack anyone caught calling it the Flying Hamburger, the joke became: 'You want fries with that?' The brown piano was switched with a white one.

Now it was his daughter's turn at the helm.

Some tours are just difficult from day one. It was a test, really, to see if Ozzy could go the distance. Sharon had picked him up off the floor of Daddy's office in London. Don had several artists in his fold but wasn't at all excited about his little girl running off with a musician – a successful Jewish man was what he'd had in mind. He'd sent her to school in

The ELO's Flying Hamburger ... Oops! ... Flying Saucer at Wembley Arena.
(ALAN PERRY)

Switzerland, for Christ's sake! But Sharon was determined to have her very own rock star.

This is where it all began: a family war that would last over two decades. As father and daughter struggled for power, there we were, the crew and the band, stuck in the middle. Don was still trying to run things from London with the tour manager, John 'Upsey' Downing, a long-time employee of Don's required to report back to him what was going on during the tour. The only problem? Upsey had a secret unrequited love for Sharon. You can't make this shit up!

We were an excellent crew, but I think the only reason any of us lasted was due to each other. And when the band was onstage it was a tight, loud, visually impressive show – once I got used to how Ozzy moved. When I finally figured out that he moved like a toddler, somehow he was easier to watch, although I was sure that at any moment he might toddle right off the front of the stage. After he avoided the Glasgow Apollo's drop of several metres, we could breathe a little easier. This was a small miracle considering the state he was in for most of the shows.

Ozzy had pretty much been on a bender since being sacked from Sabbath, and this tour was what he needed to pull out of it. From the beginning the crowds loved him. All jokes about toddlers aside, there's something endearing about him – he is uniquely a hell of a front man. But the shining light both on and off stage for this tour was Randy Rhoads: totally professional, polite, quiet and always happy. I wondered how he did it.

A crew member's job is made more difficult when the things they rely on while touring are not provided. There's a difference between a prima donna crew and a highly professional, hardworking crew who are asking for the bare essentials to keep the tour going. Everything was a battle on this tour. Per diems, the weekly allowance that road crews rely on for meals and sundries, were non-existent at first, and a crew without per diems is never a happy crew. Only when we threatened to go on strike did they appear. Little did we know, our salaries weren't being paid either.

The itinerary is second on the list of things a crew takes very seriously. That is the tour Bible. That is how we know where the fuck we are, and – more importantly in this case – when it's going to be over. We went that entire tour without an itinerary. Even the bus drivers wouldn't tell us where we were going. I guess this was so we didn't run away.

Having said all that, no matter how much of a hard time you're having as a roadie, when the show is up and running, and the audience is loving it, this somehow makes everything okay, just for that moment. That's where the magic is.

* * *

Sharon and I hit it off at first. After a few shows she decided she wasn't happy with the lighting designer and wanted me to do it. I tried to explain to her that I couldn't take on that job as well as all the other work I was doing, but she didn't want to hear it; she kept on firing whoever was operating the show. As we were going through all these lighting designers, I was redesigning the rig, focusing it and programming it in time for the next guy to turn up and push some buttons.

I was being accommodating as I needed to strengthen my position with TASCO. I didn't want to compromise my transfer to the States. And I did like Sharon – I didn't agree with a lot of her methods, but you have to give her credit for not taking any shit.

I found her one day in a lobby bathroom, crying hard. I guess everything had come to a head, and she'd just cracked. I went to her and said, 'What are you doing? Get yourself together and don't let *them* ever see you crying like this.' This was the best advice I could give her from one woman to another. 'Never let them see any sign of weakness.' Out there on my own, I tried to live by that rule.

From then on, Sharon wanted to keep me close. But I still wouldn't be her lighting designer. I didn't want to go back to working directly for a band, and this one seemed too broken to last.

It turns out I was wrong about the longevity of Ozzy. Unlike with AC/DC, it didn't feel right for me, and I just didn't share Sharon's vision. She never doubted that it was going to happen and happen big – or else!

By the middle of the tour, all shows were sold out, including the two Hammersmith Odeon shows. The day of the first show, Sharon and Ozzy appeared wearing new, matching, full-length fox-fur coats. I was doing the lighting focus from the front-of-house console when they came to stand either side of me, all excited and wanting to chat. Meanwhile, I was trying to work. Ozzy said, 'We should get Tana one then we all three can have matching coats!' I bowed out gracefully, thinking how ridiculous a statement that was considering the entire crew were still struggling to get paid. It's seemingly so easy to lose touch with reality. The phrase *Let them eat cake!* came to mind. By the end of the tour we had been paid, but the warm and fuzzies wouldn't last between Sharon and me. She does not like to be told no.

Blizzard of Ozz Tour with Ozzy Osbourne and Randy Rhoads. (ALAN PERRY)

Ozzy enjoyed hanging out with the crew. He would often turn up in the hallway of a hotel, just wandering about looking for the party room, seeming a little lost. He was actually good fun, and on one occasion he took part in shaving off the eyebrows of a certain crew member. Note to the wise: do not pass out in a roomful of road crew – *ever*!

The frivolities didn't end there; we all decided we were hungry and went to see what other trouble we could get up to. There was no room or bar service in the hotel, so we decided it would be a great idea to raid the kitchen. Off we went, Ozzy in tow.

We couldn't find the makings of a meal, but we did find a tray of incredibly oversized kippers. The things you can do with a kipper when bored is pretty much limitless, and a lot of them unspeakable. Into how many orifices can a guy put a kipper? The answer is many! Eventually, bored with that game, we all went to bed after returning the kippers to the fridge.

The next morning as we staggered into the dining room for breakfast, we were greeted by the tour manager, Upsey, singing the praises of the breakfast – especially the kippers! 'They're huge!' he called out to us. We all ran screaming with laughter from the room, leaving behind a confused Upsey to enjoy his kippers.

* * *

The tour continued to sell out, and we continued to change lighting designers. At the second-to-last show, when we should have been celebrating a successful tour and an album that was selling well, we received shocking news: Bob

Daisley, the bass player, and Lee Kerslake, the drummer, had been sacked.

Bob and Lee had contributed to the recording of *Blizzard of Ozz* and the follow-up album, *Diary of a Madman*. A dispute had arisen over royalties and songwriting credits. There are strict rules about crediting a person who either writes or contributes to the writing of a song, and these aren't negotiable. Not only are payments to be made on a regular basis to this person, but they are also to be credited in the by-lines of whatever format the music is published in. This wasn't something that Sharon would consider, which led to a lawsuit regarding the musicians' rights.

Control is something Sharon won't trifle with, and she has often exhibited this kind of behaviour throughout her very long and successful career. 'She who holds the keys owns the castle' is apparently her motto. I was glad I'd said no to working with her.

I didn't need the drama, so I moved on and focused on making sure I kept my own keys to the lighting department at TASCO London.

* * *

This was me back in the swing of things. Nothing had changed. Nobody looked at me differently; nobody knew what had happened or why I'd been gone so long. I knew, though, and I was having trouble dealing with it. I was only doing what many of the men on tour did – they left their children at home and went off to work – but I knew I would be judged for it, purely because I was a woman. I could imagine the comments, 'Isn't it time you gave all this up?' 'You had a fair run, now settle down and do the right thing.'

Why would stopping be the right thing for me but not for them? I didn't want to find out.

Things were already getting complicated back in Australia. My mother suddenly wanted to purchase a house, and she wanted me to send her the downpayment. What? This was never the plan. I wasn't moving back to Australia – she and my child were to join me in America. She was changing the rules already, and maybe she hadn't changed as much as she'd led me to believe.

I would return to Australia each February for the next two years to see my son and try to figure out how to get my mother on the same page as me – the page she'd suggested in the beginning. It appeared that I was having my own power struggle with a parent. While I was just trying to keep the peace, she focused on keeping control of me through my son. I focused on working, sending money home, and trying to keep my line of communication open, which was becoming increasingly difficult. I wasn't ever concerned for my son's safety with her, as he was her prize. Him being perfectly cared for without me was her bargaining chip.

During every phone conversation my mother relished telling me, 'You are ridiculous to think you could look after this child nearly as well as I can. If you were to take him away, it would break my heart! You would kill me and fail both yourself and your son.'

If you hear you are a piece of shit long enough, you start to believe it.

The situation was daunting and constantly on my mind, yet I didn't have anyone in London I felt I could confide in or ask for advice. I could clearly see the battle lines she was marking out. I needed to fast-track my US plan to see if I was imagining all this or if she really was going to dig in and refuse to join me.

* * *

With the Ozzy Osbourne tour over, I'd had enough of the drama and headbanging, and the train wreck that was Sharon and Ozzy's relationship. But in all fairness, they weren't the only dysfunctional couple on that tour.

I'd jumped into a relationship with an American roadie, a Vietnam vet, good-looking with the darkest, saddest eyes I'd ever seen. They say misery loves company, so in I went. He suffered from PTSD – not that any of us knew what that was at the time. It showed if he got too drunk. Or if you woke him up, which could be a bit tricky when touring – his response would be to leap up in full commando-mode and attempt to kill anything that moved near him. I found this out one day when he'd overslept and nobody wanted to wake him; they all knew him from other tours. Finally, I said I'd try. I figured the way to go would be to sit close to him, but not too close, and talk softly to him using his name. It worked, and from that I decided he was a wounded soul who needed rescuing. I was right in the first instance only. He was one of those guys who liked to say he was separated from his wife, meaning she wasn't in the room. Idiot me fell for it because I needed to, and so there was another heartache. My picker is broken!

I needed to switch gears and find a tour that was less – hmm, how should I put this? – dysfunctional? Respectable, even? That's a funny word to use for rock'n'roll, I know, but it's all relative. I took my reprieve with a series of shows with Count Basie and Lena Horne, which were black tie and definitely the change of pace I was looking for.

I had been away for eight months in Australia, but now I was back in my seat as TASCO's head lighting person, and my next tour would be with The Police for their Ghost in the Machine Tour, but I had some time to fill before that started. I had to constantly keep working; I could not afford any more time off financially, or emotionally. Although I was well established by this time, I was still insecure. It was a hard feeling to shake.

I was in the production office at TASCO when the topic of a one-off show with Elton John came up. He was to play a concert for *who*?

15

GOD SAVE THE QUEEN

THE MORE I HEARD about this Elton John show, the curiouser and curiouser I got. This could be exactly the change I was looking for. It wasn't going to be just any one-off: this one would be special. We were to present a concert at Windsor Castle for Prince Andrew's twenty-first birthday celebration.

We'd be the first crew to put on a rock concert for the Royal Family in one of their homes. Royals had attended concerts in the past, but never anything on their home turf, so to speak. I wondered what they all thought of it. This is how I imagined that conversation going down.

The Queen: 'Andrew, darling, what would you like for your twenty-first birthday? You can have anything you want, dear.'

Prince Andrew: 'Well, Mummy, I would like Elton John, please.'

The Queen: 'Philip! Philip! Can we get an Elton John for Andrew for his birthday? He wants one!'

The Duke: 'Yes, of course, dear. Let me get right on that ... Guard!'

With that said, we set about putting together a performance for the Royal Family at Windsor Castle. There was much to be done. We had to be careful about who was to crew this show, as there would be security checks and we didn't want anyone getting arrested. There would be dress codes, and everyone would need to be on their very best behaviour. Both the tour manager, Nicky Pitts, and the lighting designer, James Dann, had British public school educations, so that lent some credibility to the rest of us. My boarding school education didn't count, I'm sure, as I was an Antipodean – possibly even a convict. Should they have even let me into the castle?

Once we'd selected the crew members, we started figuring out the logistics. First up, we had to scope out the room that was to be used for the concert, then we'd create staging, lights and sound to fit. It wasn't as though we had a choice of rooms, we weren't the only entertainment scheduled for the evening.

Credit where credit's due – these royals sure knew how to throw a bash! There was to be a Bedouin-style room (my favourite), a disco room, and a full dining hall with what they called a 'buffet' and we called a 'feast'. There were hallways that seemed to go forever, lined by rooms set up to accommodate the large number of guests. All this was in a part of the castle generally closed to the public.

Our room for the performance was the portrait gallery. The walls were covered with sitting portraits of each ruler going back to when the tradition had been started in the tenth century. This room had been added under the reign of King George IV, one of thirty-nine monarchs to reside at

Windsor Castle over its 900-year history. It wasn't a massive room, but we could organise a seven-metre stage and decent sound system without too many problems, and there was a viewing balcony on which we could position additional seating and followspots. *We can make this work*, I thought. *I mean, that's what we do!*

Obviously, no self-respecting roadie of the time had anything close to suitable clothing for an event of this stature. My work with Count Basie and Lena Horne hadn't even come close. As we'd all be in clear sight of the guests while working during Elton's performance, we needed to get seriously frocked up. The guys were sent to a high-end tux place in the Strand to rent their outfits – black tie formal – we couldn't have any of them turn up in a dinner jacket; we weren't exactly invited to the dinner. Once that was all sorted, the focus shifted to me.

Nicky Pitts took me under his wing, and off we went to the appropriate exclusive stores. We asked the various salesladies to find the correct attire that a young lady would wear for an evening event in the presence of the Royal Family. We couldn't divulge what exactly we would be doing, as Elton's performance was to be kept hush-hush. The correct outfit, it turned out, was nothing less than a full-length evening gown with gloves – much to my chagrin. We're talking about a girl whose wardrobe consisted of jeans, T-shirts, Doc Martens and Kickers. Nicky made me try on and model each and every gown presented as suitable attire. This torture went on for two days. Nicky found it all very entertaining; however, we were running out of time. Finally, I convinced him that it would be impossible for me to do my job in a full-length evening gown and heels. If something went wrong, I'd have to hitch up the skirt and run. Couldn't I just wear a suit like the guys? At the time, women didn't wear trousers in the presence of the Queen, so a formal request had to be made through Buckingham Palace.

While we waited for a response, we got on with the job of building a lighting rig and stage. We learnt that Elton was to perform, with Ray Cooper accompanying him on percussion. A full band would be too loud. The show needed to be intimate for Prince Andrew.

Word came back that I would be allowed to wear a formal pantsuit. We organised for a three-piece suit to be made from heavy black crepe, which I'd wear with a white blouse off the rack – problem solved. I would also wear my Doc Martens, as the palace staff hadn't mentioned shoes. I was told to keep a low profile so my attire wouldn't cause a 'distraction'.

* * *

Now that all the formalities were out of the way, we could get on with the show. We were all shipped off to a hotel in close proximity to Windsor Castle, which would become our home for the duration of the event. They didn't want to risk any of us going missing or mentioning the upcoming event, especially to the press – this was absolutely under no circumstances to get into the papers.

We would have three days to prepare the room for the show. Did we need three days? No, but everyone was erring on the side of caution. After all, we were breaking new ground here. We needed to make sure the power provided was enough, and clean. We needed to take extra care not to damage anything, especially the portraits, as we brought the equipment into the room and got the lighting trusses into the air. There wasn't anywhere from which we could rig a sound and lighting system, so the PA needed to be stacked and the lighting system ground-lifted. And, last but not least, we needed to make it all fit.

Before we could get the set-up in any semblance of order, Elton turned up. He was obviously very nervous and kept demanding that everything be made perfect – like we were going to do a half-arsed job in front of the Queen? The last thing I wanted to hear was 'Off with their heads!' But you have to keep the star happy – it's part of the job – so we made all the right fussing noises in his general direction while he got in the way, until he was reassured enough to be whisked away. Then we carried on working.

This is a classic example of why when asked what it is we roadies actually do, often our response is 'babysit'.

We'd been working all day and the lights were hung and at about chest height while I was testing the system, when we had our second visitor. It was Diana Spencer. She'd come down to check on us for Andrew; he was 'ever so curious', as she put it. She thought our work was all very exciting and wanted to know if the lights were going to go any higher, so I explained that we were just testing the system at this height, as it was easier to fix any issues at ground level. I then showed her the lighting console, let her push a couple of buttons, and explained that once the rig was at its maximum height, we would then focus the lights. She left with a big smile, heading off to give the princes an update. She was very sweet, and extremely good at putting everyone at ease.

Around this time, we were all called in to the production office for a meeting. This office was a sleek silver Airstream travel trailer, just outside the entrance we'd used to bring the equipment into the castle. Guarding the trailer door was one of the royal guards. The Windsor Castle Guard is made up of a resident regiment of foot guards from what's called the Household Division; these are the ones in the red tunics and bearskins – and, oh yes, they carry rifles. We came to a dead stop upon seeing this one, unsure if he was there to keep us out of the production office, or keep us in. To let us enter he graciously stepped off to the side with flashy steps and turns and the repositioning of his rifle, and this became the little dance he did each time we entered or exited the trailer. Waiting inside was a rather large mirror with several lines on it. Don't judge, it was the 1980s; everyone from bankers, to lawyers, to doctors – and, yes, supposedly even Princess Margaret – were doing it. So, with the door guarded, and the Queen's flag flying above to announce she was in residence at the castle, some of us did a line. Mad if you didn't.

I was then off to find the cigarette machine I'd noticed the day before down in the staff dining hall. I found Windsor Castle quite mind-boggling, not only because of its size but also the artworks and artefacts that adorned almost every inch. While I was at the Glennie School, I'd won a book on the rococo period for my talents in the fine arts. I'd never really liked this period in art, had always thought it pretentious, and now it surrounded me.

I was thinking of that while wandering down a hallway I could have sworn was the same one I'd used the previous day, when suddenly, *boom!* I walked right into a wall.

A voice behind me said, 'Can I help you? You appear to be lost.'

I'd vaguely noticed a man behind me, and I remembered a red stripe running down his trouser leg. I assumed he was a fire marshal. So, without turning around, I responded, 'I could have sworn I came this way yesterday, and there was no wall here.'

The man said, 'It can be confusing at times. You should try finding your way around as a small child.'

That's when I realised my fire marshal was none other than Prince Andrew. *Uuugh!*

Firstly, you do not turn your back on members of the Royal Family; secondly, you address them as Your Highness. I was mortified – and still very high, I might add.

As I turned to face him, he must have seen the terror on my face. He showed mercy, smiled and pointed for me to continue down the hallway to the right. As he walked away, he was probably wondering who had let this Antipodean loose in the castle. I followed his directions to the other end of the hallway; lo and behold, there was the cigarette machine. I managed to get back to the stage without any further royal encounters.

Rumour had it there were moving walls in the castle for security purposes, which made me feel a little better.

* * *

That night we focused the lighting rig and had everything ready for sound check the following day when Elton reappeared, this time with Ray. The room was then closed for sound check.

Ray's a quiet, unassuming kind of guy – that is, until he gets on stage. This tall, thin, sallow-looking man in a well-worn black mod suit turns into a manic wizard. He was contorting himself as he reached across his percussion instruments arranged in a semicircle about twenty-five centimetres in diameter and a couple of metres high. Quite the sight! His sound check was easy.

Elton John with his band leader Davey Johnstone; they have played over 3000 shows together. (DANNY CLIFFORD)

Then it was Elton's turn. We could tell he was still a little on edge, and his way of dealing with any situation in which he wasn't 100 per cent in control wasn't always gracious, to say the least. He played several songs for sound check, which was more than he usually did. The next few years would become known as his 'difficult' period, and at Windsor Castle he was just getting started.

All the hard work, planning and other calisthenics we'd gone through were to culminate in a one-hour performance, as that was the time he'd been allotted. Elton, we would find out later that night, had other plans. It seems he was a little starstruck by royalty and didn't want his performance to be overshadowed by any other part of the evening.

Elton also had an ulterior motive: he wanted an OBE. If the Beatles could each have a Most Excellent Order of the British

Empire, then Elton could have an Order of the British Empire. The OBE is an honour bequeathed on an individual by the ruling monarch for services to the Empire. It is announced once a year to coincide with the Queen's Birthday Honours List and allows recipients to use the title of Sir or Dame before their name, among other perks. This is what Reg had set his sights on, so he saw this concert as his means to that end.

That evening, Charles, Diana, Andrew and Fergie were in their seats along with other members of the Royal Family, but not the Queen. Oh, well, the show had to start. House to black, off we went.

Halfway through the first song, I heard through the intercom, 'Got a light, doll?'

What?

'You want one? Want a cigarette?'

Oh, shit! I thought. *There's no smoking in this room. We've been through this!*

I looked up to the balcony and saw Rivett our truck driver/followspot operator with an as-yet-unlit cigarette in his mouth – and who was he talking to? Princess Margaret! Now, she had a bit of a reputation for being the wild child of the Royal Family. The last thing we needed was for one of our own to lead her astray; she'd been doing so well of late, or at least keeping it out of the papers. We didn't want to be responsible for adding 'roadie' to her list.

The lighting designer yelled for me to get the hell up there, shut Rivett up, and hopefully stop him from lighting anything on fire, including the Princess. Here's where the pantsuit came in handy – imagine all this going on if I'd been a gown and heels!

Off I ran until I got to the main entryway to the room, where all traffic had ground to a halt. At that very second,

Elton John and the princes, William and Harry, at a memorial concert for Princess Diana in 2007. Elton's royal fetish lives on. (DANNY CLIFFORD)

the Queen had decided to make her entrance. The procedure was for all of us to step aside, line up either side, wait, then bow or curtsey depending on gender as she passed by. There I was, waiting for the Queen, with a view of Rivett up on the balcony and off to my left, laughing and joking with the Princess. God knows what he was saying. I was also trying to figure out if I should bow or curtsey – yes, I was a girl, but I was wearing pants, and I'd been told not to draw attention to myself.

While addressing my quandary, suddenly there she was in front of me: the Queen of England. This snapped my attention from the goings-on upstairs, as I did not want the Queen to follow my stare up to her sister and Rivett. I executed a hodgepodge of a curtsey and a bow, hoping she wouldn't notice. She stopped in front of me, slowly looked me up and down, then held my gaze for several heartbeats. She once again lowered her eyes to rest on my Doc Martens, I think to confirm what she was seeing. She looked back up, her head tilted slightly to one side, and made what I swear was a *hmmmph!* before she moved on. I don't think it was a bad *hmmmph!* as she had a somewhat quizzical half smile on her face. Her eyes are what I remember most. There was a depth to them that hinted at way more knowledge than I could ever hope to accumulate in my life's journey. Somehow, they still seemed kind.

With the coast clear, I bolted upstairs to rescue the Princess from a very chatty Rivett, who had visited the Airstream just before show time.

What else could possibly go wrong? The star performer could refuse to get offstage, that's what. We were now way past the setlist we'd been given, with no end in sight. Everyone from his manager on was trying to make him stop, but he wasn't going until he was ready. Would someone just throw an OBE at him so we could all go home?

After two hours, it was done.

Just as he'd made the audience wait for him to finish, Elton ended up having to wait until 1998 for his honours. For 'services to music and charitable services', he received a Commander of the Most Excellent Order of the British Empire (CBE) and a Knight Bachelor, a step up from an OBE. All good things come to those who wait, I guess.

Once the show was finally over, we got to have a bit of a wander through the castle. I'd always considered myself a hardcore partier, but some of these guests left me in the dust.

They are different, the royals and their extended family. They wear entitlement and belonging as casually as a coat thrown over one's shoulder. This sets them apart from the rest of us, and I think is foremost in how we perceive them. Even their skin is different; the next time you get up close to a member of the Royal Family, check out their skin – it's amazing.

In our world, who cares who's seventeenth in line to the throne? In their world? Whoever is eighteenth in line, that's who!

There is a traditional title given to mere common folk who provide a unique service to the Queen: 'By Appointment to HM'.

I think I now qualify.

16

GHOST IN THE MACHINE

THE GOLDEN LION PUB in Fulham was notorious as a hub for touring crew and musicians. Long before us, it was frequented by William Shakespeare, but now the likes of Boz Burrell from Bad Company lived down the road, while Mitch Mitchell, Hendrix's drummer, lived across the road with Polly Palmer. Manticore Studios was on the adjacent corner, a favourite rehearsal space for Led Zeppelin that was owned by Emerson, Lake & Palmer. In the mid to late 1970s on any given night you could find Robert Plant pouring a pint at The Lion, or the likes of Jimmy McCulloch and Roger Chapman hanging out or jamming on the stage. The crew members who called The Lion home included those working with bands such as Genesis, Zeppelin and Wings. This lot hung out at the end of the bar, and you didn't step into their domain unless you were invited.

I was first given access to their domain by Trevor Jones, who was Paul McCartney's personal assistant. Like Jimmy, he'd stayed in touch since the Thai stick party, and the three of us were mates. Trevor once helped me out by giving me one of McCartney's cars to get around London in. I even slept in it a few times. It was very posh, a Vanden Plas with leather seats, walnut detailing, a fold-out bar with crystal glasses (somewhere to put my toothbrush), and custom plates: MPL1. Did I keep it? No! Not only did I not have a licence yet, I had nowhere to park the damn thing. I ended up just leaving it somewhere. One of many priceless items I've discarded over the years.

Also making up the regulars at that pub in those days were the villains, the East End's bovver boys. Not all of them hailed from the East End proper, but they aspired to its mentality. You needed to handle those boys with care. It's like having an exotic animal for a pet – chances are, you will get bitten eventually; they just can't help themselves.

Johnny Bindon, a local Fulham boy and notorious East End thug, worked his way in with Led Zeppelin for a while doing security – until he almost killed a guy at a Bill Graham show in San Francisco. This incident pit Bill against Peter Grant, Zeppelin's manager. While Bill didn't have an East End thug on his payroll, he did have some Vietnam vets who had gone to war for him. He had the home court advantage, and the peaceful outcome was a rare instance of Peter backing down and reeling in his goon. Johnny was reputed to kill people ... allegedly. He also contributed to Princess Margaret's scandalous phase – and for that there was evidence, in the way of photos. The authorities never found enough evidence for the murder rap.

I knew of two other regulars: Terry Draper and Johnny Miller. In 1977, they'd decided to try their hand at owning a music club, and they had rather quickly taken over the

Vortex Club on Wardour Street from Andy Czezowski. With this acquisition being hailed as ground zero for Punkdom, off I'd gone to check it out. I'd missed the birth of punk in New York, spending those years on tour with AC/DC in Australia, and the Boys had no time for punk. Finally, here was my chance.

Some good bands came out of the London punk scene, and between the Vortex, my old friends Tony Selinger (who worked for Siouxsie and the Banshees), and Steve Sunderland (who owned his sound company, Audiolease, which specialised in alternative bands), the scene was wide open to me. I was already dressing in tight-leg jeans, band T-shirts, leather jackets and Doc Martens, so I fit right in. The Clash and The Damned were my go-to bands.

Punks were mostly my age group, which was something I'd been looking for. All the bands and crews I'd worked for since AC/DC were at least ten years older than me, and I wanted to cut loose with my peers. But once the fire had been lit in the London punk scene, in a very short time it ran its course, snuffed out by its own apathy. What had it really achieved? 'Nothing!' say some. Me? I don't think it came close to achieving its potential, but it did force wider society to take note of the palpable change in the air. And punk was as much about political discontent as it was about music – how can that be considered a bad thing? What stood out to me most was that male punks were relatively inclusive of women. Well, they had to like you, but there was none of that 'you're a girl' bullshit, which I found refreshing, and was another reason I stood up for them to work associates who just didn't get it.

One Sunday morning I was wandering down the Kings Road, minding my own business, when up ahead I saw a

London punk band The Depressions. (DANNY CLIFFORD)

group of four punks harassing punters as they tried to pass by along the footpath. The punks were charging them money to walk past – nice scam if you can pull it off. These were the image punks, not the real ones who were out creating things and changing the world one squat at a time. These I had no respect for: I called them the 'fuck everything punks'.

I was still very hungover from the night before, so I wasn't in the best of moods. The joker who had pegged himself as ringleader of this ragtag bunch was a tall, skinny kid with a Britannia hairdo that stood a good thirty centimetres –

I must admit, it was impressive. Unfortunately for him, that was his only impressive feature. I noticed he had several facial piercings that ran from different points in his left ear to a ring in his left nostril. Well, this was going to be fun!

When my turn on the footpath came, I suggested he reconsider harassing me. In response, he jumped about laughing to his mates, slapping his thigh, yelling and generally being a dick. This was my cue to stop dead still, put my head down and mumble incoherently. As if he'd read the script, he came right up to me, held his face near mine and snarled, 'Do *what*?'

Perfect! I hooked my little finger through his piercing chains, led him into traffic and gave him a swift kick in the arse. Then I continued down the road as if nothing had happened. Not as 'well hard' as he'd thought.

* * *

In September 1981, I was about to go on tour with The Police, and my introduction to the band members was at a rather flash party for their record launch in a trendy London hotel. That was when Sting's last thread of pretence about being a schoolteacher happily married to his first wife collapsed and toppled with him into the atrium pool, along with nearly every guest at the party – once someone decided they were going to jump in, everyone was either jumping or being pushed in. This tour would rocket The Police to stardom. Even at this early stage, though, the band members' egos were rearing their ugly heads, never again to be kept in check.

A support band on this tour was the new all-girl group The Go-Go's, also managed by Miles Copeland. I was looking forward to working with them, as I'd done some shows with The Runaways back in 1976, and I thought The Go-Go's might be similar girls.

The Runaways had come to England for a short promotional tour of only nine shows. I'd been hanging out in The Marquee when the club manager, Barrie, came up to me. 'Tana, we've got a bit of a problem. I've got The Runaways here as we want to book them for the club. Well, they've had a misunderstanding, and one of them has gone MIA.'

I was a little confused. 'Okay, what does that have to do with me?'

'As you're a girl it might be better if you go talk to her – she doesn't trust guys. Please!'

That was all well and good, but I didn't really know what any of them looked like, or which one had taken the band name to heart and run away. But I didn't have to go far. I found her next door in The Ship pub, trying to use the payphone at the back of the room while having a panic attack, surrounded by fans. With a little coaxing, I managed to get her reunited with her band. For that I was asked to stay with them for the remainder of their tour dates in the UK to make sure they were okay and there were no more MIAs. We travelled around England in a transit van, keeping ourselves entertained with detours to see the sights. When there's no money on a tour, you find fun things you can do for free.

On one drive down the A303, we pulled over to the roadside as Lita needed to pee. We all got out, and I noticed some rectangular rocks in a field. 'Quick, get back in the van. Let's go have a look!'

'I'm peeing,' said Lita.

'Hurry up, then, I think it's Stonehenge.'

251

We all jumped back in the van and followed a side road from right where we'd stopped, and lo and behold there it was! Soon we were running around joking about who we should put a witch's curse on – the first choice was their manager.

The gigs were small, mostly at university venues like the one in Leeds. That didn't stop the girls from giving it their all on stage. The tension they were feeling offstage spilt into their performances and made for aggressive, tight shows, probably some of the best that line-up played live. In the downtime, my job was to lighten the mood a little and keep them distracted. They were burnt out, and you could tell they were hanging on for some sort of paydirt to hit. I'm not sure it ever did.

That tour took Joan Jett, the rhythm guitarist for the band, out of her summer camp baseball tomboy look to embrace the get-up of the British punks. Almost overnight she donned her tight jeans, leather jacket and Converses. We could have been twins.

I had no idea at the time of Joan's standing as one of the first 100 LA Punks, and I think I would have appreciated her company all the more if I'd known that. It was too early in my career for me to feel comfortable working with an all-girl band. I saw the flak they got in the press at times, not being taken seriously by bands and crews alike just because they were girls. I wasn't ready for that. But I did end up enjoying the company of Joan and also Lita Ford, the lead guitarist for the group.

The Go-Go's were another story. They had a completely different attitude from The Runaways and were going through what I refer to as their Brat Phase. Both Belinda Carlisle and Jane Wiedlin were members of that first 100

When one of The Runaways did exactly that in 1976, I found her and ended up finishing the rest of the tour with them. (PA IMAGES VIA GETTY IMAGES)

LA punks club, but the only sign of this was the way they trashed hotel rooms and were generally obnoxious. And I would suffer the fallout from these antics.

It's usual for roadies to check in to a hotel much later than the band. By the time we the crew would arrive, there would already be drama from the girls and an irate hotel staff refusing to register any more women with the entourage. That meant I had to sneak in to many of these hotels. I spent a significant amount of time swearing in a foreign language that I wasn't with the girls nor like them. Still, I'd end up sleeping on the bus.

One time I was in the middle of convincing a German hotel receptionist that I had nothing to do with 'those girls' when a belligerent Belinda crashed through the lobby, knocking over indoor plants and side tables in her path. She came to a screeching halt right next to me, looked me in the eye, smiled, knocked over a tall glass vase and yelled, 'Fuck 'em!' Then she left. As the vase smashed into tiny pieces, the receptionist looked at me sternly and pointed to the door. Yep! Another night on the bus for me.

When not trashing hotels, The Go-Go's had a party trick. It involved picking a male fan from the audience, taking him to their dressing room and collectively debasing him as much as humanly possible. This they would find amusing. I guess it wasn't any different from what a lot of male bands got up to, but it made me uncomfortable. For me as the only girl in an all-male crew, it was a whole different set of rules than for an all-girl band with a hit song. So I kept my distance.

* * *

Those girls weren't the only ones misbehaving on that tour.

At the end of a very late night off, I was barely standing in the lobby of the five-star hotel that I'd managed to get into, waiting on the lift to take me to my bed. *I give up*, I thought. *I need sleep*. The doors opened with a calming *ping!* followed by a swishing sound. And there he was! I was looking at a precariously propped-up crew member gripping the back corner of the highly polished brass rail in the mirrored elevator. He was pissing – and that wasn't the worst of it. He was naked.

The couple standing next to me, up until this moment, had surely thought I was a mess. Little did they know.

I turned to them, put my finger up to my lips and winked as a long *shhh* came out of my mouth, followed by, 'You might want to get the next one! I've got this.' With that I stepped in and hit the button for our crew's floor. It wasn't the first time and wouldn't be the last.

This is what happens after too much alcohol and too much cocaine is combined with too rigid a touring schedule and too little sleep. The body will go on automatic pilot shortly before it shuts down. It rarely shuts down in a bed, but when it does it's called an overdose. While that doesn't happen every day, it happens more than anyone wants to admit.

The next day the crew member thought he'd gotten up in the night and gone into his bathroom to piss. What should have been considered a loud shot across the bow, a warning sign, went ignored.

This was the era of cocaine. It was widely accepted, done publicly and considered the *good* drug, as opposed to heroin (whose latest victim was the London punk movement, seemingly in its entirety). What had started out in the early 1970s as a means to stay awake was now seen as 100 per cent acceptable. Christ, they were even writing songs about it.

I was now fortunate enough that what had once been luxuries had become staples, like tour buses, hotel rooms, catered meals at the venues and showers after the shows. It had been a long haul getting here, and none of us were going to sleep through it. At this level, people want to give you stuff – usually a trickle down of what the band was getting, and usually cocaine. It gets tricky because you're no longer limited by a budget, and a lot of the touring personnel would hit a wall at some point. But instead of others drying them out, they would be given more.

Cocaine really is a fun drug – in the beginning. The fun doesn't last. Luckily for me, I'm one of those who can stop cold turkey and never go back. If I'd only realised this years

Sting of The Police deep in thought before soundcheck for *Rockpalast*; Andy Sommers, a kind of serious litle guy. (MANFRED BECKER)

sooner than I did, I would have been in a much better place. But that can't be changed.

Did I act like an arsehole at times? Yep, we all did! It's incredible the behaviour you will excuse from a crew member that you wouldn't even consider taking from a partner. None of it mattered, as long as you did your job.

As the job was extreme, so was the downtime. One of the sound guys on this tour had the unusual habit of getting high, stealing commercial buses and taking them for joy rides around London. My pet pastime was getting into a taxi after a night out at some London club and asking the cabbie if I could drive home. It was amazing just how many drivers said yes. I got to drive five black cabs, with my pièce de résistance being the rare white cab, newly on the road, which marked number six. I retired the undefeated champion after that cab. I did all of this without a driver's licence and high as a kite. I'm not sure if I was having an early version of FOMO, or if I felt I had to party harder like I worked harder. Whichever it was, I wasn't going to be outdone. Others on the crew gave up trying to out-drink or out-drug me. I was 100 per cent running with the big dogs. By now, this was the only world I knew; everything else had long been left behind.

The tour rolled on through Europe like a well-oiled machine. Onstage The Police kept it together, with a new brass section, 'The Chops', camouflaging any disgruntlement from the original three.

When a tour is going smoothly, you have time to think of other things. For me, it was one of the crew. I'd stopped putting myself out there on tour, as it just never seemed to work out. But it was bound to happen again eventually, and there he was with his good physique, his dark hair and eyes that always had a sparkle to them, complementing his smile. He was quiet but not in a weak way.

Part of my job was to direct the focus of the lighting for the show. His job was to look after the lead singer's guitars and needs during the performance. This delegation of tasks meant that for at least an hour every show day, we would get to do a little dance of flirtation on a darkened stage while we went about our jobs, with no one else in earshot. Over time this took on a life of its own. It was something I looked forward to. I thought he did too.

Stuart Copeland of The Police, definitely the jokester of the group but still a serious drummer with a unique style. (MANFRED BECKER)

There's a lot of peer pressure involved in a situation like this. The band wants to know what was going on. The crew wants to know what was going on. Maybe I should have just posted it on the catering-room wall and be done with it. But I was fiercely protective of my personal life for just this reason. Rejection, I'd had my share. It was the worst pain I could suffer. It had happened all my life. For it to happen now was almost too much.

Then it did. One night off we were all in the hotel bar, way too many drinks into the evening. Not the ideal situation for baring your heart, although it seems these are the moments we choose, shored up by Dutch courage. Now it had all changed – there was no going back, the secret was out. We couldn't innocently flirt any longer, as that could be misinterpreted as something more; he was now distant. I didn't care to ask what had changed – it was obvious, and I needed to get away.

* * *

Thankfully, I could run to *Rockpalast*, a live-to-air concert series for WDR German TV. That year one of its episodes took place between the last European date of The Police tour and the start of their UK tour.

Often shows were added to my schedule that weren't part of the tour I was on at the time. These were usually for TV, or to get another tour up and running out on the road. This was just one of my responsibilities as head of the TASCO lighting department.

Rockpalast was Terry Price's contract and even though he was now based in LA, he would continue to oversee this client, as it was his baby. It also meant that he and I would get to see each other. The show went live to air twice a year

Me at *Rockpalast* with multiple headliner bands on the same bill. I would need to refocus the lighting rig between bands for WDR German TV.
(MANFRED BECKER)

and was seen throughout Europe via the Eurovision TV network with up to twenty-five million viewers.

For the past couple of years I'd been doing *Rockpalast* with lighting designer Ian Peacock, so I knew what I was walking into, and it momentarily got me away from an awkward situation. The bands on the bill were The Undertones, Mink DeVille, Black Uhuru and Roger Chapman (a regular at the Golden Lion pub).

The day before the show, Black Uhuru managed to set their hotel room on fire by burning the furniture; they said something about cooking special food for a religious reason. Needless to say, they weren't invited back.

Willy DeVille had a woman on stage during sound check who just wandered from one band member to the next popping pills into their mouths. She was a skinny, pale girl with a beehive hairdo and a 1950s dress, and to bring the outfit into the 1980s she'd added smudged make-up and holes in her stockings. She looked like she'd made the trip to Germany from America on the outside of the plane. The German crew spent the band's allotted sound-check time trying to corner her and escort her off the stage, but she just kept working her way around, oblivious. Her mission was seemingly accomplished, as at the end of the sound check Willy passed out and had to be carried offstage. Situation normal, welcome back!

My first *Rockpalast* had been with Pat Travers; over a four-year time span the other bands I worked with were Frankie Miller, Tyla Gang, Patti Smith, J. Geils Band, Johnny Winter, The Ashbury Dukes, Nils Lofgren, Mitch

Patti Smith, poet, punk rocker and a woman you really do not want to mess with when it comes to her music. (MANFRED BECKER)

Ryder, Graham Parker, The Police, Jack Bruce, Rick James, Van Morrison and The Kinks. I got to know the German crew really well and I was accepted as a woman on their crew after arm-wrestling the German production manager, Willie Lang, who ran the production in a somewhat militant manner. Occasionally, feathers got ruffled.

On one such occasion, Patti Smith turned up to participate in the show, and there were problems with her sound check – well, not so much problems as she just wasn't happy with it. She asked for more time, but Willie Lang gave her a stern 'NO!' in his best ex-German Army tone. He demanded the stage go to black and everyone eat dinner, saying if there was time after dinner and before the doors opened, he would see.

About fifteen minutes into dinner, Patti appeared. She walked the length of the dining hall, now crowded with about a hundred people, and headed directly to where Willie was eating. She was wearing one of those satin army surplus jumpsuits with the zipper all the way up the front.

When she came to a halt in front of Willie, she opened the zip down to her crotch. She had the room's full attention. She reached deep into her crotch, rubbed herself, sniffed her fingers, then used that hand to scoop food off Willie's plate and eat it. Oh God, I can still see the sheer horror on his face. She said, 'So, now I've eaten, can we get on with the sound check?'

Argh, that was a NO! Patti had, however, made her point.

I think I was the only one laughing – not out of disrespect but because I remembered Fred saying, 'She takes her art very seriously.'

17

EMPTY GARDEN

HOW CAN I BEST describe behind the scenes with Elton John?
To me, it appeared a beggar's banquet of flamboyance, royalty
and expensive things that pop and sparkle. Elton loves things
that sparkle. One Christmas Eve at the house of John Reid,
Elton's manager at the time, a party was in full swing when
Elton arrived in a fabulous mood, full of Christmas cheer.
Shortly after, several brand-new shiny Porsche 911s were
delivered to the house: gifts to show his appreciation to some of
his inner circle. That generous gesture in itself wasn't enough
for Reg, however; anyone can buy a handful of Porsches, so
he'd gone one better, having the dealership replace the logos
and raised 911 insignia with 24-carat gold counterparts.
I've always wondered how long those upgrades lasted before
someone stole them – in that era, hood ornaments were fair
game. For my part, I was always content with his end-of-tour
bonuses: he could be a generous employer.

It seems the higher up in the celebrity food chain you get,
the more beautiful and/or eccentric the hangers-on become.
Somehow, in spite of it all, an amazing process happens that

creates the music. The inspiration comes from many different threads in the tapestry of life, but the threads that are woven through the majority of successful performers' most memorable hits are *love*, closely followed by *loss*. Name three songs that stir the greatest emotions within you, and I'll bet there is love or loss of some sort going on – it's just how we are.

In the first half of the 1980s, Elton and I were each careening down treacherous paths fuelled by both these emotions. While completely different circumstances ruled our fate, neither of us seemed capable of having a healthy, loving relationship, and our separate quests for love would ultimately end in great loss. Elton's picker seemed as broken as mine.

While feeling torn by my growing feeling of unrest with my mother, I knew to stop touring would mean my son and I would have nothing.

For the Jump Up Tour, Elton had brought guitarist Davey Johnstone back in the fold after an eight-year absence, to re-join the rest of the band consisting of Dee Murray and Nigel Olsson. We joked that those two were married to the same girl, but their wives were identical twins.

Elton was continuing to rebuild his inner circle. He had kissed and made up with his Brown Dirt Cowboy, Bernie Taupin. Elton's producer, Chris Thomas, travelled with us on the tour for extended amounts of time. They were all keen to move forward musically. The critics were relatively happy with the reunion, and the album *Jump Up!* sold significantly enough to launch a world tour in 1982.

No matter how I felt about Elton at times over the years, I was always fascinated with his songwriting process. Bernie wrote lyrics that somehow encapsulated Elton's persona, and Elton added the music while never being in the same room for the process. Still, the two men were opposites in seemingly every way.

* * *

With rehearsals underway, a pre-tour get-together for everyone to become better acquainted was arranged. We were invited to a private screening of the 1922 German noir classic silent movie *Nosferatu* at the Gate Cinema, which dated back further than the movie – the perfect setting in which to watch such a film. Elton's flair for the dramatic served us well in this case.

I didn't think I'd enjoy a silent movie, but when these events are put together by whoever you're working for in the industry, it's pretty much a given that if you're invited, you turn up. I got myself to the Notting Hill Gate high street where the theatre was located with time to spare, so I decided to pop into a pub and grab a pint.

I took a seat towards the back end of the long, polished wooden bar. The pub was nearly empty, and apart from a couple having lunch at a small round table across the dusky room, there was only one other customer, an older man sitting alone two seats further along from me.

For some reason, strangers tend to strike up conversations with me. Apparently, I can be an imposing person, even intimidating at times, so these random encounters have never made sense to me. Yet it was happening again. After hearing me order a drink, the older man said, 'You are not from these parts … neither am I – I am an American.' He paused. 'I lived here a while back. But no longer.'

I wasn't sure if I was supposed to take part in this conversation, so I remained silent.

He raised his glass, took a sip, then asked, 'What brings you here?'

It was too late for me to get up and move, so I responded with a slightly curt 'A horror movie', realising too late he'd probably meant to the country, not the pub.

This made him smile. 'All our lives can be considered a horror movie.'

I liked this perspective – it seemed a little twisted. Now I could see he was an interesting character, obviously well educated, albeit somewhat peculiar. I relaxed into conversation. 'No. Well, sometimes, but today it's an actual movie.'

We kept talking. He spoke mostly about the occult, inspired by my description of *Nosferatu*. When he discovered I was in the music business, he talked of famous artists he'd crossed paths with, from David Bowie to Jimmy Page (who shared his fascination with the occult). He didn't talk about these people as celebrities, and he wasn't name-dropping; they just came up in the conversation.

As I reached the end of my pint, he said, 'You should go see your movie. You may find it interesting, and maybe your situation isn't so far from the things movies are made of.'

I laughed as I stood up to leave, then realised we hadn't introduced ourselves. 'It's been a pleasure talking with you,' I said. 'My name is Tana.'

He smiled as though he knew something I didn't, then said, 'Yes, it has. My name is William ...' raising his hand for me to take '... Burroughs.' We clasped hands before I smiled, turned and hurried off, as I was now late for the screening.

Years later, I was watching the movie *Drugstore Cowboy* when I recognised a voice from my past, and there was William S. Burroughs playing a junkie priest. Matt Dillon's character, a scruffy street kid, thief and drug addict, says to Burroughs's, 'You talk like a professor.' Yes, he did – part of his charm.

I wonder if I ever got a mention in one of his passing conversations.

* * *

The tour was ready to start. Our new lighting designer was Ian Peacock, who I'd worked with at *Rockpalast*, and multiple other bands. Instead of a full TASCO production we had the US audio company Clair Brothers taking care of the front-of-house sound – the same company that had abandoned the game-changing sound system in Australia all those years back. My responsibilities while working for Elton would be stage manager, lighting crew chief and tour electrician.

Elton's performances were always exciting. He's the consummate performer, with an over-the-top stage presence. I enjoyed Elton the most when he was just fiddling around at his piano during sound check – what he played at those times would reveal his mood. He was usually more relaxed onstage in the afternoons, before the audience came in, and he'd often joke around.

But while the business side was going to plan, it seemed that in private Elton was on the verge of self-destructing. Fractures were starting to show in his long-term relationship with John Reid, his manager. Although these cracks were small at first, hardly visible, before long there would be a trail of irreparable rubble where once had thrived an old friendship and business relationship. I thought it was a shame. John was always a gentleman and such good fun to hang out with, but you can't get in the middle where money is involved. You need to remember your position, and some crew members find that harder to do than others.

This was the only tour from which I had to send home a crew member for forgetting his position. That may sound a little *Upstairs Downstairs*, but when push comes to shove that's just how it is, and it's always best roadies don't forget that fact.

This unfortunate situation arose when a lighting crew member accepted Elton's invitation to come to his suite for after-show revelry. Now, Elton went hard when he partied, and a newbie needed to be careful just how long he stayed in that particular playpen. Elton played by different rules – there's no 6 a.m. call for Elton.

Within a matter of days, I had a crew member who couldn't make it to the load-in on time and was useless when he did. Worse, he seemed to think he should get a pass; after all, he was hanging with Elton. After the third time this happened in as many load-ins, I requested he be replaced. Unexpectedly, this was met with resistance from Elton, who wasn't done with him yet. That would have been fine if he wasn't part of a crew that relied upon each member to do their job. My response was if he couldn't do his job, we wouldn't carry him on the crew. The workload is too hard with long hours, and you're usually under-crewed to start with. You make it work, but only if everyone is pulling their weight. I guess Elton didn't want him that much either. Home he went.

While the 1980s heralded lots of change – big hair, pastels, Jane Fonda workouts and the end of disco – it didn't become any easier to be a gay man in the public eye. Especially where Middle America was concerned. While Elton hadn't officially come out, I'm not sure who he thought he was fooling. He was going through an identity crisis that wouldn't end quietly. Vast quantities of cocaine did not help him with his inner turmoil.

Elton had paid his dues from the 1960s, starting out with Long John Baldry, to Pinball Wizarding with The Who, to his big break at the *Troubadour* club in Los Angeles. Then getting up to no good with his glitter sisters Freddie Mercury and Rod Stewart, and finally his friend John Lennon. Elton was now in charge of his own destiny and holding court with his celebrity friends. All this can make a tour more interesting but also more difficult as you need to tread lightly around these special guests.

For example, when Rod Stewart insisted on dumping his champagne bottle in the top of my dimmer racks as he headed to the stage with Elton – not once, not twice, but three times. The third time, I cut him off and slapped him on the wrist. Imagine if I'd had to say, 'Sorry, Elton, no lightshow tonight because your friend Rod is an idiot and blew up the system.' Somehow it would still be my fault, so I decided to take my chances and slap him like you would a puppy that keeps pissing on your rug. It worked, and the look on his face was a combination of sheer indignation and pouty child – priceless.

Elton always got what Elton wanted. When Elton wanted his British promoter's parents, Ma and Pa Bush, to do the catering for the tour, we got stuck with what can only be classified as post-war fare: the worst food I have tasted to this day. For a man of expensive tastes, he ate some nasty shit, like pies upside down in mushy peas. *Eeeuuuw!*

When Elton wanted the same British promoter's brother to be both his cohort and security chief for the European tour, Bev came on board. Now, Bev's only job – as far as I could tell – was to keep Elton amused and to say no to us the crew. For example, I'd asked him a dozen times to put security at the location where the power for the show connected to our mains through a junction box. I'd explained how dangerous it was to have it just lying there outside in the dark unattended. I'd also suggested toilets backstage for the crew. Bev said no to all that. And there was never any consideration given to the difference between girls and guys peeing. Then, one fateful eve, all these things came together.

Just as it was getting dark, Bev arrived with Elton and the band. We were in the middle of the sound check when there was a huge flash. *Bang!* The power went out, throwing the room into darkness. What the hell?

Bev had stepped outside, and, without looking down, pissed on the three-phase power distribution. We found him passed out on the ground with his pants around his ankles. I still laugh just thinking of it – couldn't have happened to more deserving soul.

He recovered in time to rejoin the tour down the road, where I was waiting for him. I got my chance just before a sound check. In walked Bev, acting as though nothing had happened. I was onstage focusing lights, and I turned to the mic and announced through the PA for all to hear, 'So, Bev, is it true when a guy starts to pee he can't stop?' Everyone on the crew squirmed and laughed. Bev yelled, 'Fuck off!' then did just that. But not before checking on the security guard at the power distribution location, and possibly using our recently added backstage toilets.

Shortly after that episode, we started the German leg of the tour with local promoters and hopefully decent catering. The Americans who worked for Clair Brothers were having difficulty with all food that wasn't American. On one occasion they demanded that the promoter take away our meal and replace it with McDonald's – good old American food that they could recognise. This was my first ever encounter with US fast food; until this time, it had been from the corner chippy or kebab place after the pub. To me McDonald's was a whole new animal, and upon close inspection its patties appeared to consist of a never-before-seen meat sources, scary sight to a once-upon-a-time vegetarian.

Once again, my revenge was sweet. At the end of the meal break, many of the fish patties were left on the table, as they'd been ordered for the vegetarians on the crew. (Yes, that's right, it took a while for 'vegetarian' to be correctly translated into many languages, including English.) Hungry as I was, I wasn't about to eat any of this shit. I decided that if the Americans liked McDonald's so much, they could have it 'to go'. I stuffed the Filet-O-Fish patties in any and all parts of the sound system that would heat up during the show; as it was winter, only then would the fish defrost from being in the trucks overnight and start to smell really, *really* bad.

It took the Clair crew about a week to figure it out. Needless to say, McDonald's was removed from the menu, at least for the remainder of that tour.

But I shouldn't have laughed so hard, as karma can be a bitch. We'd completed our European leg and were back in England, and now it was my turn to be taught a lesson.

* * *

Remember that 'check your equipment' thing from way back in the beginning?

We'd arrived late to the load-in and needed power straightaway for the riggers to start getting our sound and lighting systems into the air. The power for this venue was two floors below the stage level, and after feeding our mains cables through a hole in the stage that dropped directly to the distro panel in the basement, I started heading down to tie in our tails.

Our production manager stopped me, telling me to let the house guy do it. 'You're needed onstage to direct the rigging gear.'

I'd recently added the title of electrician to my list of chores. This had come about on an earlier tour: I was doing the load-in one day when the electrician for that tour called me over to where he was tying in the tails for the rigging. Tours use three-phase electricity to compensate for the sheer amount of power needed to run a show, provided through five heavy-duty cables. Each is colour-coded so you know where to connect it to the house supply. That morning, the electrician was holding up two different-coloured tails, and he asked me which was the green one. I laughed and started to walk away, thinking it was electrician humour, until I realised, he wasn't kidding. He explained that he was colour-blind, and it got worse when he was hungover. That day, he couldn't tell the difference between green and blue! He brushed it off as not a big deal, as lots of guys are colour-blind. That was my cue to start tying in the tails on all my tours, as I knew I wasn't colour-blind.

At the Elton show in England, I'd seen the house electrician on the way in, and I'd mentioned to the production manager that he looked a bit worse for wear. I was told to shut up and go onstage. 'We don't have time for a discussion!' I wanted to check the tie-in before turning on the power but again was told, 'We don't have time. He is the electrician. Let him do his job!'

The main breaker for my system was built in to a flight case that was luckily still on its wheels when I went to throw the switch. The case shot off in one direction, while I landed several metres away, tangled up in the fly-wires for the theatre.

I untangled myself, grabbed the closest object – which turned out to be a scaffolding pipe – and headed full speed downstairs to kill the electrician. But why was everything so quiet? I got to the basement with the distro panel, and there was the electrician holding the disconnected cables in his hands as he realised what he'd done, the mistake he'd made. I took a swing at him just as I passed out. Adrenaline alone had got me down the stairs to the basement. Was he colour-blind also? I know he was hungover as I could smell the alcohol on his breath.

The next thing I remember, I was standing outside the venue next to the lighting crew's tour bus, but for some reason I couldn't get on. Everything was still unrealistically quiet; the two people holding me up were talking, but I couldn't hear anything. My arms wouldn't go down by my sides, so every time I went to step onto the bus my arms kept hitting the doorframe. Finally, they turned me sideways and got me through.

I'm not sure how long I was out for, but I remember later managing to focus the lights for the show.

The power to the building was three-phase 200 amps: that was the strength of the jolt I'd received. I should have been dead. My hair started to turn grey that very day.

I don't remember being taken to hospital or being seen by a doctor. Oh, that's right! That's because it didn't happen! There were no health and safety procedures in place. The rule of thumb was still 'if it doesn't kill you, you're good to go'. This sort of work-related accident came in many shapes and sizes, and most crew members who toured in the 1970s,

'80s and even the '90s have their own stories to tell. With our productions expanding on an almost daily basis, there was now a need for tighter safety guidelines to protect us from our jobs and ourselves.

From that time on, nobody told me I couldn't be present while my tails were being connected, and I did it myself whenever possible.

* * *

My next stop was the United States of America, where I could hopefully get a decent catered crew meal and not get electrocuted. Throughout my years based in London, I'd found out one thing for sure: I most definitely wasn't built for the cold. While I would miss the Brits and their self-deprecating humour, my getting to tour the States was long overdue. Better late than never! Off I went, wide-eyed with anticipation.

My USA experience started in TASCO's new Los Angeles warehouse prepping the Elton John tour rig and meeting for the first time the LA division of our London office. It was a fifty-fifty ratio of familiar faces, the balance being Americans. Steering this new shiny ship were Paul Newman and Terry Price, who made it clear they were breaking away from TASCO's founder, Joe Brown, to make this their own separate endeavour. They added it was time for me to come on board. They wanted me to transfer to LA after this tour. Finally, I could start to implement my family's move. I was excited!

My first Elton show in the States was on 12 June 1982 at Red Rocks Amphitheatre in Colorado, which might just be the most beautiful venue in the world. It looks as though it was built to be lit and featured as part of a show. The stage area is nestled in a perfect acoustic basket of sandstone unlike that of any other natural amphitheatre. It made a grand first impression on me, not unlike the country as a whole. Only upon closer inspection would I come to see the flaws that could bring it all tumbling down. At the time, I wasn't looking for faults – I was enjoying everything being bigger, brighter, shinier. I wanted to see cowboys like the SHOWCO sound crew I'd worked with. I'd caught up with a lot of them in the UK and Europe, but now I could watch them in their natural habitat. Bring it on!

The America I got up close and personal with on that tour wasn't the America of today. So much has changed. At the risk of sounding like someone's parent, there was a naivety about it, with just a touch of petulance that has been long lost. That unfathomable pride – which could be simultaneously grating and awesome – has been replaced by a seemingly endless stream of arrogance and anger. Sad, really.

In 1982, I was ready to soak up America, and it seems Elton was ready to soak it all up too, although in a totally different way from me. He'd toured the country several times since getting his first big break playing the Troubadour Club in Los Angeles, back in 1970. He was a fixture in the US gay scene, so an array of young, usually blond, companions accompanied him throughout the tour. This didn't restrict Elton's voyeuristic eye to gay people. Beware the unsuspecting young concert goer that accepted an invitation to an after-show party. Whether it was a couple of college kids fresh out of that John Mellencamp song 'Jack & Diane', or someone else who caught his eye from the stage, they would be the prize and entertainment for the evening. Most ended up leaving with their sexual horizons somewhat broadened. This set the theme for the rest of the tour, as we headed off down the road to see what havoc we could create at the next port of call.

* * *

While Elton was tackling nasty rumours in the press, my biggest dilemma was coming to grips with never getting my breakfast order at truck stops due to my accent. The average *Middle America* waitress in those days just shut down when she heard an Australian accent – smiled and nodded and pretended to write something down, then quickly left. If I got really bored, I would order something complicated that wasn't on the menu, as chances were I wasn't going to get it anyway.

But my restaurant adventures didn't stop there.

We had a day off in Biloxi, Mississippi, which seemed like a nice enough town. It had a pier with a large seafood restaurant at the ocean end, and this was where we crew decided to congregate. The old-style seafood joint had probably been considered quite grand in its heyday. On entry there was an oyster-shucking station to the left, with a bar that ran on from there, across the back of the place. Towards the front there was a row of round, high bar tables set with bar stools, each good for seating two to three patrons. Then at the very front of the place were big old booths with traditional overstuffed, couch-like pleather seats; these ran along the glass front of the restaurant with ocean views, and were reserved for patrons interested in a full sit-down meal. That wasn't us – we were there for the drinks. And some of us for the oysters.

Not me, I'm an oysters Kilpatrick girl; I'll eat them all day long, but not raw. This didn't stop me from having fun with the staff shucking the oysters. These guys showed me how, and even let me try it for myself. The rest of the crew took this as a sign that now I should try at least one of the oysters I'd shucked. Their pleas went on and on, and I could see I wasn't going to get out of it – you can just tell when there's no point in arguing. After several shots, it didn't seem like an impossible feat, so I conceded, if only to shut everyone up so we could get back to enjoying ourselves.

Well, they took this to mean they could douse the poor mollusc in anything they could get their hands on: Tabasco, horseradish and Worcestershire sauce! Being a good sport, I put it in my mouth, but couldn't bring myself to swallow it. Sound familiar? It's all about the texture for me.

Right at that moment, the truck driver sitting beside me turned to me and sneezed. Out flew an oyster that he'd shoved up his nose.

Without even thinking, I spat out my oyster, which hit one of the guys shucking square in the face – along with all its additives. He yelped and fell backwards into the wall of oyster shells that was like a monument to their day's work. A chain reaction was set in motion, and it seemed to take forever. Why is it that good things never run in slow motion, only disasters? When the dust settled it looked like a hurricane had torn a path through the restaurant. There were upturned tables, patrons covered in food, staff yelling and a waitress crying.

The bill was substantial, but luckily covered by an understanding tour manager. Oysters, from that time on, were also off the menu.

* * *

This US tour was when I first had to deal with the International Alliance of Theatrical Stage Employees (IATSE) labour union crews. They were certainly something to behold. There were no unions in other parts of the world. Thanks, Jimmy Hoffa!

I had to get used to being told I couldn't load my truck. I couldn't touch my equipment or tie in my power unless the union crew deemed it okay. Well, hell, I may as well go back to the hotel! Once I got used to that, I just knew they would have a fifteen-minute break to wash their hands before their mandatory one-hour meal break any minute now. Drove me nuts. What would take five minutes to finish before a break could take thirty by the time everyone got back together and picked up where they'd left off.

All wasn't lost, though, as Elton was travelling with his own stage that went on top of the venue stages. What it lacked in height, it made up for in girth and weight. It allowed me to mess with the union guys, as most of them couldn't fit in the space beneath. I would get to negotiate what I was and wasn't allowed to do, as I would be the one shimmying through the partitions.

My favourite union crew story is from this first US tour. It took place in the hallowed Madison Square Garden, the Holy Grail for musicians and road crew alike. If you can make it there, you can make it anywhere!

During the load-in for the first of four shows, I was once again waiting on a union electrician so we could run our mains onto the stage to power up the rigging. One electrician had done the tie-in, but a different electrician was needed to run the cable. I was getting upset at the ridiculousness of this dilemma. I pleaded my case to the head of the union crew, a thick-set New Yorker with the accent to match, who

A touching moment with Elton John, Sean Lennon and Yoko Ono at our show at Madison Square Gardens in 1982. They were paying tribute to John Lennon, remembering his last ever public performance in this venue, with Elton in 1974. (THE LIFE PICTURE COLLECTION VIA GETTY IMAGES)

explained that no exceptions would be made. Hoping for a consolation prize, I asked him to say 'Thirty-Third and Third' for me. He laughed and obliged. It was *sooo* good, and made me giggle. *Toidy-Toid and Toid.*

When we went to black to break for lunch, the steward summoned me to his office and told me that he and another crew member wanted to take me somewhere. Had I pushed too far this time? Was I about to swim with the fishes? They bundled me into the pick-up truck and drove me to ... guess where? *Toidy-Toid and Toid.* Very funny, guys!

At the second Garden show, Yoko Ono turned up with a very young Sean Lennon to join Elton onstage for a tribute to John Lennon. The song was 'Empty Garden (Hey Hey Johnny)', written by Elton and Bernie to John after his death. Security was tight, with a gaggle of very large, ominous security *men in black*. Sean was in the midst of it all, looking very confused and a little scared, and Yoko was on the side of the stage.

Just as a security guy was about to bring Sean up the steps to the stage, I noticed Sean's shoelaces were undone; he was about to trip on them. I'd picked him up, placed him on a flight case and started to tie his laces, when the security guy freaked out. He went to grab Sean, who wriggled closer towards me while I explained to the guy that he needed to be more careful with the golden child – he wouldn't look good if the kid fell and hurt himself in front of twenty thousand punters, not to mention the band, Elton and his mum. I did up Sean's laces; he smiled at me with what I took as a thankyou and was then whisked up onto the stage.

It reminded me of Angus saying that security guys are big and bump into you and you can't see where you're going. Be careful out there, folks! Celebrities don't appreciate you breaking the things they hold dear, like themselves and their children.

Over the four days we were at The Garden, I'd built a great rapport with the union crew and would hang out with them in their office. When the last show came to an end, they had a parting gesture for me at the load-out. Every time the freight elevator came up to the stage area to be loaded with equipment, it would mysteriously be out of order for both backline and sound – however, it worked perfectly for all lighting equipment. That was the only night in history, when a lighting rig loaded out faster than both the backline and sound. Thanks, boys!

18

UNDER PRESSURE

A WEEK AFTER THE US leg of the Elton John tour had finished, I was still in LA. I was sitting by the pool in a Hollywood hotel right next door to the Tower Records store and within walking distance to The Whisky, Roxy and Rainbow clubs on Sunset Strip. TASCO LA paid for me to stay on while we finalised my transfer date from London. This was when I got to see the Los Angeles you hear about in every story from the road. The hotel was like something from a Gus Van Sant movie but with clean sheets. I liked the edge to it, the breezeways littered with as-yet-undiscovered rock stars and their clingy girlfriends wearing clingy outfits. I spent several days watching the parade go by. I was expected back in London to start yet another leg of the Elton tour, but once that was done, I would move to LA.

I was now in a relationship with an American crew member, who I'd worked with on Elton's US tour. I was hoping our relationship would bring some normalcy into my life. I'd been out there alone for a long time, and I was starting to feel it. Who knows, if all went well, maybe at some point we would move in together?

My last tour back in England was the first and only one where I got to work with another woman on the crew. TASCO was starting to hire more Australians – they liked our work ethic. An Aussie friend of mine and fellow roadie, Meri Took, had turned up in London with his girlfriend at the time, Debbie Vincent. When he explained they were looking for jobs and that she also did lighting, I put them to work. Meri was sent out on Neil Young in Europe, so I decided to take Debbie out with me on Elton. This meant giving up my single room, but it was well worth it to have another woman on the road with me.

Debbie was a country girl who reminded me of those Glennie girls I'd liked so much. She was tough, cute, smart and very likeable. We got on well and, more importantly, worked well together. It was nice to finally have another girl out there, and one who mostly knew her shit – what she didn't know, she learnt quickly. It was like having a little sister all of a sudden. We formed a long-term friendship on that tour. Even though she returned to Australia to continue touring and I headed back to America, the experience had been momentous as now I knew there was at least one other woman like me.

It was 1983 and I had been touring for nearly a decade.

* * *

In the States I hit the ground running with several back-to-back tours. A rash of Australian bands were touring the States in the mid 1980s, and I was put on Air Supply, Men at Work, Little River Band and INXS in a relatively short period. I would joke that I was the tour translator. During this time, I would work for not only TASCO, but also Delicate Productions and Light & Sound Design. I was also adjusting to being part of a couple, but with both of us working on different tours, we had no real time to work on our new relationship.

Finding the right person is hard. Keeping that relationship going is even harder. Why wasn't I happy? This was what I'd hoped for: someone to love. He was a great guy who told me he loved me, so what was wrong with me? Why was I still unsettled, nervous, restless?

I'd never lived with a romantic partner. So far, my relationship choices hadn't panned out, and, looking back, that was probably mostly my own doing. It's that broken picker again. I had serious trust issues, and it looked like I was being tested right off the bat. At the beginning of our relationship, my new partner had told me he was no longer with his ex-girlfriend, but three months later he invited her and all her friends to see Elton at the Hollywood Bowl and brought them backstage, giving them the royal treatment. This he didn't tell me until the day of the show, after we'd been together for the entire tour. I spent the dinner break crying up in the roof of the Hollywood Bowl, where nobody would see me. What else didn't I know? I felt I'd been humiliated in front of the entire crew. He apologised, and I tried to get over it.

I moved forward in the relationship, accepted his proposal of marriage and hoped everything was going to be alright. On my wedding day, I stood in an annex while the friend whose job it was to walk me down the aisle kept telling me, 'You got this!' I wasn't so sure. Suddenly, I wasn't ready. I wanted to run, and not stop running. Would London be far enough away, five thousand miles? We'd done all the things you were supposed to do: met with a priest, told each other our darkest secrets, sworn a forever love. He was the only person I'd told about my son, and he was on board about my mother and son coming to the States – if he hadn't been, we wouldn't have got this far. Yet there I was, getting cold feet. I couldn't trust my legs to carry me out of the annex. If they had in that moment, they would have diverted me into the carpark and far away. A runaway bride.

It was sheer embarrassment in the end that propelled me out of that deer-in-the-headlights moment and into the adjoining room. A room full of genuine warmth and the smiling faces of friends who had come to witness our union. The music started, and I was guided firmly by my arm towards the altar. I faltered and stopped. My chaperone was a big bear of a man, and even though he was being incredibly gentle, there was no escaping him as he led me up the aisle. The music started again, and I saw the big smile on my soon-to-be-husband's face. I relaxed a little. In that moment I thought maybe, just maybe, everything was going to be alright.

But the union sadly didn't last. What is the excuse that everyone uses? Irreconcilable differences. It was a shame, really, as I'd thought I finally had it all. And the irreconcilable differences weren't between my husband and myself: they were between myself and my mother.

It turned out she'd never really wanted a happy family reunion in the States – she'd just wanted to be in control again. She could see from my visits to Australia that my son and I were bonding. This had changed everything, in her mind. She wasn't going to give up without a fight. When I put a date on when they would move to join me and my husband in the States, that was when all communication stopped. Dead silence, no response.

I'd told my husband about my fears. He hadn't believed me. He'd wanted to believe she was a wonderful, selfless woman, right up until she finally answered the phone and said that she couldn't possibly get on a plane, and that she and my son would be staying put, confirming my biggest fears. That call not only ended our care agreement, but also my marriage. My husband had no idea of the battle about to ensue, nor would he have survived it, so it was better that he wasn't involved. For all our sakes, I had to leave.

* * *

Step one of getting my son would involve me getting as far away from my husband as possible; he wasn't dealing with it at all well. I did so by sleeping with a mutual friend. Step two would involve me getting money.

I left for Paris on a several-month contract for Light & Sound Design. I would be running the largest lighting rig ever built, so this show was going to be a beast. It was for a French performer, Johnny Hallyday. We'd be opening the new Le Zénith venue in Paris. The show would run six days a week from October 1984 to February 1985. I could be in Australia for my son's birthday.

Paris, the city of lights. The place people run to with love on their minds. Me, I was running there to, once again, escape.

People travelled from all over Europe to see Johnny's 'spectacle', as the French called his shows. That's how much his fans loved him. The rig consisted of three thousand par cans, sixty Vari-Lites (the new motorised, multi-colour single light source), fourteen followspots and ten 5k Fresnel lanterns, attached to 250 metres of trussing, suspended from two hundred rigging points with ninety-eight moving motors and a maximum load of thirty tonnes. Not only was it the largest lighting rig ever assembled, but it also had a huge mechanical fist that appeared through the rear of the stage and would rotate to a palm-up position over the audience. Once opened, it would reveal Johnny standing inside singing as it moved from left to right over the crowd, before it deposited him safely back onto the stage. Between that effect, the rigging harnesses that would fly various members out over the audience, fire, and a thirty-member dance troupe, it was quite the production.

I'd taken the job for a few reasons. Of course, there was the professional challenge of the sheer size of the rig, but

What a 3000-lamp system looks like, the biggest ever and designed for the Johnny Hallyday shows in 1985. (LIGHT & SOUND DESIGN)

being in Paris also got me away from prying eyes at TASCO and gave me time to pull together additional funds for my eminent return to Melbourne. The most important reason, though, for escaping to Paris was that I could be miserable there, and nobody would notice. This stable job gave me a chance to lick my wounds, while keeping my looming battle with my mother a secret from my work. In Europe I was more relaxed, more self-assured; everything was more familiar than in America. And I knew Johnny Hallyday as I'd done two previous tours for him – in fact, he'd requested me.

Johnny was a megastar in Europe, loved by rulers of countries and the working man alike. We had got on well

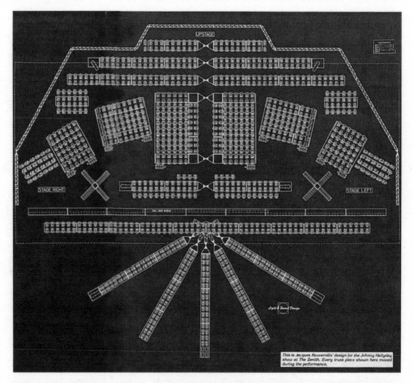

The overhead section of the largest lighting rig ever assembeled – for French megastar Johnny Hallyday, 1984. (JACQUES ROUVEYROLLIS)

in the past, so now after the shows, when he'd decide it was time for a formal dining experience in a restaurant kept open just for him and his entourage, or for a night out to a club in the VIP section, I was frequently invited to attend and sit at his side.

On one of these occasions Johnny said, out of the blue, that I should become his mistress.

Well, I laughed! Out loud! It wasn't as though we were in any sort of relationship. We'd never so much as alluded to anything of that nature: it had always just been work. I was very confused when I realised I was the only one laughing, I had to say something quickly so as not to embarrass him, so I said, 'Johnny! It couldn't possibly be. You will grow tired of me and leave for some girl better equipped for the Parisian lifestyle. You hate it when I dump my Grand Marnier in my coffee, order my steak *bien cuit*, or take control. It would all be too much – I would drive you crazy!'

Johnny's response was simple. He looked at me directly with those beautiful ice-blue eyes and said, 'Tana! A Frenchman never leaves his mistress. He leaves his wife.'

I guess he was speaking the truth – when he died in 2017, he'd been married five times, twice to the same woman.

I still passed on his offer. That would have been all I needed, adding *that* into the mix. My life was about to get complicated enough. I just had no idea how complicated.

* * *

It was becoming obvious to me that I wouldn't be able to achieve anything significant in my life or accept any proposals until I resolved my position with my son. He needed to be with me – with or without my mother.

What I'd once naively hoped was my mother finally stepping up to help me had turned into a war that ended up in the courts. When I arrived in Australia, I moved in with them, hoping we could resolve our differences and get on a plane back to the States, all forgiven. It got much uglier than even I could have imagined. Instead, she took my son and disappeared. I came home from working a show one day to find them gone. I panicked, thinking they'd been in an accident, so I called the police – who, after a couple of hours, got back to me to say that she'd removed the child for his safety as I was a dangerous person. What? Oh, yes, and I had to leave the premises immediately and not return. This time in my life became a jumbled nightmare.

Whatever allegations she made against me were accepted by the authorities, no matter how extreme. I was guilty until proven innocent. All this because the legal system couldn't get its head around the fact that I was a female roadie. I must truly be a whore, as my mother told them, and a good one at that if all these different bands had been willing to take me all over the world for years. Yep, one of those groupies you hear about. Definitely, absolutely, 100 per cent unfit. I was ordered to stay away and pay alimony, with limited access; all visits were to be supervised.

Now, roadies are alpha personalities, which doesn't always work in our favour. In this case, though, it gave me the strength to not give up. Through a friend I got a lawyer who *got* me. He saw through all the bullshit and the rough edges to a person who was being wrongly judged. God bless him.

In the end, it was the supervised visits that I hated so much that shifted the judge in my favour. A friend who had accompanied me to collect my son was a witness to my mother saying, 'Do not touch or kiss this person.' Me! 'If you do, you will get AIDS and die.' Among other things. Who says such things to a four-year-old? That's how far it had to go before anyone would even consider what I was saying had any foundation.

It turned out that from the time my son was old enough to listen, she'd been warning him that I wasn't his mother, and that I would hurt her and take him away. He never really recovered from this. I don't think either of us did. There were no winners here.

After a long hearing, my mother's words became a self-fulfilling prophecy when she refused to stay away as ordered by the courts. She would turn up at his school and take him at lunchtime. When his teacher was asked why she'd gone against specific legal instructions, her response was, 'She's a little old lady. What harm can she do? She's the child's grandmother.'

It was time to put an end to this once and for all and return to the States, just the two of us.

* * *

While I was in court battling for custody of my son, INXS were in a recording studio in Sydney with their producer, Chris Thomas. They were working on *Listen Like Thieves*, the first of what would become a three-album partnership that would also include *Kick* and *X*. These albums would establish the band's international stardom. I received several calls as an extended invitation to join them so I could witness firsthand the fruits of the creative union I'd put in place back in Los Angeles.

It had all come about after I'd got a call from one of the INXS crew members asking if there was any way I could get Chris, who was Elton's producer, to come to their show at the Palladium in Los Angeles. It was the end of the Elton USA tour and the next night was the INXS show.

Chris had asked me out several times throughout the tour – I'd always said no. As the tour was now over, I thought I could help INXS by finally having that dinner with Chris. He'd told me he would be staying on after the tour at the Chateau Marmont and given me his contact information, adding, 'Let's do that dinner!'

When I got another call from the INXS camp, I asked why they couldn't just call Chris at the hotel. They said there *had* been contact through the band's manager, Chris Murphy – and it hadn't gone well. It seems there had been a clash of personalities. This is something a producer doesn't want, especially before they meet the band. It looked like I had my work cut out for me. The only reason I decided to get involved was that I liked INXS, had done a few shows with them and saw real talent in Michael. I told the INXS crew person I would try to bring Chris Thomas to their show, on the condition the band wasn't told he might be coming. This was just in case I couldn't pull it off – because then, of course, it would be my fault it didn't happen.

I called Chris. 'Okay! Let's go to dinner, but first I want to catch this Aussie band at the Palladium.'

He thought I'd lost my mind. We'd just finished a year on the road with Elton, and I wanted to spend my first night off at a show?

After I'd done a lot of finagling, he finally agreed to pick me up at the venue. This didn't turn out to be the smooth scenario I'd envisioned. Life rarely is. I got numerous messages from the stage and made several runs to the box office to see if he'd turned up. It seems the bit where I'd said

'Don't tell the band' had fallen on deaf ears, so now everyone was stressing out.

Finally, Chris arrived, and I planted him in the front-of-house area and promised that after two songs we could go. Well, that's all it took, folks. The rest is history! After much celebrating and drinking of champagne later that night, and an agreement to record an album together, I'm still waiting for that dinner.

I never explained why I couldn't come to the recording sessions. My lawyer had advised me against going, as he thought that me hanging with a band during all this would only add fuel to my mother's fire and negatively affect any chance I had of getting custody of my son. INXS did send me a platinum album as a thankyou.

* * *

My time back in Australia hadn't been all heartbreak. On leave from TASCO and while briefly working for two different lighting companies, I set up my own company providing local crew to international tours. This kept me in touch with the rest of the world and connected with old friends and allowed me to make some new ones. Work kept me sane; it also allowed me money to pay alimony to my mother. Argh! My company did everything from Michael Jackson to Cindy Lauper, The Eurythmics to Simple Minds, the Australian Ballet to the Royal Ballet. I even landed the stage manager position for the Comédie-Française season in the Arts Centre. They had heard I'd just come from Paris working with Johnny Hallyday and requested me to translate their cues to English for the local crew. Funny thing was they all spoke English but they wanted to hear stories about Johnny. The French just loved Johnny.

In the end, despite my horrendous circumstances in Australia, I'd found a support system that kept me sane – Lord knows, at times I was hanging by a thread. I didn't always do the right thing by them in return, but I was in bad shape mentally by the time the court case was over. I'd even become friends with the local Hells Angel chapter, who offered to help resolve my situation. I declined – after giving it a lot of thought. God bless 'em. Their door was always open, which is a very rare thing.

After having even momentarily entertained such thoughts, it became clear to me that I couldn't stay in Australia, as an ominous presence would always be hovering over everything I would achieve. The court had ruled that there was to be no contact from her to either myself or my son. Zero. Still, the bitch just wouldn't go away, and she wouldn't die of her own accord, so it was up to me to find a way out. Hopefully, eight thousand miles was far enough away.

I'd paid a heavy price for being a roadie. I had to decide if I was to continue working in this industry, and if I could even make it work with a child.

Enter Terry Price, my friend and boss from TASCO LA. He was in Melbourne to sell an old Avo dimmer system – the one I'd toured with for The Police – to a company in town. We spent a couple of days catching up, and as was Terry's habit we talked about major changes in his life; I'd become a sounding board over the years.

It was Terry who had supported my career those several years I'd spent working for TASCO. We'd spent his last night together in London before he'd left to open TASCO LA. We'd always been close, but now, years later, he was married with a couple of kids, so I wasn't going to tell him that the young boy he was looking at was his. Instead, when he asked, I pretended that he was another guy's in London; someone who I knew wouldn't step up, as he'd turned out to be one of those pieces of glass. This I'd hoped would stop people from asking more questions now my secret was out. I used the crew guy back in London just as he'd used and hurt me. In my desperation it seemed only fair at the time. It wasn't.

Terry was now talking about changes coming up for TASCO LA, and he said I should come back to LA to be a part of it. In case LA didn't work out, I booked two round-the-world tickets, and my son and I left Melbourne: off to conquer whatever came next. Terry had said we could stay with him and his family if we needed to. I'd known his wife from the Golden Lion pub before he'd married her, so I guess it wasn't that strange, us all in one house. During the time we stayed with Terry, he continued asking me who the father was. I got the impression he didn't believe my original answer, or why would he keep asking? He would play with my son like his other kids, and I think he was starting to figure it out. I was scared what would happen if he made up his mind that he was the father, so I moved in to a place of my own.

The situation resolved itself, as situations tend to do. Sadly, Terry was killed in a road accident not long after. I was devastated, but at least my son didn't have to deal with losing a father he'd just got to meet, as I hadn't told either of them the truth. That was my final break with TASCO also. There was nothing for me there now but ghosts. I wanted a clean slate to build a relationship with my son.

Mentors and role models are two completely different things. I was lucky to have some of the world's greatest roadies as my mentors. It all started with Swampy, then Peter Wilson, Patrick Stansfield, Steve Sunderland, Tony Selinger, George Harvey, Ian Peacock, Ted Gardner, Terry Price. While they were prepared to teach me my trade, role models they weren't. My school was look and learn. It could be tricky trying to find a role model in that bunch of hard-drinking, hard-drugging, hard-mouthed, law-breaking, loveable rogues who made up the industry. There was no Big Brother Program. If they took you under their wing, the initiation (so to speak) was to get you drunk, get you high, and try to get you laid. Not unlike the Hells Angels, just without the initiation beating – although it wasn't unheard of. I would joke that I'd been raised by wolves, which wasn't far from the truth.

While I would make light of it all, I feel deep down a person needs nurturing and guidance – oh, yes, and love – to live a happy, complete life as opposed to just surviving. Up until my son came into my life, I felt as though I was just surviving. I swore he wasn't going to have to go through the things I'd gone through growing up. He wouldn't want for anything. After such a horrible start, it looked like we finally had a fighting chance.

But as the years went by, he wanted the one thing I couldn't give him: his father. When he realised that wasn't possible, he started wanting the only other staple in his life: his grandmother. I may have won the battle, but it seems she won the war. And what a terrible price to pay. I'd decided that I would never badmouth her to him or tell him of the court case. In hindsight, this was a mistake. Somehow, she became a wonderful person in his mind, a saint. I could never break that spell. I could never be good enough. I'd taken him away just like she'd warned.

It has taken a very long time, but I am finally in a place where I can't help but wonder who hurt her so badly that she decided that her only recourse in life was to pass on all that pain and anger. I sometimes wonder what might have been for her if she could have just let go of her demons. Maybe she would have seen Paris like she'd wanted – if things had been different I would have taken her. My remaining question is, 'Are you allowed to not love your mother?' From my calmer perspective, I can answer that question: the answer is yes, but only after you've stopped hating her. Then and only then will you have some semblance of peace from your past. Forgive yourself; it will set you free.

19

THERE GOES THE NEIGHBOURHOOD

IN 1988 I WAS shedding the skin I'd worn during my lighting days, and what emerged was a refreshed attitude and a totally different outlook for my career. The backbone of all lighting systems up till then had been the humble par can. It had taken lighting design from being a mere backdrop to front and centre, in your face. This elevated the lighting rig from being hidden by masses of black drapes to front and centre. With the flick of a switch, we'd changed the face of concert production. The lighting rig itself was now a featured part of the show, all shiny and screaming in your face, 'I am rock'n'roll! I am lighting! I am alive! I move! I have arrived!' This was thanks to the rock and metal bands of the 1980s and early '90s, who projected that very image and gave us the money to create these *monsters of rock*.

But now these rigs were being superseded by newer technology, with moving lights becoming the norm and video screens kicking everything up a notch. Vari-Lites were the king of the moving light and a massive step up from the stationary colour scrollers that had been our first attempt at a multicoloured single light source.

The industry was heading towards sensory overload, and an era was coming to an end. In a way I felt a little sad, as I'd devoted so much of my life to helping bring the industry to this point. But change, for me, had become almost second nature; it wasn't something to be feared, as it had always meant survival. I just wasn't sure I wanted to go through it all over again.

I started working in film to see how that would suit me. You have no idea the sheer volume of films that never see the light of day! I then did a season of the Freddy Krueger TV series mainly doing lighting/grip work, although I appeared in one episode as a scientist – I only agreed to that as my character wore a hazmat suit so you couldn't tell it was me. I found it all very interesting and gravitated towards the assistant director position, but I couldn't stand the 'hurry up and wait' mentality. This mentality is peculiar to the film industry. You're told to turn up somewhere at, say, 6 a.m. Then you aren't allowed to do anything until 10 a.m. Or you finish shooting at 2 a.m. but they won't cut you to go home until you've had a meal break, so you have to sit and wait for food to arrive before you can leave – you don't have to eat it, you just have to see it. Drove me nuts! Don't get me wrong, I will work from 6 a.m. to 2 a.m. the following day without complaint, provided I am working. If you want me to just hang about for that time, you've got the wrong person.

I never really stopped working in production, I just drifted away from lighting. I specialised in events such as the *Grammys*, *MTV Video Music Awards* and the *Guitar Player Magazine* 25th Anniversary Gala in San Francisco. This way

I wasn't gone from my son for long periods. I was looking for a niche and found it, funnily enough, with these events, which entailed logistics.

By now the term 'roadie' had taken on negative connotations, as it dated people in a time where everyone needed to feel current and had to have an official job title. I never really understood this, but apparently if you came from the era of 'roadie', you weren't in step with new technology – weirdly, the same technology we'd paved the way for. Whatever! I was going with the flow. My new title would be logistics specialist, and I found that I was good at it.

My first encounter with the logistics of getting equipment from A to B had come very early in my career, while I was still based in the UK. One afternoon we were loading the lighting truck out of TASCO's London warehouse for the start of a tour the next day in Dortmund, Germany. There we were, about halfway to finishing, when the call went up to break for lunch. The Brits have a habit of going to the pub at lunchtime, and my desire to finish the load first was outvoted as the pub would be closed by then. As we were still living in a democracy in those days, off we went.

The yard guy took advantage of our absence to clean and sweep the warehouse. In doing so, he moved the Avo QM 500 lighting console around a corner, out of sight from the rest of our equipment. We got back from the pub and loaded the truck, which now had a tight schedule to catch the ferry, then sent everyone to get their luggage for the flight.

There it is. That 'check your equipment' thing again.

I was sitting in the office, happy with myself for a job well done, when in walked the yard guy. 'I moved a lighting desk when I cleaned the warehouse, and I just saw you didn't take it. Where do you want me to put it?'

I shouted rather loudly exactly where I would like him to put it, and that I would be more than happy to give him a hand.

Yes, there was yelling! Yes, there was panic! Then there was a long silence while I figured out how to fix it. No way to communicate with the truck. Too risky driving it to the ferry in case we were too late. We just had to get it on our flight out of Heathrow – that was our only option.

Into the warehouse van it went and met us at the terminal. Here goes nothing!

Upon arriving at check-in, I waited for my turn, then casually stepped forward to the counter, smiled and greeted the attendant. She asked me to put my luggage on the scale, so I signalled to the driver to wheel over the console. I hefted its front end onto the scales, looked at her and smiled again. She now had an expression of terror that slightly resembled mine from earlier in the day. I just stood there with an idiot smile.

She asked, 'What on earth is this?'

'My toolbox,' I responded – still smiling, with eyebrows raised.

As it was too big to get properly weighed on that scale, she asked, 'How much does it weigh?'

Um … I'd lifted one a hundred times, but I didn't know the exact weight. Still smiling, I said, '465 pounds?' a little hesitantly.

A larger scale had arrived, so on it went. She turned to me, starting to show her doubt in this fiasco, and said, 'It only weighs 455 pounds?'

Quick as a flash, I went, 'Damn! I forgot the hammer,' raising my arms from my sides and shrugging.

She started to laugh. We were in!

A few tense moments with the loading, then we were finally away. An AVO console measures 210 by 90 by 40 centimetres and weighs 201 kilos (455 pounds, without a hammer). Imagine trying to pull that off today.

For the *Guitar Player* event, I was responsible for getting sixty musicians, their assorted personnel, equipment and instruments from their homes and other locations, around the country and internationally, to the hotel in San Francisco. I also needed to coordinate all of the ground transportation to and from the airport, venue, restaurants, and any other scheduled and non-scheduled events over a three-day period. You wouldn't believe how many assorted things sixty people will want to do that aren't on the schedule when a free limousine is involved.

As each one of these people was a famous guitarist, some of them couldn't be in the same room as each other. In fact, I was under strict instructions that certain performers weren't to bump into each other under any circumstances. They sometimes can be quite ... um, how should I put it? Critical of each other?

It took a fleet of a hundred limousines broken down to three eight-hour shifts over four days to enable the movement of all those involved. Although it was a one-evening event with a three-day pre-production call including rehearsals, I worked on it for over a month. The show was a thing of beauty and went off without a hitch.

I got to catch up with Carlos Santana, as he was one of the performers. I'd last seen him when he played the Hammersmith Odeon in December 1976, and his band and crew were up to their shenanigans. They were always such a fun group to hang out with.

As part of a prank to mark their last show for both the

tour and the year, Bill Graham had ordered in jungle animal costumes for himself and the crew. During the final song they were to rush the stage dressed in these costumes, throw an unsuspecting Carlos into a large cargo net lowered from the roof, then raise him up into the roof for the end of the show. Bill had chosen a gorilla outfit.

During the rehearsal without Carlos, a situation came up that Bill needed to deal with, and he removed the gorilla head and held it under his arm while he yelled at the cause of his discontent. It was made of soft rubber with fur attached, and when he placed it under his arm it contorted into comical expressions that had us all laughing hysterically. Whenever Bill moved, the gorilla's expression contorted as though it was mocking him.

Carlos arrived shortly after this incident and wondered why Bill was wearing a black furry onesie – he found out later that night.

After that show, I wished Carlos a Merry Christmas. He said that I needed to come to the States, and when I did, I should come say hi to him in San Francisco.

Now here we were, our paths crossing after all these years. Carlos took my face in his hands and looked deeply into my eyes, his usual greeting for me. 'So nice to see you, Tana. Are you here doing the lights?'

'No! I'm one of the organisers of the event.'

He smiled. 'It is beautiful – everyone here is having a wonderful celebration. You should be proud of yourself.'

'Thank you, Carlos! Enjoy yourself on stage. It's a party up there!'

It meant a lot that he'd called me over to speak with him, but the show was in full swing and you have to keep everyone on track. Logistics is a bit like herding cats, really.

* * *

With my new career up and running, it was time for me to get a little out of control. On my birthday the plan was to blow off a bit of steam, and party! Some friends were flying in to LA, while others were already in town on tour, and then there were some Angelenos. We were starting the festivities mid-afternoon at the Cat & Fiddle Pub & Restaurant on Sunset Boulevard, an iconic music industry hangout. It was owned by my old friends Kim and Paula Gardner, who'd offered to close off half the pub for my festivities.

But all wasn't well elsewhere in Los Angeles. The city was ready to blow. Serious social changes were needed, but they wouldn't come without a fight. When it came, it came hard, and in the shape of the LA riots. It was 29 April 1992.

At the same time my party was getting started, unbeknownst to us another group of people were starting their own get-together just eight miles away on the corner of Normandie and Florence avenues in South Central. This intersection became known as ground zero, and within twenty-four hours this group's actions would affect the entire country. The riots they started were to become the biggest wake-up call to the establishment in over thirty years. The rioting wouldn't be contained for five days and only after enlisting the help of the National Guard.

My first inkling that something was up was when the pub's phone started ringing off the hook around 6 p.m. Friends flying in from SFO were cancelling, then my neighbour in Venice Beach called to say she was too scared to leave her home. There were already about thirty early birds at the pub, so we had no idea of the intensity of what they were talking about. Kim finally figured it out from people coming in to the pub, and he put the TV news on.

What did we do? *Fiddled* while Rome burnt! The pub was shut down for safety reasons with all of us inside. It was a pretty good place to be locked up: there was good company, good food, plenty to drink, and plenty of party favours. But the more out of it we got, the more restless we became.

We were on the guest list for a concert down the road at the Palace Theatre. It was only about a mile away, so we ignored a lot of protesting from the saner members of our group, and two carloads of us headed out to the show. I was in the front car of the convoy – and, of course, it was a convertible with the roof down. In what else do you drive through a riot?

The street was eerily quiet, like when it snows. Sunset Boulevard was empty. We stopped at a traffic light, probably because the only other car on the road apart from ours also stopped. A group of maybe four guys stepped off the sidewalk and came in our direction. They had baseball bats, which at first glance I thought was strange; it took me a few seconds to register their intentions. Once it was clear they were about to start swinging those bats in our direction, I stood up on the passenger seat of the convertible and yelled, 'Whoa! Whoa! Whoa! It's a rental! We just need to get to Vineland Avenue, then you can have it! It's my birthday!'

I don't know if it was the accent or the fact we didn't care about the car, but without saying a word they changed direction, crossed the street and beat the shit out of the other car that had stopped for the light. I assume the occupants were not having a birthday.

We took that as our cue to get the hell out of there, and we soon arrived at the show, to everyone's shock. The venue was locked down, but we kept banging on the stage door until they recognised us and finally let us in. It seems *all* venues across town, from Lakers games to live music concerts, were either cancelled or in lockdown. The security guy couldn't believe we'd been out on the streets.

Around this time, I got a call from Japan on my brick of a cellphone. It was Tony Selinger, my old friend from London who was now the tour manager of the Red Hot Chili Peppers. He was freaking out because his wife and son, Loya and Sam, were staying in a hotel on the Sunset Strip. He asked me to pick them up and take them to my place in Calabasas where they would be safe. As the news of the riots had broken as far away as Japan, I realised this must be even more serious than we knew. The Peppers were clients of mine, and Tony was a dear friend, so what was I going to do?

We left the venue in just one car this time – the convertible, in case we had to sacrifice it at some point – and headed to Le Mondrian Hotel, not stopping for anything, to rescue Loya and Sam. At the hotel, after clearing an armed guard at the entrance, we set about getting an overnight bag packed and them out of there. Well, no good deed goes unpunished. Loya didn't want to leave; she was more scared of the streets. We had several calls back and forward to Tony in Japan, but she wouldn't move. We'd all been through the Notting Hill riots in London, so I agreed to stay with Loya for protection, and we spent the rest of the night through sunrise watching Los Angeles burn from the rooftop pool area. My party got moved to the hotel; the Peppers picked up the tab. The convertible survived unscathed.

The LA riots would help drag rap music into the mainstream, whether the music industry was ready or not. The Lollapalooza Festival also helped, as it provided the main environment at the time where an audience of all races could see a rap group play live. Perry Farrell and his manager, Ted Gardner, a fellow Australian, had come up with this cutting-edge, multi-stage festival with over thirty performances and an array of vendor booths.

The key difference between Lollapalooza and its predecessors, such as The US Festival and Glastonbury, was that it visited multiple cities on a country-wide tour. This entailed a complicated format production-wise, meaning the crews had to be the best. The likes of Kevin Lyman, who would go on to create the Vans Warped Tour, got their start at Lollapalooza. These crews were young, hardworking and as diversified as the performers.

One of the goals of Lollapalooza was to integrate different elements of social and political opinions and introduce these alternate styles of thought to the world. We were also about to witness the birth of grunge, which quickly grew from a foetus to a full-grown angsty teenager. Flannel had never looked so good.

Ice-T and Ice Cube each played the main stage consecutive years. As I was now specialising in logistics, many of my clients played Lollapalooza, and both these rap groups became my clients. My major competitor was Rock-it Cargo, and they weren't willing to work with rap groups at the time. As I was already working with Lollapalooza, I had no problem; we would just have to negotiate some ground rules. I really liked both clients, but they didn't like rules. I was the token white girl, and these guys were hardcore back then.

Ice-T played the inaugural Lollapalooza in 1991, so they were my first rap group. This was OG shit! I've met people from many walks of life, and many of them were those that the general public frowned upon. I'm at home as easily with

One of many fans enjoying the mosh pit at Lollapalooza, 1991.
(STEVE EICHNER/WIREIMAGE/GETTY IMAGES)

a roomful of Hells Angels bikies as I am with the Royal Ballet of Covent Garden. I found working with Ice-T's crew and likewise being accepted by them easier for me than some of my competitors. They were street, and both bands' crews consisted of their homeboys who were mostly gang members – allegedly. These guys didn't mess around.

The way Ice-T performed at Lollapalooza that first year was a more polished version of their home-grown style in South Central. I was invited to a show in the Compton area. I went because I needed to see what equipment Ice-T and his thrash metal band Body Count used, as opposed to Ice-T with his rap line-up, so we could combine one set of documents for customs. Going to a show also helped me get a feel for a client and allowed me to socialise with my new work partners.

The venue was a club that looked like it had been converted from a 1940s dance hall, with low ceilings, bad lighting and no AC. The room was packed with several hundred punters, and popping up through this crowd were two massive champagne glasses, a naked girl taking a bubble bath in each one. Nobody was paying much attention to these girls; the crowd were too into Ice-T. Production such as lighting wasn't a priority yet, but a good loud sound was. I had a lightbulb moment: *This guy is going to be big!* People were coming to see *him*, not some fancy production.

After the show I was introduced to Ice-T and some of his group. There were wall-to-wall OG supporters, most of them wearing gang colours, and I realised that while I was there to do a job, that didn't mean I got a free pass from the room. I was the only white face, so I figured it was best to keep a low profile, do my job and get out of Dodge. I noticed the crew worked differently from what I was used to, and that I needed to establish ground rules on how international touring worked when it came to customs and shipping of their equipment. Ice-T and Body Count would turn out to be slightly more understanding of the rules than Ice Cube's posse.

International touring with these groups became a constant game of hide the salami – only the salami, in this case, was contraband hidden in the equipment being shipped either by air or sea under a document called a carnet: basically a passport for all the equipment a band needs to perform their show, including sound, lighting, backline, wardrobe, sometimes even the stage. You're required to take out a bond guaranteeing that everything listed on the carnet is declared and will remain the same. These bonds run into the hundreds of thousands of dollars, up to millions, and can be forfeited if you don't follow the rules – no additions, no deletions, absolutely no changes, and nothing undeclared. Like a passport, a carnet can be revoked. The stashed contraband ranged from alcohol to illegal substances to, in one instance, a gun.

I would search through the equipment for contraband prior to tending it to customs. I soon learnt not to call my clients and yell at them when I found something; they weren't really in any position to call me and complain that their illegal shit was gone. There was a healthy paranoia from both camps regarding the police, as these artists were being publicly targeted for both their lyric content and alleged gang affiliations. I used this to my advantage, making them aware that customs was more powerful than the police, and not to be messed with.

Around this time, I discovered an AM radio station that broadcast the flight tower at LAX. You could listen to all the airwaves chatter about planes in holding patterns and being cleared for take-off and landing. Now, I thought this would be perfect for the office phone system whenever a client called and we had to put them on hold. This happened to the tour manager from Ice-T's entourage, and he hung up. He called back and got put on hold again. He hung up. He called back saying our phones were bugged (the LAX flight tower chatter), so he was coming straight over. We dried our tears of laughter and came up with a story that if we were in fact being bugged, his group would have to be even more careful about what they considered putting in their equipment. Problem solved, plus you never want to make a client look stupid.

Out of necessity, I'd come up with a system for penalising clients for undue hardship inflicted upon me. Unfortunately, I had to use this for about 30 per cent of my clientele. It was the ASC surcharge that would appear on their itemised bill –

ASC stood for Aggravation Sur-Charge, but no one ever asked. It seemed that once the tour was over, nobody wanted to pay for the services that had got them there. They would make constant demands, then once they had their gear back? Crickets!

One example was the group that had hidden the gun in their equipment. After about ninety days of trying to get paid, I decided to return their weapon. I explained how bad it would be for their *gangsta* image if some crazy white girl shot up their offices with one of their own guns. I was paid in cash later that day; we exchanged brown paper bags. Problem solved. You just have to get creative at times.

* * *

Grunge, seeping out of the Seattle area, was the other music phenomenon that Lollapalooza played a hand in launching to the mainstream. Pre-Lolla, grunge bands like Sound Garden, Pearl Jam, Alice in Chains and Mudhoney had all pretty much evolved from the band that started it all, Green River. While Green River never played Lollapalooza, most of the other major grunge groups did. Nirvana was an exception because Kurt Cobain died the year they were to headline – another wasted talent. The industry, sadly, hadn't got any better at handling these unpredictable musicians. In general, the mid to late '90s was a great time for new music; getting discovered had a lot to do with playing Lollapalooza. Bands would start on the side stage and two years later be topping the bill.

There was such a buzz about Lollapalooza that musicians from all walks of life came out to take a look. I even ran into Iggy one year. He was in the backstage area about thirty yards from the stage, trying to get there but surrounded by people vying for his attention. He looked cornered, a little desperate and in need of saving, so after a moment of deliberation I decided to both forgive and rescue him.

I went up to him, pushing my way through the crowd, and said, 'So! There you are, James. Let's go, they want you on stage now!'

He looked at me for a moment, either trying to recognise me or thinking I might deck him if I was still pissed off. Then he just squinted, smiled and followed me.

Once he was safely on the side of the stage, I turned to look at him and said, 'You still owe me a fucking leather jacket!' I smiled and walked off. (And if you're reading this, James Osterberg, you still owe me a leather jacket.)

Lollapalooza was all about breaking down boundaries. The likes of Maynard Keenan from Tool getting onstage with Rage Against the Machine, the Dalai Lama playing basketball backstage, or the Jim Rose Circus in catering. What more could you want? It made for great parties on days off.

Lollapalooza was also socially conscious and each year the festival organisers made substantial donations to various charities. With its success, Lollapalooza became a template for festivals around the world, including the Big Day Out in Australia.

After Kurt's death, grunge was given the back seat to a heavier sound with an industrial rock edge. The bands included Nine Inch Nails, Tool, Korn, Porno for Pyros, Marilyn Manson, A Perfect Circle and Evanescence, and I quickly took on clients from this market. Fans adapted quickly too, possibly even feeling a little relieved, particularly because the novelty of wearing flannel had worn off.

Another change was the arrival of girls in the industry. In the 1990s women were finally tour managing and running the production and box offices. Pearl Jam, another client of mine, had a female sound engineer, and the band were big supporters of gender equality in the industry. There were girls doing the load-ins and operating followspots. Among crews there was a show of acceptance for women, albeit in small numbers. This would make me smile whenever I saw it.

These women had no idea I'd been in their situation three decades earlier, just starting out, full of wide-eyed expectations. Hopefully, their road would be easier to traverse, paved with a greater understanding that, yes, a girl can do that!

20

ARE YOU GONNA GO MY WAY

TOURING IS HEAVILY RELIANT on freight forwarding to meet restrictive timeframes. Time is money! I thrived on the challenge of making it all happen from both the road and my offices in Venice Beach, California. Several tours were always going at any given time, which kept me on my toes. I was helped by my in-depth knowledge of many aspects of live production. I knew the equipment and knew how to handle it.

In 1995, Lenny Kravitz was recording his fourth studio album, *Circus*. He had started the album in France but had chosen Compass Point in Nassau, Bahamas, to complete this venture. Impossible! That is, unless you knew Mike in Miami.

Mike owned an old DC-3 airplane for haulin' cargo. Haulin' isn't a typo – that's just how he did it, rough and ready. He was, however, the only pilot available for our tight timeframe who could land a cargo plane on the short Nassau airstrip. He assured me that after three tours of Vietnam, this was a walk in the park, and the runway was longer than some he'd used in South America. I figured it was best not to respond to that one. We loaded the equipment into his plane, tucked away at the far end of the runway. When the doors were closed, a forklift truck appeared with one of those demolition-style balls resting on the forks. Mike attached this ball to a huge eye bolt protruding from under the tail area of the plane. With it firmly attached, he pulled out the forklift, and the ball dropped along with the tail of the plane.

I was astounded. 'What the hell are you doing?' I asked him.

'Balancing the load,' he casually responded, like it was the most natural thing in the world.

Miraculously, nothing was damaged. We flew off right as the control tower was calling a plane tail number and saying the airport was closed on a hurricane warning, abort take-off! There I was perched on a milk crate between the pilot and co-pilot as we flew into gale-force winds – evidently that tail number was ours – when Mike yelled over his shoulder for me to 'be careful!' Just then, the front landing gear came up through the floor and flipped both me and the milk crate that I'd thought was for me to sit on during the flight. Silly me, the crate was there so I wouldn't step in the hole when the landing gear was in the down position. Mike explained he didn't usually carry passengers – I was beginning to understand why. Somehow, we made it safely through the gut-churning turbulence.

After two days in paradise passing my time between a very pink bungalow and the studio, watching Lenny in action, I bowed out to return to my other commitments via a commercial flight. It was a small SAAB propeller plane that seated maybe fifteen passengers, and I had no better luck than with the inbound flight! This one did have alcohol, though, which came in handy when I had to subdue a passenger: a very large woman who tried to open the exit door mid-flight, mistaking heavy turbulence to be a sign from God, who she suddenly wanted to meet. The little flight attendant was no match for her. When it grew serious, with the woman throwing the attendant, I got up and, hanging on to the seat backs, lunged towards the woman and knocked her out. I wasn't going to die because of some crazy person! The flight attendant sat on the woman for the remainder of the very rough flight while I helped myself to the drinks trolley.

So much for paradise. Don't get me wrong, the couple of days in the studio were good. But Lenny's next album, 5 – which was thankfully recorded on the mainland – would become his bestselling album with sales of six million and garner him two Grammys for 'Fly Away' and 'I Belong to You'.

I would get to watch his rise through the charts as he'd been a client since 1993 when he had his hit 'Are You Gonna Go My Way' that was supported by a sold-out tour. It started in Australia, then the States, with Canada before Europe. Portland had been the last show in the States before we headed into Canada.

Blind Melon was the support band for that leg of the tour, and on that night the lead singer, Shannon Hoon, got naked, climbed on top of the tour bus and refused to come down – in subzero weather! This was the beginning of a downward spiral. During the show in Vancouver, he would pee on the audience.

Upon arrival in Vancouver, at the venue, General Motors Place, I woke up on the bus well before anyone else. I wandered into the venue to have a look. All the trucks were lined up in position, and a bunch of guys were standing on the loading area. Perfect, I'd have the trucks unloaded to get the boys off to a good start for the day.

I grabbed the guys out of the venue and put them to work. Now, they weren't the best stagehands I'd ever had, but they were in good shape, and not bad looking most of them, so I was happy just rolling along.

We were two trucks in when this guy came out of the building waving his arms and telling the crew to stop working.

I told him, 'No, no, no, we're good here, they're doing a good job!'

He said, 'No, No, NO!!! This is the champion NHL hockey team, the Vancouver Canucks! Your stagehands are in catering.'

I thanked them for their service, gave them a tour T-shirt and invited them to the show.

* * *

In 1995, my old buddy Carlos Santana decided that, for his birthday, he wanted to play Lima, Peru. This was going to be interesting!

I got the call that Carlos's management company was having a hard time getting the sound and lighting equipment from the States for a one-off show in Lima. Rock-it Cargo was Santana's freight company, but they didn't want to touch the sound and lights as the promoter was paying that bill, not Santana. Now, I understood their concerns – my outlook, though, is if you're doing the job, do the job; if you're scared, stay at home. While I was still a relatively new kid on the block, I never shied away from a challenge.

I took on the job for two reasons. One, I was looking forward to seeing Carlos, as it had been a few years since the

Guitar Player Magazine event. Two, I wanted to show my competitor Rock-it Cargo that I could do what they were too scared to do. Was I taking a chance? Absolutely! But if you don't push outside of your comfort zone, you will never grow.

Getting the equipment into the country wasn't too difficult, but that was to be expected. The flight into Lima did include flying over an active volcano, not something I would recommend for the faint of heart. But the trickiest bit would be getting paid and out in one piece.

There had been a changing of the guard in 1991 after Bill Graham, Carlos's manager and Bay Area promoter, had sadly died in a helicopter crash. The new guard left a lot to be desired and they made it very clear they were true Rock-it supporters. I said, 'Oh! You mean the company that was too scared to bring your sound and lights into the country. Here's your gear!' I'd never had that response before, and later found out that Rock-it had been concerned about me stealing them as a client, so they were stirring the shit.

This was when I buddied up with one of the promoter's reps to make my life easier. However, he was possibly the highest (meaning under the influence of drugs) person I have ever met. And that is saying something.

I spent most of the show chasing the promoter as I tried to get the $40,000. After being given the run-around by the promoter's money man, I made it clear I knew Carlos personally, and this wouldn't end well if he came offstage to find I'd not been paid. That seemed to work, as the promotor finally said he would meet with me.

The venue was an old bull-fighting arena – large, but in serious disrepair. For our meeting, the promotor chose a part of the place as far away from the stage area as you could get. He put me in a damp, dimly lit room with one of his bodyguards on the door. Then he came in with two bags full of US$20 bills, dumped them in front of me and said, 'Count them!'

Two more bodyguards, obviously armed, entered the room and stood looking at me while I counted the sweaty cash. It's amazing how you can understand a language without a word being said. Once I'd finished counting, the guards were standing directly in front of me; they'd closed ranks. The original guy was still guarding the door. It was as if they were daring me to pick it up.

As if on cue, Carlos and the band, talking and laughing, walked by the door. This confused everyone, as their dressing rooms were in the opposite direction – they'd gone the wrong way after coming offstage. Seeing him, the guards all left.

There I was, sitting alone in a dingy tunnel in Peru with $40,000 bundled into $1000 lots held together with rubber bands. That was the scariest part of the night, as I couldn't see my opponents – they'd disappeared into the dark. I knew they would be back.

Then I heard it. Faint at first, then louder and echoing off the walls. 'Where are you, my love? I am coming.' (I had visions of the cartoon Pepé Le Pew). Again and again his voice called to me, until he was standing there in the doorway, my crazy Peruvian buddy, the promotor's rep. He looked at me, looked at the cash and said, 'Come, we go NOW!'

You don't have to tell me twice!

The next morning, after loading the equipment onto a plane, I had just enough time to return to my hotel room, gaffer tape the cash to various parts of my body and run back to the airport to catch the last flight out of Lima. A political coup had started, and the country would be in lockdown for weeks to come.

* * *

By the end of the '90s, my company was doing well – we'd just added offices in London and New York, plus a network of exclusive agents in Australia, Japan and South America. We were chartering 747s to handle the freight of clients such as Luther Vandross and En Vogue, which kicked our profile in the industry up a notch.

However, two battles loomed in my personal life that would take precedence over my work, because they had to. Both were out of my control. Both would be gruelling. Both would become life-or-death fights. One I would win, the other I would lose. Of all the struggles life had put in front of me, these would be the most difficult. These I couldn't just fix or run away from.

While my son was struggling, he wouldn't live with me or even let me know where he was unless he wanted something. It was hard and it was wrong, but it never changed. With a successful international company to call my own, and a righthand person, Dianna Pedersen, who I could trust with my life, I thought I was finally in a position where I could focus on trying to rebuild my fractured relationship with my son. I felt I was in a place where I now had more to offer him than the last time I'd tried and he'd rejected me. Our ongoing struggle wasn't getting either of us anywhere.

But this attempt at a reconciliation was brought to a screeching halt when I was told I needed surgery immediately – possibly from climbing around all those old theatre roofs back in England filled with asbestos. Who knows? Extended periods of touring around the world with bands will eventually take a toll on either your mental or physical health. Or, if you're unlucky, you get both. For me it manifested in a physical manner, and this would eventually cause me to close my company right when my major competitor was on the verge of offering me a buyout. Once again, I found myself having to diversify. You can't take any of it too personally, or cry over the *what-ifs*.

After surgery and months of recuperation, I was ready to start again. But there was to be no reunion, so I returned to work.

* * *

This next segment of my life started with an unexpected phone call. The question put to me was, 'Would you like to meet with Bill Ward, the drummer from Black Sabbath? He's looking for someone to manage him. He's been working on a solo project, and he wants to take it to the next level.' Bill had been rehearsing with a band and was starting to do live shows, and he needed a business partner/manager. It was July 1997, and rumours had been circulating for decades about his drug problems. With this at the forefront of my mind, I agreed to meet with him at his house in Seal Beach, California.

The address I'd been given wasn't flash at all, not like what I'd come to expect when going to a famous musician's house – in fact, more low-key than I felt comfortable with. We met in the living room of the front cottage: an informal meeting with his band and crew, all of us seated on folding chairs arranged in a semicircle, set up the way you would some sort of group therapy class or AA meeting. Bill explained he'd made a lot of mistakes but had been clean and sober for years and was taking his sobriety very seriously. It was apparent that he needed music in his life, and that he badly missed performing live. I felt for him and agreed to come to a show, not sure what, if anything, I could do to help him.

The show was in the Long Beach area, in an old theatre. The band was tight, the audience packed full of Bill Ward fans. What really stood out to me was that the crowd reacted differently when he was fronting the band and singing from when he was playing drums. The audience loved him at the front – they just wanted to be near him. But when he got behind that drum kit, they really, really loved him – they lost their collective minds. Bill also seemed more natural drumming.

After the show, I agreed to work with him. But I had no idea how I was going to proceed. What I did know was he loved and missed Sabbath, and what I took from that show was that the Sabbath fans loved and missed him. What Bill thought he wanted and what Bill really needed were obviously two completely different things: he wanted his own band because he couldn't have his first band, his real band, the one he'd been longing to be allowed back in to. I set about seeing if I could find a way to get him what he needed.

How would I pull this one off? A reunion of Bill Ward and the rest of Sabbath – a reunion that had been fraught with disaster since his first departure from the band in 1980. All reunions after that date had been in the hands of Sharon Osbourne, and had either been short-lived (1983–85) or failed (1994).

I was going to have my work cut out for me. All the stars would need to align if I was going to pull this one off.

At the time I had an office in BMI Music, on the Sunset Strip, and I was helping the Australian Promoter Michael Chugg pull together a music industry business conference, to be held in Sydney from 21 to 25 September 1997, that would be called the Pacific Circle Music Convention. It was to be the first of its kind in the southern hemisphere and based on the SXSW (South by Southwest) model, a conference held annually in Austin, Texas, which was proving to be very successful even in those early years.

At that exact moment, Ted and Nikki Gardner from Lollapalooza/Larrikin Management were in a lift across town at a record company, coincidently with another passenger by the name of Sharon Osbourne. Now Sharon being Sharon, with no regard for her fellow lift riders, was having a rather loud and heated phone conversation with a promoter in the UK about a Black Sabbath reunion to be held at the end of that same year in Birmingham, England. The yelling was to do with the fact that the person on the other end of the phone was obviously asking about Bill Ward – would he be attending? Sharon's response was NO!

As you can imagine that information was just too good for Ted and Nikki not to share with me. I got a call. 'Tana? Aren't you handling Bill Ward?' The conversation from the lift ride was relayed to me.

Suddenly, it all fell into place and I knew what I needed to do. It took me one phone call to find out which promoter was putting this reunion together: Harvey Goldsmith. All I needed now was to get to talk to Harvey about Bill and the reunion.

As if on cue, into my office walked one of Michael Chugg's employees. 'Michael wants you to bring Bill down to Australia for the convention.'

'Will Harvey Goldsmith be there?' I asked.

'Yes.'

'Yes!' was my quick response.

Could it really be that easy? Less than a week had passed since I'd thought about pulling this off, and suddenly all the necessary pieces were just throwing themselves at me. It was time to get Bill on board.

I called him at home and told him an opportunity had come up for him to go to Australia, attend the music summit as a guest, do a couple of interviews and a couple of drum clinics for his fans, and all would be paid for. It was the sort of publicity he needed right then – the sort of publicity you just can't buy – to let the world know he was back, and I suggested he accept. This seemed to make him nervous; maybe things were happening too fast for him. But after some thought, he said he would go.

Upon our arrival in Australia, everything was going well. Bill was being kept busy, happily mingling with his fans, while I set up impromptu jam sessions with Australian musos alongside press coverage. I was still figuring out how to get Bill and Harvey in the same space so they could casually bump into each other. I didn't want to take the chance that if I called Harvey, he might not want to get in the middle of a she-said, she-said situation. Rumours are nasty, and it's difficult to unhear something. I figured it would be best for me to keep it casual and let him make up his own mind.

We were staying in a different hotel from Harvey's, so I got hold of the transportation schedule for the limos that were moving the higher-profile attendees around. Harvey had his own limo on call, due to collect him from his hotel later that day. I called in that there was a change to his pick-up: the car needed to swing by our hotel and get Bill Ward before collecting Harvey. Here's where my earlier work for *Guitar Player Magazine* really paid off: I knew how to get a limo driver to do what I wanted. With me and Bill safely tucked away in the limo, off we went to the Sebel Townhouse Hotel to meet Harvey.

This would be a one-shot deal, so it had to go smoothly. I positioned Bill on the far side of the back seat – the side away from where Harvey would get in – while I sat on the near side on the bench that ran the length of the car. My idea was that when Harvey got in to the limo, he'd be looking in the direction he was moving and see Bill first. However, Harvey is a rather large-framed man, and instead of going in headfirst, he slightly backed into his seat and ended up looking directly at me. It clearly took him by surprise to find a woman in his limo.

'Hi, Harvey!' I said as casually as I could. I could see he was trying to figure out who I was. 'Harvey, I have someone here for you to see. Look to your right.'

'I know you,' was his response. Still trying to place me. It had been several years since I'd seen him, and a lot longer since I'd lived in London. The penny dropped, and he said, 'Tania? Tana?' I'm sure he was wondering why there was a roadie in his limo.

'Yes, Harvey, but look to your right! It's Bill, Bill Ward, the drummer from Sabbath.'

He turned, saw Bill, and the ice was broken. We started talking about how long it had been, how Bill was, and how it would be just wonderful to have all four members of Sabbath back together again – brought together by Harvey Goldsmith, the man who made it happen! It was short, it was sweet, Harvey had somewhere to be, it was all that we needed. Bill was in!

Now the real battle was about to start: getting Sharon on board. Having seen her in full flight over the years, and watched her devour her opponents on many occasions, I knew I needed legal representation, especially as contracts would need to be drawn up.

I had an acquaintance who was married to an up-and-coming attorney who until recently had represented none other than Sharon Osbourne. When going into battle, know your enemy. I set up a meeting and brought Bill with me so he would be aware just how much work this was going to take – and that he would need to follow directions, as we didn't have a lot of time to pull this off. This sort of negotiation can easily take twelve months; we had six weeks.

The attorney explained that he could only represent one of us, as representing both of us would be a conflict of interest. I looked at Bill and knew that if I didn't have him represented right now, this reunion would never happen. I told the attorney to go ahead and represent Bill. And I told Bill not to do anything without a signed contract.

Weeks later, he called me from backstage *so* excited they were about to go on to start the first show, and he was back with his mates and just so happy! You guessed it: without a signed contract!

Sharon had taken great delight in calling me at three or four in the morning (my time) to bitch about Bill and how unreasonable I was in thinking I could actually pull this off. My response was to point out that the fans came to see *them*. SABBATH! The band!!! The fans had no fucking idea who Sharon was. To them she was nothing! An unknown!

In true Sharon form, however, she would have the last laugh. She did the shows in Birmingham, collected the cash, briefly fired Bill (again), flew to New York, and pitched a show to MTV – yes, you guessed it! *The Osbournes*, the show that made Sharon Osbourne a household name. You're welcome!

21

FOR WHAT
IT'S WORTH

IT WAS 1999 AND a new millennium was on the horizon. I was going through a reflective phase after yet another failed reunion with my son. This one ended up with him moving back to Australia. Just as I'd moved halfway around the world to get away from my mother, so it seems would he. Had I been this difficult as a child? Probably! Could I see some similarities in behaviour? Probably more than I cared to admit. And is trauma passed down through the generations? It seemed so.

I decided I needed to do something for children. If I couldn't help my own, then I would try to help others. What did I know? I knew music. I started a not-for-profit to help schoolkids by showing them the importance of music in their lives. I would network with the resources I'd gathered over the years to see what I could pull together.

The project's first recipient was Venice High School in LA. The plan involved a full day of interaction with the students to give them an up-close-and-personal look at different aspects of the music industry. After working my way through all the red tape required by the Los Angeles Unified School District, I got the go-ahead.

During my discussions with the school staff, I discovered they also needed computers in the school. An ex-employee of mine who was now at Digital Domain, James Cameron's visual effects company in Venice Beach, let me know they were in the process of upgrading all their computers, so they donated the entire design department's thirty-plus computers to me – problem solved.

Then a relatively new band, the Black-Eyed Peas, agreed to play a lunchtime concert and afterwards go into the classrooms to speak with the kids – live entertainment, solved.

To enable the students to see what it was like to record music, a competition was held in advance; students were to submit original works of music with the chance to record their own pieces. Six children got to record that day on the John Lennon Educational Tour Bus, a mobile recording studio funded by a not-for-profit established by Yoko in 1998 – recording, solved.

Then there was a request from the school for assistance with equipment for their marching band. *How difficult can that be?* I thought. I'd briefly played drums in a primary school marching band; there were about ten of us, max, in the whole band. *This should be a doddle.* Then the list arrived. Holy shit! I'd had no idea that America took the whole marching band thing so seriously. There were upward of seventy members. You could have knocked me down with a feather. This proved the hardest of all the tasks, but with help from a friend, Mike Morse, who was working for

Zildjian, my mission became a lot easier – marching band, solved.

This not-for-profit was the forerunner to the very successful VH1 Save the Music Foundation, which runs music education in public schools. Doing good makes you feel good. But I was no closer to fixing my own family crisis.

* * *

It seemed that something was always going to be keeping me and my son apart. Although contact was sporadic between us, we were at least talking. We even started trying to get a plan in place for our relationship to have some sort of future.

On the heels of this decision, I was again diagnosed with a need for immediate surgery. This time for cancer. Jesus Christ, can a girl get a break? Apparently not.

While it was a serious matter, for some reason I wasn't scared. I was more reflective about what I'd done with my life to bring me to this point. This, funnily enough, took me back to those early days in Lansdowne Road, with the Boys, AC/DC; for some reason, maybe to justify what I'd done with my life, I wanted to see them. Maybe I was looking for some sort of validation that I hadn't completely fucked up my life and what I'd done had somehow mattered.

I made a call. It had been a while since we'd last seen each other.

Malcolm and Angus said they'd be in Los Angeles a few days before their upcoming show and invited me down to the Guitar Center on Sunset Boulevard – where they were being inducted into the RockWalk by placing their hands in cement for posterity.

On the day I arrived at the hotel, I jumped into the van with Phil, Brian and Cliff, and we took off to the Guitar Center. It was the first time I'd met Brian, and he made a point of sitting next to me. He said he'd heard stories, and it was nice to finally meet me. It was that natural. We played a silly game on that drive: we matched a song to each billboard on the Sunset Strip that we passed along the way and changed the words to suit. Most of it was very inappropriate, and very funny. I could see how Brian was the natural replacement for Bon – similar energy. I could also tell that something just wasn't right with Phil, but felt it wasn't my place to ask.

Once we arrived at the venue, I peeled off to join Malcolm and Angus. Angus had spotted a Crème Gretsch guitar that he knew Mal would love. So, while they were getting

Catching up with AC/DC at the RockWalk, 2000. (JACK EDWARD SAWYERS)

inducted and doing the whole press/fan thing, Angus handed me his Amex card so I could buy the Gretsch and hide it in the van where Mal wouldn't see it. Angus presented it to him back at the hotel, and Mal fell asleep that night alone in his room playing his new guitar. We laughed the next day on the tour bus when he told us how he'd woken up pinned by the Gretsch and couldn't move as it was so big. But he loved it and said thank you again with a big smile. Perfect! Mal at his happiest.

The next day was the Glen Helen Blockbuster Pavilion concert in the Inland Empire, east of Los Angeles. I would travel to the show with Malcolm and Angus in their bus. 'No need to sound-check,' they said, 'after all these years.'

We didn't leave the Hollywood hotel until 7 p.m., which threw me into a panic because access to the venue is a single-lane road. I still get on edge not being in the venue before the doors open. I always feel I should be doing something. I got my chance as, sure enough, the entrance road to the venue was packed with punters, and when we finally got into the carpark it all just ground to a stop. The bus couldn't go any further. This was a good two hundred metres from the backstage entrance, with several thousand punters tailgating in the carpark. I suggested that the Boys stay put, while I would get security to escort them backstage.

Angus said, 'Let's just walk.'

Wait. What?

Next thing, there's Malcolm, Angus, his wife Ellen, a photographer and me. Oh, yes, and several hundred AC/DC fans between our bus and backstage, with more starting to show interest in the bus.

I said, 'Wouldn't it be better if you had security?'

They looked at each other and smiled, and Angus said, 'Why? We've got you, T.'

I grabbed Mal's guitar, took the lead, and off we went. Some things don't change.

I sometimes wonder what would have happened if I'd taken Mal up on his offer to become their lighting designer. I never told Malcolm and Angus why I'd made that call to catch up. Just catching up was enough.

Always pay attention to the details. (ALAIN LE GARSMEUR)

EPILOGUE

IF YOU WANT IT done, leave it to a roadie. Whether it's getting Chris Thomas to produce INXS after he'd said no, or Bill Ward back in Black Sabbath after Sharon Osbourne had said no, or even smuggling $40,000 out of Peru in the middle of a coup.

How do you think Malcolm and Angus ended up on stage with the Rolling Stones, playing together as if they'd known each other all their lives? A crew member who'd worked for AC/DC and was touring with The Stones made a call to the right person, Fifa Riccobono, and it happened. If one manager had called the other, they'd still be trying to figure it out.

Yep, if you want to make something happen, ask a roadie. It's what we do.

POSTSCRIPT

SINCE THE TIME OF WRITING, there has been a catastrophic disruption to the music industry's touring workforce. COVID-19 has decimated our industry. Touring worldwide is at 100 per cent lockdown without any signs of starting up again. The most positive outlook is for a gradual recommencement by 2022; I hope for this. The ripple effect is devastating to the touring professionals, with an estimated 50–60 per cent of our workforce not expected to return to our industry after the end of 2020.

Before this happened, women had built up participation in the industry to an estimated 10 per cent and growing. Growth will come again and we must hold fast to our beliefs and be prepared for the day when once again we can call 'house to black' without a fear of it being for the last time.

I would like to thank the following organisations for supporting women in the industry: SoundGirls in the US (www.soundgirls.org) and Women in Live Music (WILM) in Europe and the UK (www.womeninlivemusic.eu). Also thanks to CrewCare (www.crewcare.org.au) and SupportAct (www.supportact.org.au) in Australia for their tireless support of the industry as a whole through this time of crisis and beyond.

IN MEMORIAM

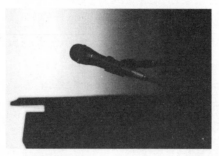

WHEN YOU GO ON tour with a bunch of people, some friends and some strangers, they will be strangers no more. There is a bond that comes from living every day in each other's pockets. A bond that doesn't fade with time. A bond that persists through the good days and the bad. A bond formed from doing a job that if you aren't careful will kill you. A job that has claimed many casualties along the way but still we line up for more. A job well done.

R.I.P. for AC/DC

     Bon Scott, you were so much better than you ever knew

     Malcolm, two thumbs up! You are sorely missed

     Goodbye, Brother George

R.I.P. Bill Joseph, 'The Rajah'

R.I.P. Peter Laffy, your music is with you

R.I.P. Ron Blackmore, thanks for taking a chance on me

R.I.P. Bill Graham, a man ahead of his time

R.I.P. Steve Kahn, Bill's friend and helicopter pilot

R.I.P. Patrick Stansfield, friend and sage

R.I.P. Swampy, my best china

R.I.P. Douglas Russell Douglas, father of mine

R.I.P. Rick Parfitt of Status Quo

R.I.P Mal Kingsnorth, Status Quo front-of-house and one of the nicest men in rock

R.I.P. Fred 'Sonic' Smith, you left a great legacy

R.I.P. Janis Joplin, a girl after my own heart!

R.I.P. Keith Moon, crazy fun, crazy talent

R.I.P. Jimmy McCulloch, I miss your laugh

R.I.P. Stevie Marriott, shine on

R.I.P. Jon Lord, a true gent

R.I.P. George Harrison, a likeable rogue

R.I.P. John 'Upsey' Downing, he got on the ferry but never got off

R.I.P. Davey Kirkwood and Gungie, my two favourite front-of-house sound guys

R.I.P. Brian Hendry, TASCO monitor engineer extraordinaire

R.I.P. Randy Rhoads, who fell victim to a joy ride in an airplane

R.I.P. Debbie Vincent, you rocked, 'little face'

R.I.P. John Lennon, peace

R.I.P. Johnny Hallyday, *une étoile jusqu'au bout*

R.I.P. Alan Rogan, Pete Townshend's roadie for forty years

R.I.P. Dee Murray, Elton John's bass player

R.I.P. Terry Price, I should have told you

R.I.P. My Lost Boy, my heart went with you.

This list is only related to this book. To all those who remain unnamed, we salute you!

PLAYLIST

'We Gotta Get Outta This Place'   Eric Burdon
and The Animals

'Father of Mine'   Everclear

'Summertime'   Janis Joplin and Big Brother
and the Holding Company

'School's Out'   Alice Cooper

'The Long and Winding Road'   The Beatles

'Happy Together'   The Turtles

'White Rabbit'   Jefferson Airplane

'Darling Nikki'   Foo Fighters
(written by Prince)

'Born to Run'   Bruce Springsteen

'High Voltage'   AC/DC

'Where Did You Sleep Last Night'   Nirvana
(written by Lead Belly)

'Black Magic Woman'   Santana

'Girl, You'll Be a Woman Soon'   Urge Overkill
(written by Neil Diamond)

'California Dreamin''	The Mamas and the Papas
'Time on My Side'	The Rolling Stones
'London Calling'	The Clash
'You Can't Always Get What You Want'	The Rolling Stones
'She Came in Through the Bathroom Window'	Joe Cocker
'Crimson and Clover'	Joan Jett & The Blackhearts
'Alison'	Elvis Costello
'Rockin' All Over the World'	Status Quo
'Lust for Life'	Iggy Pop
'I Don't Like Mondays'	The Boomtown Rats
'Who Are You'	The Who
'What is Life'	George Harrison
'Crazy Train'	Ozzy Osbourne
'Cocaine'	J.J. Cale
'Spirits in the Material World'	The Police
'Because the Night'	Patti Smith (written by Bruce Springsteen)
'Empty Garden'	Elton John
'Under Pressure'	Queen and David Bowie
'Never Tear Us Apart'	INXS

'Don't Come Around Here No More'	Tom Petty and the Heartbreakers
'April 29, 1992 (Miami)'	Sublime
'Last Wordz'	2Pac featuring Ice Cube and Ice-T
'Dark Necessities'	Red Hot Chili Peppers
'Jeremy'	Pearl Jam
'Killing in the Name'	Rage Against the Machine
'Are You Gonna Go My Way'	Lenny Kravitz
'Story of My Life'	Social Distortion
'For What It's Worth'	Buffalo Springfield

ACKNOWLEDGEMENTS

IT ALL STARTED WITH a phone call from a young American who wanted to write my life story for the movies. After several discussions, it became apparent that the only person who could really do that was me. With all the naivety of someone who had already been through it once, I thought it should be simple enough. This is where my acknowledgements come in, because, as I started to find out, it is never simple. It has been quoted on many occasions that if you remember the '60s you weren't there. Well, I'm here to tell you the same thing goes for the '70s, '80s and possibly even parts of the '90s if you spent it touring around the world with a rock band.

Without the support of those crew and band members in the very beginning, my story would have been a very different one. To the following people I say a sincere thanks. Wane 'Swampy' Jarvis, as he is where it all started. Adrian Barker and the band Fox for giving a young girl her first band job. Angus Young and AC/DC for sharing their journey and teaching me a solid work ethic. To the ACT crew, who gave me the means to learn what it takes to do it right. And then to all those who came along after and remained in my life through the highs and the lows. Here's my village:

Danny Clifford (dannyclifford.com), photographer extraordinaire, who selflessly opened his catalogue of images to me while encouraging me to ask for what I needed Robert Ellis (repfoto.com), another brilliant photographer, who broke his unwritten rule and likewise generously permitted me the use of some of his images. Also Manfred Becker for wonderful *Rockpalast* images. Additional photography provided by Alain le Garsmeur (alainlegarsmeur.photoshelter.com/archive), Philip Morris (itsalongway.com.au), Alan Perry (concertphotos.uk.com), Bob Young, Tracy and Noeleen at Glennie School, Jack Edward Sawyers, Vicki Marks, Christina Hutchence, Lynne Cox, Michael Wickow, Peter Burke, Nathan Brenner and Nicky Campbell.

Additional photographers' information can be found on my website: www.tanadouglas.com.

Fact-checking was entertaining to say the least and for that, and further support, I would like to thank the following people: Mark Evans, Michael Browning, Stuart Coupe, Simon Austin, Sheila and Roger Searle, Lorraine Walters, the Jarvis Family, Diana Pederson, the Cutler extended family, Ian Peacock, Johnny Hallyday personnel Didier Schrieke, Roger Abroil, Jacques Rouverollis. A special thankyou to Richie Steffa. To Train for starting the ball rolling and Jeff Apter for inspiring me to keep it rolling.

My agent, Jeanne Ryckmans, who took me on with a full plate. My editor, Kate Goldsworthy, who taught me so much about letting go. My publisher, Jude McGee, at HarperCollins who believed in me.

And to the countless others who are not named but have patiently listened while I talked LOUD for years, I thank you!

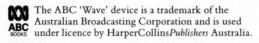 The ABC 'Wave' device is a trademark of the Australian Broadcasting Corporation and is used under licence by HarperCollins*Publishers* Australia.

Australia • Brazil • Canada • France • Germany • Holland • India Italy • Japan • Mexico • New Zealand • Poland • Spain • Sweden Switzerland • United Kingdom • United States of America

First published in Australia in 2021 by HarperCollins*Publishers* Australia Pty Limited ABN 36 009 913 517 harpercollins.com.au

A catalogue record for this book is available from the National Library of Australia

ISBN 978 0 7333 4090 1 (pbk)
ISBN 978 1 4607 1234 4 (ebook)

Cover design by Hazel Lam, HarperCollins Design Studio
Front cover image by istockphoto.com
Back cover images: (left to right) © Manfred Becker; © Alain le Garsmeur
Author photo by Lisa Johnson
Typeset in Sabon LT Std by Kelli Lonergan

Printed and bound by CPI Group (UK) Ltd, Croydon, CR0 4YY